The "Who Is Johnny Dollar?" Matter

A CHARACTER PROFILE
AND PROGRAM SYNOPSIS
OF "AMERICA'S FABULOUS INSURANCE INVESTIGATOR,
THE MAN WITH THE ACTION PACKED EXPENSE ACCOUNT"

"YOURS TRULY, JOHNNY DOLLAR"

BY JOHN C. ABBOTT

THE "WHO IS JOHNNY DOLLAR?" MATTER

A CHARACTER PROFILE AND PROGRAM SYNOPSIS
OF "AMERICA'S FABULOUS INSURANCE INVESTIGATOR,
THE MAN WITH THE ACTION PACKED EXPENSE ACCOUNT"
"YOURS TRULY, JOHNNY DOLLAR"
VOLUME THREE
© 2010 JOHN C. ABBOTT

Published in the USA by:

BEARMANOR MEDIA
PO BOX 71426
ALBANY, GA 31708
www.BearManorMedia.com

ISBN-10: 1-59393-091-7
ISBN-13: 978-1-59393-091-2

BOOK DESIGN AND LAYOUT BY VALERIE THOMPSON.

Table of Contents

VOLUME THREE

Section 5:
Robert Readick

After the move of CBS radio to New York, Robert Readick became the fifth actor to play Johnny Dollar.

Bob was an established motion picture, radio and television actor. Other than some basic biographical information, very little is known about him.

Bob Readick was a capable actor, and portrayed a softer Johnny Dollar, similar to that of John Lund. Many give Bob short shrift because he followed Bob Bailey, but Bob Readick was a solid actor, and his portrayal is a good one.

The following are the Robert Readick Johnny Dollar programs.

SHOW: THE EARNED INCOME MATTER
SHOW DATE: 12/4/1960
COMPANY: NORTHEAST INDEMNITY
AGENT: TOBY TETRICK
EXP. ACCT: $ $418.15

SYNOPSIS: Toby Tetrick calls, and Johnny is glad to hear from Toby. Glad because he likes the large fees Toby's company passes out on his cases, and he can use one right now; he is running a little short. Toby tells Johnny that the case is a robbery, $5,000 cash. Johnny is worried about the commission he would get on 5Gs. Toby tells Johnny that the case just happened in Hartford, so grab a cab and come on over.

Johnny cabs to Toby's office because he could use some extra dough. Toby tells Johnny that he should have had him go straight to Mercy Hospital. The client is Phillip Standish, who lives alone at the Ashley Arms Apartments. Last night someone broke in, beat him and took the $5,000. He thought he had the money concealed well—it was on the wardrobe in his bedroom—that is, the urn was on his wardrobe. It was a brass funeral urn and he kept his money in it. It was heavy and had a tricky lock on the top. Standish has an interest in an import business in New York that gets goods from the Orient. His policy covers loses up to $5000, and he wants Johnny on the job. Toby urges Johnny to go easy on the expense account, but Johnny tells him that "Oh, but who knows. Pursuit may take him to the furthest corners of the earth . . ."

Johnny goes to Mercy hospital and meets Standish, who does not want the police involved—only Johnny. He wants Johnny to run the man down, because he knows who the man was. He does not want the police involved because it would bring out something from his past—15 years ago he went to prison for forgery. His cellmate was a Thomas Slade, and Johnny recognizes the name. Standish does not remember what Slade was in for, but he remembers talking about places to hide stolen goods, and Slade suggested the funeral urn—a place even experienced crooks would never look. So that is where he had hidden what money he has. Standish does not trust banks because what he did. Standish tells Johnny that there is more than $5000 in the urn, and if it is returned, he will pay Johnny more than the insurance company will. Standish is sure that only Slade knew where he kept his money, and that Slade has kept track of him. Standish tells Johnny that Slade lives in Los Angeles, and gives Johnny the address, 1308 Pandora Avenue, an area that Johnny knows well. Standish is sure that Slade is going back to LA. Standish is sure that Slade will not be able to open the urn, and will not trust anyone else either. He will feel that the money is safe.

Johnny cabs to police headquarters and asks Sgt. Jimmy Wormser if he has a flyer on Tommy Slade. Jimmy has one on his desk; the boys in LA wanted him to know that Tommy was headed their way. The police watched him, but he did not do anything except for a visit to the Department of Health to get a permit to carry someone's remains back to California. Johnny is told that Tommy is going to New York to catch the Starlighter Express for LA. If Johnny hurries, he can catch the train in New York. Johnny is sure that he and Tommy Slade have crossed paths before. Johnny cabs to the airport for a plane to New York and gets a roomette on the train. Johnny tips a porter to find out if Slade is on the train— and there is a man named Slade on the train.

Johnny has a cocktail in the observation car, and then has dinner with a stranger—Tommy Slade! Tommy introduces himself, and Johnny gives him the name Harry Walker. When asked is destination, Johnny tells Slade that he is not sure that he is going all the way to the coast. Tommy goes back to his roomette, and Johnny must bide his time or figure out a way to get him out of his roomette to search it.

Johnny has drinks with a pretty little blonde, who must leave to go take care of her children. Johnny goes out onto the observation deck on a beautiful evening. Johnny dozes off and wakes up when something is thrown over his head and something knocks him out. Tommy tells Johnny that now he is going over the side.

Johnny wakes up in a roomette looking at the face of a stranger who turns out to be one Dr. Springer. Doc Springer tells Johnny that no damage was done, but his head will hurt for a while. Doc Springer tells Johnny that a conductor came onto the observation deck, and a man told him that Johnny had fallen from his chair and then walked away. Johnny asks if the conductor knew who the man was, but the conductor does not know. So, Johnny rests for five minutes and is ready to settle with Tommy. Johnny finds Slade's room and the door is open and room is empty and the urn is on the table. Johnny sees where the urn had been picked at, but it has not been opened. Slade appears and tells Johnny that he thought Johnny would try that, and pulls a gun with a silencer on him. Johnny slams the roomette door closed and dodges bullets from Slade's gun. Johnny breaks open the window and climbs out of the moving train.

Johnny takes a car, train and plane back to his apartment in Hartford. After cleaning up, Johnny goes to the hospital, makes a phone call to the police, and goes to Standish's room. Standish is glad to see Johnny and urn. Johnny tells him that he had a slight accident with the urn. A wheel on the Pullman car almost cut the urn in two. The money did not fall out, but it did jar loose the false bottom. Johnny tells Standish that he is making a fortune in one of the foulest, filthiest rackets in the world. Johnny tells Standish that he remembers what Slade went up for, and that he had turned to Slade's caper when he got out. Johnny asks if he was holding out on Slade, and that is why Slade came after him, for the kilos, two pounds of pure uncut stuff worth $8,000 - $10,000 wholesale. But once carefully cut, it would be worth over a million for that much heroin. Johnny calls him a "dirty rotten son " just as the police come into the room.

"Interesting side light on the case; I saw in the afternoon papers that the railroad company didn't look too kindly on Tommy Slade's little act. I mean when he was caught standing there blasting away at the lock on the door of his roomette. Come to think of it, I better tip the Federal boys to his having gone back to his old racket. Expense account total $418.15, and no padding on this one."

NOTES:
- RALPH CAMAGO IS PHILLIP STANDISH, RALPH BELL IS TOM SLADE, WILLIAM MASON, IS ROBY TETRICK, JACK GRIMES IS THE POLICE SERGEANT, BILL SMITH IS THE DOCTOR, SAM RASKYN IS THE STEWARD
- THE ADDRESS" 1308 PANDORA AVENUE" WAS USED IN TWO OTHER JOHNNY DOLLAR PROGRAMS; THE HARRIED HEIRESS MATTER AND THE SHADOW OF A DOUBT MATTER
- $10,000 IN 1960 DOLLARS IS WORTH OVER $68,000; A MILLION 1960 DOLLARS IS WORTH OVER $6.8 MILLION.
- I HAVE TO WONDER, GIVEN THE PAST EXAMPLES OF JACK JOHNSTONE'S SENSE OF HUMOR, WHETHER THIS PROGRAM SHOULD HAVE BEEN CALLED "THE URNED INCOME MATTER"
- IF THE DATE OF THIS PROGRAM IS CORRECT, IT IS THE FIRST OF THE NEW YORK RUN, AND BOB READICK'S FIRST PROGRAM.
- MUSIC DIRECTION IS BY ETHEL HUBER
- THE ANNOUNCER IS ART HANNES

Producer: Bruno Zirato, Jr.   Writer: Jack Johnstone
Cast: Ralph Camago, Ralph Bell, William Mason, Sam Raskyn, Jack Grimes, Bill Smith

◆ ❖ ◆

SHOW: THE WAYWARD KILOCYCLES MATTER
SHOW DATE: 12/18/1960
COMPANY: TRI-STATE LIFE & CASUALTY COMPANY
AGENT: EARLE POORMAN
EXP. ACCT: $400.00

SYNOPSIS: Earle Poorman calls Johnny from Los Angeles, and the weather is wonderful. But Earle is having a problem with all the small claims. Earle wants Johnny to come out and put a stop to a bunch of armed robberies.

Johnny flies to Los Angeles, California and arrives the next day. Johnny cabs to Earle's office where he learns that the robberies have taken place in Lamosa Beach, a new development in the area, which has a nice shopping mall half a mile long. The robberies seem to have been done by the same man, as the descriptions match. The jobs are pulled in the morning when the owners are all alone. The robber also carries an Army .45, and his timing seems to be perfect. There have been seven robberies in the past week. Earle wants Johnny to act fast, as the robber may move on. Johnny borrows Earle's car and drives to the coffee shop on Lamosa Beach. Johnny notes that Lamosa Beach is an exclusive community and the mall has a number of upscale shops. At The Coffee Nook, Mrs. Webster tells Johnny that the robber took $135 from her, and that she wishes that there were a bank around, as she has to keep too much money in the store. The police drive up and go to the nearby radio and television store where another robbery has just taken place. Johnny hangs around the edge of the crowd and after the police leave he talks to the storeowner, Mr. Marx. Marx wonders how the robber knew that he was alone and wants to close the store. Marx tries to sell Johnny a television with a remote control unit, and gives a demo to Johnny. While they are talking the television changes channels all by itself. The last time it did that was just before the robbery, Marx tells Johnny. Johnny tells Marx who he is and Marx repeats that the remote control system acted the same way just before he and Mrs. Webster were robbed, and maybe three days ago when the previous store was robbed. Johnny wonders if the remote control explains how the robber knew that Marx was alone. Johnny is told that some types of sound waves activate the remote using 44.6 to 56 kilocycles. Johnny now knows that the robber has a pal who knows when storeowners are alone and coordinates with the robber via a radio. Johnny figures he can find the accomplice if he can find a direction finder. The police arrive to investigate another robbery—two in one day again. Johnny calls Bob McKenny in North Hollywood, a radio ham known as W6BFG. Bob used to handle the engineering on Johnny's programs and Bob tells Johnny that all the robber would need is a small receiver. Bob agrees to bring down a direction finder and will be there first thing in the morning.

Johnny drives back to Earle's and then meets Bob in the morning. A direction finder is set up and they wait. Johnny explains how the remote works, but Bob tells him that the remote puts out sound waves, not radio waves, so his theory is not correct. Bob gets an idea about sympathetic resonance and thinks that the sender is somewhere along the main street. Johnny learns that on top of the shop there is a small apartment, and Bob sees and antenna on the roof. Marx tells Johnny and Bob that he has two boarders and one of them, Willard Thorson never seems to leave. Johnny is sure that from the tower Willard can see everything. The other border, Harry Williams leaves early and comes in late at night. Bob is sure that the antenna is the cause of the interruption. Johnny has an idea, and they sit down to watch TV. Three days later the TV acts erratically and the Bob discovers that the signal comes from upstairs. Outside their door, Johnny hears the voice of Thorson tell Harry that the coast is clear in the jewelry store down the street. Bob goes upstairs to grab Willard while Johnny runs down the alley to Beckham's Jewelry store with his .38 ready for action. Johnny stops Harry and his knuckles are still sore from where Harry ran into his fist.

"Yes, I guess there is nothing like modern electronics as an aide to crime, and as an aide to catching a crook. Two of them in this case."

NOTES:
- BOB MCKENNY FIGURED IN THE "THE MISSING MISSILE MATTER" DURING THE BOB BAILEY RUN.
- LEON JANNEY IS MR. MARX, LES DAMON IS EARLE POORMAN, BILL STERLING IS BOB, ATHENA LORDE IS MRS. WEBSTER

Producer: Bruno Zirato Jr.   **Writers:** Jack Johnstone
Cast: Leon Janney, Les Damon, Bill Sterling, Athena Lorde

SHOW:	THE PAPERBACK MYSTERY MATTER
SHOW DATE:	1/8/1961
COMPANY:	CONTINENTAL INSURANCE COMPANY
AGENT:	FRED BRISCOE
EXP. ACCT:	$70.00

SYNOPSIS: Fred Briscoe calls from Boston and Johnny asks Fred why no one ever calls from somewhere warm. Fred tells Johnny that he has an insurance problem that is making him hot. Come on up to Boston, and come prepared. You usually carry a gun don't you?

Johnny drives to Boston, Massachusetts and meets with Fred. Over lunch at the Union Oyster House, Fred tells Johnny that he is expecting Henry R. Girson, who is probably trying to get a free lunch. Girson is very wealthy but lives in a ramshackle apartment and is hated by everyone because he got rich by taking advantage of others. Lately he has just been counting his money, which he is trying to keep from a niece and two nephews, who are poor and could use the money. Jerry and Paul had studied for the ministry, but are just drifters now and live in Syracuse, New York just waiting for Girson to die. Nancy Trimmer lives in Boston and works at a supermarket. Girson arrives and asks Johnny if he can keep his relatives from killing him. Girson sits down and wants lunch. His policy is for $47,000 double indemnity and he would commit suicide to keep his relative from collecting. Johnny notes that the suicide clause would prevent payment, which means that the premiums would have been paid for nothing all these years. After lunch Girson wants to take Johnny to his place where he is safe.

Johnny wonders why Girson can wander all over town to get to the restaurant, but only feels safe in his apartment. Johnny drives Girson to the apartment in a horrible part of town near the railroad tracks. Girson tells Johnny that he is well off and probably has a couple of million, but there is no need to waste it. Girson tells Johnny that one of his relatives is going to kill him. Girson shows Johnny a series of notes with biblical quotations. One is from Philippians 2:12, "Work out your own salvation." Another note has a passage from Isaiah 38:1, "Set thine house in order." Another has Revelations 2:10, "Be thou faithful unto death." Another has Romans 6:23 "The wages of sin is death." Girson tells Johnny that the notes came in the mail from Syracuse. Girson tells Johnny that he let his relatives starve a little and is not giving them anything. He has to leave his money to the family because he does not want give it to charity. The quotations are threats to Girson who remembers that the boys had studied to be ministers. Johnny decides to call on Nancy Trimmer first, to see what she knows about her cousins. Johnny drives to Nancy's apartment and Nancy thinks that Johnny is from the parole board and tells Johnny that she is playing her new job straight. Johnny tells he that he is with her Uncle's insurance company, and she tells Johnny that she does not want any insurance, but will be glad to take any part of her uncle's money she can get. Johnny asks her about her cousins, but she knows nothing about them. All they ever told her was to improve her mind. She shows Johnny a stack of paperbacks she has been reading to improve her self and tells Johnny to leave. Johnny calls Fred to update him and arranges to fly to Syracuse. Johnny tells Fred that Girson will be safe in his apartment, but notes he never should have hung up the phone and flown to Syracuse, or to have left Girson alone.

Johnny flies to Syracuse and cabs to the apartment of the boys. Paul is home and does not know where Jerry is. Johnny tells him of the insurance, but he does not want the money, as he and Jerry are going to continue with their studies. Uncle Henry's money is tainted, and they do not want it. Paul tells Johnny that Jerry had left just after Fred Briscoe had called to say that Johnny was coming. The phone rings and Fred is calling Johnny to tell him that it is all over; Girson is dead. As Fred tells Johnny that Girson committed suicide, Jerry comes in. Both of the boys tell Johnny that they do not want the money. Johnny calls Fred again and is told that Girson committed suicide by turning on the gas in his bedroom. Also, all the windows and doors were locked. Fred tells Johnny that Nancy had been there to beg for some money and left after he had given her some. Johnny tells Fred that he is sure that Nancy killed Girson. Johnny flies back to Boston and Fred meets him at the airport. Johnny and Fred go to Nancy's apartment and invite themselves in. Johnny shows Fred a mystery magazine that Jack Johnstone, who dramatizes his cases, writes for occasionally. Johnny finds a story called "Death by Jets." Johnny tells Fred that Nancy did not know that he was a special investigator, so Johnny's talk about the money she would get reminded her about the story. She figured this was the answer, so why waste time. Nancy rips up the magazine as Johnny explains that the jets refer to gas jets. He tells Fred that Nancy had gotten into the basement and turned off the gas line to the apartment and then went to see Girson. When he was not looking she opened the valve on the heater, and then went downstairs and turned the gas back on when Girson was asleep. Johnny tells Fred that Nancy probably did not even wipe her prints off the valve, but Nancy tells him that she wiped them off real good. Call the police Fred.

"So it looks as thought the boys will get the old man's fortune whether they want it or not, and his insurance. You can build a lot of fine churches with money like that."

NOTES:

- THE FIRST COMMERCIAL BREAK IS FOR CBS NEWS AND THEIR EXPANDED COVERAGE.
- THE SECOND COMMERCIAL BREAK IS FOR COMMANDER CIGARETTES.
- EDGAR STEHLI IS MR. GIRSON, RALPH CAMAGO IS FRED BRISCOE, TERRI KEANE IS NANCY TRIMMER, JOHN THOMAS IS PAUL, RICHARD HOLLAND IS JERRY

- MUSICAL SUPERVISION IS BY ETHEL HUBER
- THE ANNOUNCER IS ART HANNES

Producer: Bruno Zirato, Jr.   Writers: Jack Johnstone
Cast: Edgar Stehli, Ralph Camago, Terri Keane, John Thomas,
             Richard Holland

◆   ❖   ◆

SHOW: THE VERY FISHY MATTER
SHOW DATE: 1/15/1961
COMPANY: GREATER SOUTHWEST INSURANCE COMPANY
AGENT: THEODORE JARVIS
EXP. ACCT: $245.50

SYNOPSIS: Theodore Jarvis calls from Las Vegas and asks about the weather in Hartford. The weather is nice and warm in Nevada, can you fly on out? Johnny agrees to come if he can be guaranteed time to drop a fishing line at either Lake Mead or Lake Mojave Resort. That is exactly what Jarvis wants Johnny to do, among other things, like escorting a very lovely and wealthy young lady. And the expense account is virtually unlimited. Johnny is on his way!

Johnny senses that there is something fishy with this case. Johnny flies to Las Vegas and cabs to Ted Jarvis' office, about the only place in Vegas without a slot machine, besides the offices and churches. Ted tells Johnny that this case is about the Lisa Birdwell fortune. Jarvis wants Johnny to go fishing with Lisa at Lake Mojave. Lisa used to be a schoolteacher in Salt Lake City, and considered becoming a Mormon. When her father died he left her $10,000-$12,000 and she decided to have a little fling. When she came to Vegas she discovered the roulette wheel and won over $400,000 and stopped gambling. Lisa bought a small ranch and brought her foster brother Tony to manage the ranch. Now she is just enjoying life by cruising around on her 52-foot yacht. Ted is afraid that if anything happens to Lisa, Tony will get all the money. Get down to the lake as Tony has already arranged for Lisa to be murdered.

Ted is sure that Tony has planned the murder because when he called the ranch last night, he accidentally got connected to a phone call in which Tony promised someone $10,000 to kill Lisa. Ted tells Johnny that he gasped and Tony hung up. Ted is sure that someone on the boat is going to kill her. Ted called Lisa, who pooh-poohed the idea. She is fishing with a crowd that includes: Jim Furee, a dealer in town with a bad reputation; Sadie Reese, a B-girl to put it kindly; Clara Hinkley a visiting school teacher Lisa picked up somewhere; Charles Shroder, an elder in the Mormon church, and Paul Holder, who runs the boat for her. One of these people is going to kill her. Johnny rents a car and drives to Lake Mojave Resort and meets with Ham Pratt. Ham tells Johnny that Lisa left about an hour ago, and that the boat will not be hard to miss. They were probably headed for the Big Basin area. All of the guests arrived last night at the same time, except for Paul who runs the boat. Johnny asks for a boat, fishing gear and a string of big fish. Johnny takes the boat up the lake, finds the yacht and fakes a running out of gas by Lisa's boat. Johnny comes on board and Lisa invites him to stay as long as he likes after she sees the string of fish Johnny has. Johnny spends the day and shows Paul where to take the boat to catch fish. Johnny is invited to say with them and he accepts so that he can survey the guests. Paul holder is a friendly young man. Jim Furee is tall, dark and suave, and who would kill his own mother for a prize. Sadie Reese is happy as long as Jim is there to bait her hook. Clara Hinkley fished alone because of her shrill voice and incessant talking. Charles Shroder spent most of his time talking to Lisa from the Book of Mormon. Johnny joins them and the conversation ends. Johnny offers cigarettes and both Charles and Lisa accept. Lisa tells Johnny that she has had an uneasy feeling and is afraid, and wants Johnny to look after her. After a fish dinner, everyone goes to bed. Later Johnny switches cabins with Lisa and puts a rolled up blanket in her bed. Johnny goes on deck to wait and falls asleep. Later there are shots and Johnny runs down to Lisa's cabin where everyone is gathered. The dummy is discovered and Charles is glad that Lisa is ok. Jim notes that Johnny's boat is missing and Johnny tells them that he used the boat just to get on board. Paul is told to make coffee and they talk. Johnny tells the group why he is there and that one of the group is a phony. Johnny's tells them that his boat had been cut loose to mislead the others. Jim is told that he is a gambler and a likely suspect because he has a prison record, and there is nothing phony about Sadie or Clara. Johnny tells Paul that he is not the phony either. Johnny points to Charles as the phony and Charles pulls a gun and tells them that there is a bullet in it for each of them. Paul breaks a pitcher on Charles' head and Johnny gets the gun away from him. Johnny tells Lisa that Charles claimed to be an Elder in the Mormon Church, and that he had accepted a cigarette earlier that day. But Morons do not smoke or drink coffee.

"Well, he talked all right, plenty. And of course he implicated Lisa's foster brother Tony. So now it is all up to the courts.

NOTES:
- THERE IS NEW JAZZIER MUSIC DURING THE PROGRAM NOW, WITH THE SAME THEME AT THE BEGINNING AND THE END.
- THE FIRST COMMERCIAL BREAK IS ABOUT RADIO FREE EUROPE FUND.
- THE SECOND COMMERCIAL BREAK IS FOR THE "ARTHUR GODFREY TIME" SHOW WITH THE KIRBY STONE FOUR, DICK HARMON AND SINGER KING LING.
- MANDEL KRAMER IS TED, TERRI KEANE IS LISA, JIM BOLES IS HAM, DANNY OCKO IS CHARLES, BILL MASON IS PAUL, JOAN LORRING IS SADIE, ROBERT DRYDEN IS JIM
- MUSICAL SUPERVISION IS BY ETHEL HUBER
- THE ANNOUNCER IS ART HANNES

Producer: Bruno Zirato, Jr.   **Writers:** Jack Johnstone

Cast: **Mandel Kramer, Terri Keane, Jim Boles, Danny Ocko,
Bill Mason, Joan Lorring, Robert Dryden**

◆   ❖   ◆

SHOW:	THE SHORT TERM MATTER
SHOW DATE:	1/29/1961
COMPANY:	NEW JERSEY STATE MUTUAL LIFE INSURANCE COMPANY
AGENT:	BILL TILTON
EXP. ACCT:	$82.80

SYNOPSIS: Bill Tilton calls and Johnny is terrible. Johnny asks Bill if he wants to buy a pair of skis. Johnny is terrible because of the North Slope over on Chickapee Mountain in New Hampshire. Johnny tells Bill that he and Doc Hubble were skiing when his chair broke loose and he fell on his back. The doc is making him wear a corset, a sacro-lumbar support, and Johnny can hardly breathe. Bill tells Johnny that he will find someone else, even though it is Larry Moody that he has a line on. "Fingers Moody," the safe operator? Johnny tells Bill that he will not let anyone else have a crack at him—Ohhhhhhh!!

Johnny moves slowly with the corset, but feels better with the prospect of getting Moody. Johnny flies to Patterson, New Jersey to meet with Bill, who chastises Johnny for trying to be superman and tells Johnny that he will not handle the case. Bill relents and tells Johnny that Moody pulled a job 4 years ago in Chicago. Johnny recalls how he had followed every false lead Moody left until a state trooper picked him up. Bill tells Johnny that night before last $33,000 was taken from a store in Patterson, and Bill is sure that it was Moody because of the modus operandi, three witnesses and a trail of $5 bills leading to an alley. Bill gets a call from the police and they tell him that Moody has been picked up in Pemberton, New Jersey but the money was not with him. Bill tells Johnny to find the $33,000.

Johnny walks to police headquarters and meets with Lt. Walter Ivin who gives Johnny directions to Pemberton. Johnny is told that Pemberton will not let Moody loose until they get him for running down a citizen with his car. Irvin is sure that Moody will not get out on bail, so they have all the time in the world. Johnny asks about the jail and is told that it is adequate. Johnny notes that he has a little stunt that, if it works, might lead to the money. Lt. Irvin remembers the Merryman case in Chicago, and is sure that Moody will tell them nothing about the money. Lt. Irvin asks about the stunt, but Johnny tells him that he would not let Johnny get away with it. (Ohhhh! This darn corset!) Johnny goes back to Bill's office and empties his pockets and leaves his cashmere jacket. Johnny borrows Bill's car and tells Bill he will see him in jail. Johnny buys an extra key to the car and some other things. In Pemberton, Johnny looks for a police officer and fakes an accident by running into him. Johnny is thrown into a cell with Moody. Johnny tells him that they will not keep Johnny in that jail, as he will break out. "Alone?" asks Moody. "That depends," Johnny tells Moody.

Johnny tells Moody that for a price, he will take Moody with him. Johnny tells Moody that the man he hit has died and Moody gets anxious and begs Johnny to take him for $5,000, no $10,000 and then half of the money, then $20,000. Johnny tells Moody that in the corset he has some hacksaw blades and an extra key. Pretty Smart, eh? After midnight Johnny and Moody cut their way out and drives to New Lisbon. Along the railroad tracks Johnny is told to stop at a tool shed. Moody goes to the shed and Johnny watches him get a sack and return with the money and a gun. Johnny is told to "get out of the car, Mr. Johnny Dollar!" Moody tells Johnny that he knows that Johnny had chased him all over the country four years earlier, and that he recognized Johnny's voice. When Moody aims to shoot Johnny tells him that a car is approaching without it's lights, and that means the police, and Moody runs away shooting.

"You know something? That was a police car. It had been following us all the way from the jail in Pemberton. And the only reason they let us break out was because Bill Tilton, reading my mind I guess, had called the chief of police and told them who I was. And the chief figured out why I had gotten myself locked up and what I was up to. He and his boys nabbed Larry Moody with no trouble at all. The moral of the story? Don't ever underestimate the ability of a small town cop. Oh, I uh beg your pardon, police officer."

NOTES:
- THE FIRST COMMERCIAL BREAK IS FOR DONES PILLS FOR BACK ACHES.
- THE SECOND COMMERCIAL BREAK IS FOR COMMANDER CIGARETTES.
- MUSICAL SUPERVISION IS BY ETHEL HUBER
- THE ANNOUNCER IS ART HANNES
- ROBERT DRYDEN IS BILL, SANTOS ORTEGA IS LARRY, LAWSON ZERBE IS LT. IVIN, JACK GRIMES IS THE OFFICER

Producer: **Bruno Zirato, Jr.**   Writers: **Jack Johnstone**
Cast: **Robert Dryden, Santos Ortega, Lawson Zerbe, Jack Grimes**

SHOW: THE WHO'S WHO MATTER
SHOW DATE: 2/5/1961
COMPANY: WESTERN INDEMNITY COMPANY, GREATER SOUTHWEST
AGENT: TED BECKHAM
EXP. ACCT: $306.25

SYNOPSIS: Johnny is called by a man who had trouble getting Johnny's number and finally had to call Pat McCracken at the Universal Adjustment Bureau. He thought Johnny was going to drop by and pick up his check for his services on that oil refinery case he handled last week. The caller is Ted Beckham in Fort Worth, and he has approved Johnny's expenses for the investigation. Johnny tells him that the only case he handled last week was in Hartford, and the week before he was in Little Rock, Arkansas, and the week before that he was also in Hartford and before that in Los Angeles. Ted gets angry and tells Johnny that he is not Johnny Dollar, but an imposter who is impersonating Johnny Dollar.

Johnny is upset by the phone call accusing him of impersonating himself. The phone rings again and Pat McCracken asks if Beckham has called? Pat tells Johnny that Beckham heads up a new company, but Pat wants Johnny to go to Dallas, Texas and look into an arson case for Al Pinker at Greater Southwest. Johnny tells Pat that he will handle both cases; he will kill two birds with one stone. Johnny flies to Fort Worth, Texas and cabs to the Western Indemnity office. Johnny bullies his way into Beckham's office and shows him his credentials. Beckham admits that he is Johnny Dollar. Beckham tells Johnny that another young man had done some investigations for him and said that he was Johnny Dollar. He did a good job for Beckham, but the size of expense accounts made him suspicious. Beckham called about the expense account because the other Johnny Dollar had agreed to come in to pick up the check. After talking to Johnny in Hartford, Beckham was suspicious because of the amount of the check. Al Pinker comes to the office and greets Johnny. Al tells Johnny that he has a real problem with the Geary Brothers Department Store fire. Beckham tells Al that he also has a policy on that building, and the other Johnny Dollar is investigating the fire. Johnny tells Al that he is there to run down two people; a firebug and a guy named Johnny Dollar.

Al and Johnny drive to Dallas, Texas and Johnny updates him on the double. Al describes the fire, which Johnny does not think is too complicated a matter for the police, but agrees to look into it for Al. Johnny gets a room at the Statler Hilton and drives to the department store to look around. Johnny sees that the fire was on the second floor of the building and hears a voice cry out "Who's there?" and then there are shots. Suddenly the scene is silent and then the voice tells Johnny to give up and there are more shots. Johnny tries to move to another spot and ends up falling through the floor. When Johnny wakes up he is on the floor and his gun and his ID are gone. The police arrive and slug Johnny so he will not shoot anymore.

Johnny wakes up in police headquarters with a police guard. The guard is sent to look at the papers that were just brought in from the scene and the sergeant tells Johnny that the other investigator found the clues to pin the arson on Jerry Springer, a professional torch man. Just when their investigator was going to come in and report, you show up and try to shoot him. The sergeant tells Johnny that the other man is named Johnny dollar. The first policeman brings in Johnny's real ID and the police are confused. Johnny decides to run the other man down for the police. Johnny drives to the Western Indemnity office Ft. Worth and picks the lock to get in. Johnny sees the envelope addressed to Johnny Dollar and the check on the desk. The door opens and the secretary enters and tells someone that she wondered when he was going to get there. She turns on the light and sees Johnny sitting at the desk as she reaches to give the other Johnny his check. Johnny tells him that he should have taken a better look last night and the impostor pulls a gun. He tells Johnny that he is going to leave and Johnny asks him how long he was going to try and get away with his act by solving crimes he had set up? The impostor tells Johnny and the secretary to get into a closet. Then Beckham arrives causing a distraction that allows Johnny to slug the impostor. Beckham tells Johnny that he suspected the man as soon as he got the expense account. He knew all about Johnny, but the expense report was so small Beckham knew the first man could not be Johnny Dollar!

"OK, then Mr. Beckham, on the strength of that last remark, I will not expect you to question this expense account."

NOTES:
- THE FIRST COMMERCIAL BREAK IS FOR HEART MONTH IN FEBRUARY AND THE DRIVE FOR RESEARCH FUNDS.
- ETHEL HUBER DOES THE MUSICAL SUPERVISION.
- IAN MARTIN IS TED, BILL STERLING IS AL, LAWSON ZERBE IS PAT, BILL LIPTON IS THE OFFICER, ROSEMARY RICE IS CAROL, ROGER DE KOVEN IS THE SERGEANT, LEON JANNEY IS THE MAN
- THE ANNOUNCER IS ART HANNES

Producer: Bruno Zirato, Jr.   **Writers:** Jack Johnstone
Cast: Ian Martin, Bill Sterling, Lawson Zerbe, Bill Lipton, Rosemary Rice, Roger De Koven, Leon Janney

SHOW:	THE WAYWARD FIREMAN MATTER
SHOW DATE:	2/12/1961
COMPANY:	MASTERS INSURANCE & TRUST COMPANY
AGENT:	HARRISON HADLEY
EXP. ACCT:	$227.00

SYNOPSIS: Harrison Hadley calls Johnny from Buffalo and his problem is two fires. One occurred yesterday and one is still burning. Harrison will arrange for a room at the Statler for Johnny. So far the total insurance coverage is $400,000. "Then you can afford my expense account for two," Johnny tells him. "I don't understand," answers Hadley. "You will when you see me," replies Johnny.

Johnny is sure that a lot of people think that most crimes are solved by a lot of Sherlock Holmes type deduction, or by the equally mysterious scientific razza-matazz that goes on inside some of the fabulous crime labs. But most of Johnny's crimes are solved by hard work, and information from stoolies. Johnny calls Smokey Sullivan, who is working in Syracuse, but is on vacation. His new job is working for the city as a special consultant for the arson squad. Smokey is sure that all the firebugs have left town since he got there. Johnny tells Smokey to go to Buffalo and wait for him at the Statler. Johnny flies to Buffalo, New York and is met at the airport by Harry Hadley. Harry tells Johnny that the police are sure that the first fire at a small department store was arson, and that the owner has had problems paying his bills. That fire was worth $200,000. The second fire was at the Strath Rubber Company warehouse.

The owner is named Morley and has been having financial troubles. The police are sure that the same method was used in both fires, but they do not know how they were set. Johnny is sure that his friend will know. Johnny and Harry go to his hotel room and hear a window close. Inside they find Smokey unconscious on the floor.

Johnny gets a bottle of brandy for Smokey, who was beaten badly. Smokey comes to and tells Johnny that he does not want a doctor. Smokey tells Johnny that he was beaten by "Bottles" Burton who uses chemicals to set fires. He is a bad one, and a pyromaniac since he was a kid. They put Burton into an institution and let him shovel coal into the furnace to try and cure him, but he is still sick. He does not set fires for money, only for himself. Smokey tells Johnny that Bottles always sets three fires on three days in a row. Smokey is sure that Bottles knows Johnny is in town as he was surprised to see Smokey in the room when he came there. Harry tells Johnny that he did call the police, and Johnny surmises that if a reporter was there, Burton must know that Johnny is in town. But Smokey tells Johnny that Burton thinks Johnny is dead. Smokey is sure that Burton will not set the fire tonight. Smokey tells Johnny that Burton always gets a job around fire, like as a fireman or at a powerhouse or a blast furnace; somewhere where there is fire. Johnny tells Harry to get the word out to the press that Smokey is dead and his body is in the morgue, but Smokey will stay in the hotel.

Johnny cabs to police headquarters to get a mug shot of Burton and then checks all the firehouses until he finds one where a fireman named Charlie Smith works, or used to. He seems to have disappeared a couple days earlier. He was a good man and always seemed to enjoy his work. Johnny returns to the hotel and moves Smokey to an adjoining room. Smokey tells Johnny that Burton may go nuts waiting for Johnny to leave town, and Johnny has an idea. Johnny goes to radio station WBEN and talks to Bill Peters, the program manager who had made the announcement that Johnny was in town. Johnny is sure that Burton keeps tabs via the news broadcasts, so Johnny writes an article for the newscaster Jack Ogilvy to read. Back in his room Johnny listens to the broadcast as Jack reports that Johnny Dollar is leaving the case due to the death of his colleague Smokey Sullivan. "Dollar has checked out. But is he afraid of the pyromaniac killer?" Smokey comes out and tells Johnny he is fine and then collapses "Oh, fine." moans Johnny as he carries Smokey back to bed. Later there is a knock at the door announcing a telegram, but Burton is there when Johnny opens the door. Burton pushes his way in with a gun and makes Johnny sit facing away from him. Burton is going to kill Johnny so that he can set another fire. Burton take's Johnny's gun and knows he has to kill him. Smokey comes in and breaks a chair over Burton's head, and collapses again.

"Well, it is up to the courts, naturally. This time I'm betting there will be no parole for Burton, ever. Not only because of the fires, but the murder attempt on Smokey. And, come to think of it, on me! As for the insurance money, that will have to be paid out. Well, you can't win 'em all."

NOTES:
- BREAK #1 IS FOR THE HEART FUND AND THE NEED FOR MONEY FOR RESEARCH
- BREAK #2 IS FOR COMMANDER CIGARETTES
- NAT POLEN IS SMOKEY, BILL SMITH IS HARRISON, BERNARD GRANT IS BURTON, GEORGE PETRIE IS GEORGE PETERS, ROBERT DRYDEN IS THE CHIEF, JACK OGILVIE PLAYED HIMSELF
- MUSICAL SUPERVISION IS BY ETHEL HUBER
- THE ANNOUNCER IS ART HANNES

Producer: Bruno Zirato, Jr.   Writers: Jack Johnstone
Cast: Nat Polen, Bill Smith, George Petrie, Bernard Grant, Robert
            Dryden, Jack Ogilvie

SHOW: THE TOUCH-UP MATTER
SHOW DATE: 2/26/1961
COMPANY: STAR MUTUAL INSURANCE COMPANY
AGENT: TERRY HOLMES
EXP. ACCT: $0.00

SYNOPSIS: Terry Holmes calls Johnny at 2 AM from a party and needs Johnny to come over right away to the Chadwick residence on Weathersfield Avenue. No one has been murdered, but the company will murder him if they have to pay the claims on the biggest jewel robbery ever pulled in Hartford. Terry wants Johnny to come out.

Johnny dresses and drives to the Hartford, Connecticut residence of Bruno Chadwick, a local showplace mansion. In the library, Terry tells Johnny what has happened. The party was for the Chadwick's fortieth anniversary and the guests are most of the local wealthy people of Hartford including Mr. and Mrs. Lloyd Augustus Brownfield, the Fritz Melchiors, the Lawrence Comstocks, Kenneth Gordon Hodge, Mary Ann Hooper and a bunch more. A Mr. Thompson B. Thompson barged in to the party and said he was up from New York and wanted to discuss a business deal with Mr. Chadwick. He was young and handsome, so Mrs. Chadwick told him to stay, and he became the life of the party and the old women all tried to occupy his time while he cased the jewelry the ladies were wearing. They were in the music room listening to Mrs. Jackson Lee Kenworthy Price squawk out an encore of "Sweet Mystery of Life" when the lights went out. Mrs. Chadwick screamed about her necklace, and then all the other women screamed about theirs, and when the lights came on, two million worth of jewels and Mr. Thompson were gone. Lt. McQuaid walks in and tells Johnny that they have sent a police officer to the motel where Thompson was staying. He was registered there, but his car had Connecticut plates. Officer Conroy calls from the motor court and reports that the car was stolen as Thompson drives in. Lt. McQuaid shows Johnny a snapshot of Thompson taken with one of those new instant cameras, and tells him that Thompson did not object to having his photo taken at all. Officer Conroy calls back and he is sure that Thompson is there as he sees his shadow moving in his room. Officer Conroy is told not to disturb Thompson unless he tries to leave. Lt. McQuaid and Johnny leave for "an easy kill." At the Pearson Motor Court they meet officer Conroy and go to unit 7. Lt. McQuaid knocks at the door and gets no answer. They break in the door to find no one there. Johnny notices a pinwheel device on the lamp that is making the shadows on the window shade. Officer Conroy finds an open window and gets a chewing out from Lt. McQuaid. Johnny finds all the missing jewelry lying on the floor under a table. Officer Conroy is sure that Thompson knew the police were there, so he left the jewels and ran. Lt. McQuaid tells Officer Conroy his stupidity paid off, and Johnny tells Officer Conroy that he left his squad car parked right where Thompson could see it when he came back.

Back at the Chadwick Mansion, everyone was happy to get the jewels back, and Terry is relieved that he will not have to pay the claims. Everyone thanks Johnny for finding the jewels so quickly and he tells them that it was the police who did the work. Terry and Johnny talk about how Thompson will need to be captured. Johnny notes how Thompson seemed to use makeup to make himself look younger and how he made sure that everyone knew where he was staying and wonders why he went back to the motel. That all adds up to a hunch. Johnny borrows the jewelry to play his hunch.

Next morning Johnny takes the jewels to a jeweler named Caldwell, who tells Johnny that they are beautiful, but paste, imitations. Johnny knows now that no one would suspect anything until the jewels were cleaned, so Thompson had all the time in the world to disappear quietly. Lt. McQuaid walks in and Johnny gives him the all the jewels but one to return and leaves telling Caldwell to give Lt. McQuaid the good news. Johnny is amazed at how neatly things fell into place. Johnny returns Mrs. Chadwick's necklace and Johnny asks to borrow the instant camera. Johnny also asks where the jewelry is cleaned and Mrs. Chadwick tells him she uses Rickter's, as they would trust no one else. All the ladies use Rickters. Johnny goes to Mr. Rickter who takes Johnny to the back room where the jewels are cleaned and mounted. Johnny takes a number of pictures, supposedly for a magazine story, and stops at the bench of a lean middle-aged man who is Ernest, a new employee, but their best stone setter. Johnny is told that Ernest is leaving for a new job in Philadelphia next week. Johnny asks to take a photo of Ernest standing up straight. Johnny asks Mr. Rickter to have the photo retouched. When Rickter says "Of course, Mr. Dollar," Ernest knows who Johnny is. When Mr. Rickter tells Ernest he does not look well, he tells Rickter that Mr. Dollar knows why. Johnny tells Ernest that he would get the jewels in for cleaning and make copies of them. Last night he stole the real jewels, and left the copies in the motel room for the police to find. Ernest tells Johnny that, as they say in the movies, he will go along quietly.

"The gems he had stolen, we picked them up in his apartment and then took them along to police headquarters. It's funny. Lt. McQuaid even forgot to bawl me out for keeping that first picture of Ernest. Expense account total, what expense account? But believe me, I want a nice fee out of this one!"

NOTES:
- THE ANNOUNCER IS WALLY KING
- MUSICAL SUPERVISION IS BY ETHEL HUBER
- THE CAST IS LISTED IN ORDER OF THEIR APPEARANCE.
- JACK JOHNSTONE LOVED TO RECYCLE NAMES. NAMED IN THIS EPISODE ARE: AUGUSTUS BROWNFIELD WHO WAS A CHARACTER IN "THE CANNED CANARY MATTER"; FRED/FRITZ MELCHIOR WHO WAS THE AGENT IN "THE HAIR RAISING MATTER" AND "THE MYSTERY GAL MATTER" AND A CHARACTER IN "THE DEADLY CHAIN MATTER"; LAWRENCE COMSTOCK WAS A CHARACTER IN "THE LAMARR MATTER"; KENNY HODGE IS NOTED AS AN ASSOCIATE DIRECTOR OF THE PROGRAM IN "THE FIVE DOWN MATTER"; AND MARY ANN HOOPER IS THE NAME OF A CHARACTER IN "THE HARRIED HEIRESS MATTER" AND "THE MISSING MATTER MATTER" THE NAME CHADWICK APPEARS IN NUMEROUS CONTEXTS BOTH AS CHARACTERS AND CREW.

Producer:	Bruno Zirato, Jr. Writers: Jack Johnstone
Cast:	Jim Stevens, Carl Frank, Lawson Zerbe, Bill Lipton, Elsbeth Eric, Jean Gillespie, Guy Repp, Raymond Edward Johnson, Luis Van Rooten, Bob Dryden

◆ ❖ ◆

SHOW:	THE MORNING AFTER MATTER
SHOW DATE:	3/5/1961
COMPANY:	AMALGAMATED LIFE ASSOCIATION
AGENT:	TIMOTHY HANDLEY
EXP. ACCT:	$0.00

SYNOPSIS: Timothy Handley calls and needs Johnny's services. Johnny tells him he is heading out to go fishing in South Carolina. Handley tells Johnny that he is waiting for him at 500 Fifth Avenue. Goodbye.

Johnny is ready for a vacation at the Arundel Plantation in South Carolina, but he flies to New York City and goes to Penn Station to catch his train to South Carolina. Sucker that he is, Johnny takes a cab to Handley's office where Handley tells Johnny that Mrs. Brownberg should be there soon. She had insisted that Johnny be brought into the case. "Brownberg? Hmm." Johnny is told that she is the wife of Thaddeus Brownberg who flew his own plane, and disappeared after he lost his fortune on Wall Street. Brownberg lost his memory just before he left, and his plane was found in the Alleghenies. The insurance payment of over $600,000 has been held up. Mrs. Lita Spencer Brownberg comes in and barks at Johnny to "Sit down and let me tell you something. You must find my husband, and you must find him before this Wednesday." Johnny is told that on Wednesday there is a hearing, and if he does not come back, he will be declared dead. She could really use the money, because when he disappeared there was less than $100,000 in the joint bank account, and she has had to scrape and scrimp ever since. Johnny tells her that things will not be so bad if he is declared dead, and she gets indignant. She tells Johnny it was the cold-blooded insurance company that ordered the hearing. Handley tries to weasel his way out by saying that there is no hope because the police have not been able to find him. Mrs. Brownberg knows all about Johnny and the miraculous way he solves his cases and she gives him a picture of Thad. "Now you have to find him," she snarls and storms out of the office. Handley implores Johnny to do something. Johnny looks at the picture and wonders.

Johnny tells Handley that he is not sure about the picture, but thinks the face looks familiar. Johnny leaves to go to the police 18th precinct and talk to his friend Randy Singer. Johnny asks their artist Billy Cross to copy the picture and make it up with over 50 different hairstyles and beards. Johnny thinks one with a head looks familiar. Later that night Billy tells Johnny to give up like everyone else. Johnny rushes to Mrs. Brownberg's penthouse apartment at midnight and listens to her yammer on about poor old Thad. She is sure that he would not kill himself. He loved to fish, and would just take off and go. Suddenly Johnny sees a mounted fish and knows just where it came from. Johnny calls Handley and tells him he is going fishing!

The lunker bass could have only come from one place. Johnny flies to Los Angeles and on to Las Vegas where he rents a car and drives to Lake Mojave Resort. Johnny talks to Ham Pratt and shows him a picture of a man with a beard. Ham recognizes the man as Ted Bennam, who has been fishing here for 6-7 years. He does not seem to know much about his past, and hangs out at Cottonwood Cove up the lake. Johnny and Ham drive up the lake in Ham's boat to Cottonwood Cove. At the cove Johnny spots Ted Bennam and calls him Mr. Brownberg. Ted knows who Johnny is and tells him he has been expecting him to show up sooner or later. Over drinks they talk, and Johnny likes him. Ted stubbornly maintains his identity until Johnny asks for fingerprints. Ted tells Johnny that he knew Thaddeus Brownberg and that he never suffered from amnesia, and that he lost most of his fortune deliberately. He could make money but his wife's extravagance kept demanding more and more. She only wanted his money. Ted gets Johnny another drink and tells him that the wife only wanted him to be there so he could build up another fortune for her to go through, and he finally realized this and that she did not love him. He realized he could be free of her and the nerve-wracking fight to make money for her by disappearing and providing for her. After the hearing tomorrow, Thad will not exist. He will be free and she will be well off. "Don't you see Mr. Dollar?" Johnny suddenly feels woozy and tries to fight the drugs in the drink but loses. Johnny wakes up to the smell of coffee. Johnny tells Ted that he knows all about the woman, but he has to get him back. Ted tells Johnny that it is Thursday, and that Thaddeus Brownberg is dead. Ted suggests that they go out on the lake and talk. Johnny has a better idea. "Let's go out on the lake and fish, Mr. Bennam!

"And so we fished, and it was great, all three days of it. Right? Wrong? I don't know. Who is to judge? As for the expense account, forget it."

NOTES:
- THE FIRST COMMERCIAL BREAK IS DENNIS JAMES FOR ALL BRAN CEREAL.
- THE SECOND COMMERCIAL BREAK IS FOR COMMANDER CIGARETTES.
- GERTRUDE WARNER IS LITA, CARL FRANK IS THADDEUS, ROBERT DRYDEN IS TIMOTHY, BILL STERLING IS BILLY, JIM BOLES IS HAM.
- ART HANNES IS THE ANNOUNCER.
- MUSICAL SUPERVISION IS BY ETHEL HUBER

Producer:　Bruno Zirato, Jr.　　　**Writers:**　Jack Johnstone
Cast:　　Gertrude Warner, Carl Frank, Robert Dryden, Bill Sterling, Jim Boles

◆　❖　◆

SHOW:　　THE RING OF DEATH MATTER
SHOW DATE:　3/12/1961
COMPANY:　SURETY MUTUAL INSURANCE COMPANY
AGENT:　　DON PINKLEY
EXP. ACCT:　$389.00

SYNOPSIS: Don Pinkley calls Johnny from New Orleans, and he has a small problem as long as Johnny knows a little about boxing. Johnny remembers winning $20 from Tom on a boxer named Touchy Tarantino, a fighter with a future. "Not any more, Johnny" Don tells Johnny. "It is suicide or murder. Fly on down and I'll tell you."

Johnny flies to New Orleans, Louisiana, gets a room at the Roosevelt Hotel and explores the town, "The most interesting city in the country" it's called. The next morning Johnny meets with Don, who tells Johnny that Tony Tarantino is insured for $25,000, and was a promising fighter, with a nice wife named Angie. He has done well physically, but has a crooked promoter named Raul Martinez. Recently in Los Angeles Tony fell out of the ring, and Raul left him flat. Now Martinez has another fight for Tony, but a doctor in Los Angeles told Tony that one blow to the left of his head would kill him. The fight is tomorrow in Mexico, but Don does not know where. But Johnny will try to find out. Johnny calls his friend Johnny Ortez at police headquarters and finds out where Tony was taken from a stoolie named Miguel Andrati. For $50 Johnny gets the name of a small town in Mexico, withheld for diplomatic reasons. Johnny flies to Brownsville, Texas and cabs to the small town in Mexico. Johnny sees the posters for the fight between Tony and Pancho Gutierrez. Johnny finds Tony's wife in a hotel. She had discovered where Tony was, and wants Johnny to save her husband. She tells Johnny that Raul has Tony tied up in the coliseum, and Tony will believe everything Raul says. Johnny is sure that there is no way that Tony can beat Pancho. Angie tells Johnny that the odds are on Tony for the fight, and Johnny realizes that Raul's money is on Pancho. A man named Jose enters the room and tells Angie that she had better sit or he will kill her. Jose tells Johnny that he had better forget about this matter if he wants to live. Jose slugs Johnny to keep him quiet.

Johnny wakes up on top of a rubbish heap in Brownsville, minus his gun. Johnny cabs back to the town and goes to the coliseum and Tony's dressing room. Johnny meets a punch-drunk Tony who is convinced he is ok, because Raul says he is. Tony tells Johnny that he is going to take a dive in the fourth round, but Johnny suggests that is it not like Tony to do that. Tony tells Johnny that this fight will be enough for him to make some money and make a new start. Tony had gone back to Raul after Los Angeles because he was broke and had told Raul he had to help him. That is why he is there. Johnny asks if Tony knows for sure if the fight is fixed. Johnny tells Tony that he is being set up for a sucker, but Tony does not believe him. Johnny tells Tony that Angie is there and will be in the area tonight. Tony is worried because she will know it if he takes a dive. Jose meets Johnny in the hallway and tries to slug Johnny again, but Johnny gets the best of him and locks him in a closet. Johnny overhears Raul talking to Tony, and Raul tells Tony that if Johnny comes back he will be shot, just like Pancho will kill Tony if he does not take the dive.

Johnny rushes to the police and talks to the chief, but the name of Martinez elicits only a shrug, and eventually gets Johnny kicked out of the office. Johnny realizes that Martinez must have the town under his thumb. Johnny goes back to see Angie and is told that she has left with Jose. Johnny searches the town but cannot find her. Johnny buys a ticket for the fight and spots Angie in the back of the arena. Johnny goes to her but Raul puts a gun in Johnny's side and they watch the fight. The fight starts and the Tony starts to tire quickly, and by the fourth Pancho is trying to set Tony up, but Tony lasts out the round. Pancho constantly tries to hit the left side of Tony's head, but Tony fends him off. In the sixth round Tony manages to nail Pancho with a right uppercut and knocks Pancho out. The crown goes wild, but Johnny senses the gun moving as Raul aims it at Tony. Johnny swings at Raul and the gun goes of in Raul's face.

"Yes, Martinez was dead. And of course, the police moved in. And when they realized that he was definitely, finally out of the way, I'm sure they all breathed a deep sincere sigh of relief. And believe it or not, Angie and Tony and I got a formal escort back to the border that was fit for royalty."

NOTES:
- THE FIRST COMMERCIAL BREAK IS DENNIS JAMES FOR KELLOGG'S ALL-BRAN
- THE SECOND COMMERCIAL BREAK IS FOR COMMANDER CIGARETTES
- ROBERT DRYDEN IS TOUCHY, JOAN LORRING IS ANGIE, RALPH CAMAGO IS MARTINEZ, MANDEL KRAMER IS DON, DANNY OCKO IS JOSE
- ART HANNES IS THE ANNOUNCER.
- MUSICAL SUPERVISION IS BY ETHEL HUBER

• THIS IS A REMAKE WITH VARIATIONS OF "THE SQUARED CIRCLE MATTER."

Producer: Bruno Zirato, Jr.   **Writers:** Jack Johnstone
Cast: Robert Dryden, Joan Lorring, Ralph Camago, Mandel Kramer, Danny Ocko

◆ ❖ ◆

SHOW: THE INFORMER MATTER
SHOW DATE: 3/19/1961
COMPANY: PHILADELPHIA MUTUAL LIABILITY & CASUALTY INSURANCE
AGENT: HARRY BRANSON
EXP. ACCT: $115.20

SYNOPSIS: [The opening is missing.] Johnny notes how informers play a big part in solving of crimes, and this caller was one of those. But Johnny did not keep him on long enough to make him tell what he knew. Johnny calls Pat McCracken and Pat tells him he will have to call all the companies they cover. The name was Phillip, or Phil Bernesconi, and the caller says he was murdered? Johnny tells Pat that the caller was named Fred Ackerlloyd, and had told Johnny what he had told Pat, and hung up. Johnny had tried the local directories and the operator, but could not find a number for anyone named Ackerlloyd. Pat tells Johnny to forget it, but Johnny has a hunch. Johnny remembers seeing a stack of phone directories in Pat's office and arranges to come in and look at them. Johnny cabs to Pat's office and looks through the phone books. Pat picks up a phone book from Vineland, New Jersey his hometown, and discovers the name of Fred Ackerlloyd in it at 2424 E. Elmer Street. Johnny rushes off to Philadelphia and wonders if Pat is right. Johnny rents a car and drives to Vineland, New Jersey, gets a room in the hotel and starts to look for Mr. Ackerlloyd. The clerk at the desk gives Johnny a telegram from Pat that tells Johnny he was right. "It was murder. You are on expense account."

Johnny is told to contact Branson at Philadelphia Mutual. Johnny asks the desk clerk if he knew Bernesconi, and Johnny is told that the clerk is not a bit surprised that he was murdered. He kept to himself, but no one could figure out how he could retire, as he was in his mid-fifties. Then they learned that he had been in the rackets and had not done well by his friends. Johnny makes a phone call to Harry Branson who, in spite of several interruptions by Johnny, tells John to "come right down and go to Vineland, New Jersey as Phillip Bernesconi, insured for $30,000, has been murdered. The police thought it was an accident, which would have made it $60,000, but the chief tells me . . . what did you say? Johnny tells Harry he is in Vineland. Johnny asks who the beneficiary is, and Harry tells him it is Harvey Renzolli, the chief of police. Johnny tells Harry that he does not want to see him yet, as Renzolli had promised Bernesconi protection from his old gangster pals. Johnny drives to the Ackerlloyd house on Elmer Street where he meets an old man who is the landlord. Johnny knocks and a tall young man with black hair and a hat opens the door. Johnny asks for Ackerlloyd and is invited in. After confirming who Johnny is, the man tells Johnny that they will have to kill him the same way they will kill Ackerlloyd. Johnny and draws his gun, a shot is fired and Johnny is hit and knocked unconscious by the man. The man calls for Lucy to tell the landlord the shots were a backfire while he goes to get Ackerlloyd and they can leave town.

Lucy tells the landlord that the noise was a backfire, and that the other man had left out the back. Lucy gets rid of the man, and Johnny manages to grab her, even with a gunshot to the ribs. Johnny turns out all the lights and Lucy tells Johnny she is not part of the gang. Tony killed Bernesconi because the gang found out he was going straight and hanging out with cops. Fred Ackerlloyd was a friend of Phil's from the old days and had come down to warn Phil. Johnny rips Lucy's skirt and ties her up with it. Johnny watches Tony bring Ackerlloyd in and throw him on the floor. Tony turns on the lights and Johnny fights with Tony. Johnny goes down because of his wounds and Tony starts to shoot Johnny when the police enter. There is gunfire and Tony is hit. The chief comes in and tells Johnny to stay still as he does not look too good. The chief tells Johnny that Ackerlloyd used to be the bookkeeper for a mob in Philadelphia. When he came here and started hanging around with Phil, who was going straight, the chief had been keeping an eye on him. When Phil was killed the chief knew Ackerlloyd was innocent, but would not talk. The chief knew who Johnny is because Harry Branson had called. The landlord had called the chief and told him something funny was going on. The landlord comes in, sees what is going on, and faints. Johnny suggests they let him rest for a while.

"I understand that Tony recovered well enough to be tried and convicted in Bernesconi's murder. Lucy, his girl friend gave enough evidence against the mob in Philly to enable the police there to round them up. Where she is now, I don't know. Like Fred Ackerlloyd, she moved away, a long way away."

Johnny will welcome a big fat fee on this case.

NOTES:

- THE FIRST COMMERCIAL BREAK IS DENNIS JAMES FOR ALL BRAN cereal
- THE SECOND COMMERCIAL BREAK IS FOR COMMANDER cigarettes
- THE THIRD COMMERCIAL BREAK IS FOR BUICK SPECIALS THAT PLACED FIRST AND SECOND IN THE CLASS C US AUTO CLUB ECONOMY run
- JOHNNY IS SHOT FOR THE 11TH TIME
- WILLIAM REDFIELD IS TONY, LAWSON ZERBE IS PAT, RALPH BELL IS FRED, TERRI KEANE IS LUCY, BILL LIPTON IS THE CLERK, LARRY HAINES IS THE CHIEF.
- ART HANNES IS THE ANNOUNCER.
- MUSICAL SUPERVISION IS BY ETHEL HUBER

Producer: Bruno Zirato, Jr.   **Writers:**   Jack Johnstone
Cast: William Redfield, Lawson Zerbe, Ralph Bell, Terri Keane, Bill Lipton, Larry Haines

SHOW: THE TWO'S A CROWD MATTER
SHOW DATE: 3/26/1961
COMPANY: WORLDWIDE MUTUAL INSURANCE COMPANY
AGENT: PAUL FERRIS
EXP. ACCT: $379.50

SYNOPSIS: Paul Ferris calls Johnny from New York. Johnny has not spoken with Paul since the affair with Tony Valentine, who made a lot of noise about getting Johnny before Johnny could get him. Paul tells Johnny that Valentine has escaped with a man named Sandy Rhinehart. They pulled a red-light robbery the other night and killed the driver of the car; a man named Barton Osborne. Johnny is sure that Valentine is not a killer, but Paul tell Johnny that Osborne was a policyholder with coverage of $75,000 and the heirs want the company to investigate. Paul wants Johnny to investigate because he knows Valentine's habits.

Johnny recounts to Paul how Valentine was not a killer, but would pose as a highway patrol car to stop drivers at night and rob them with a pistol. Paul tells Johnny that Randy Singer thinks that Rhinehart pulled the trigger. Johnny flies to New York City and cabs to the 18th precinct. Johnny talks to Randy about Valentine, and Randy tells Johnny that they want Rhinehart. They have found the gun used in the robbery, and Rhinehart's prints are all over it. Also, a man matching Tony's description was seen boarding a plane to Oklahoma City hours after the robbery. The airline clerk identified Valentine from a picture. Officer Conroy enters and gives Randy a message. Johnny reminds Randy that Valentine was supposed to go to Overton, Oklahoma, as that is where Johnny thinks Valentine's money is stashed. Randy reads the message which is about Sgt. Mike Thomasson, who is the nephew of Osborne, and who does not know that Rhinehart is the killer. Thomasson has taken a vacation and gone to Oklahoma to follow the lead on Valentine. Thomasson is a crack shot and is really mad over the murder. Randy is sure that he will kill both Valentine and Rhinehart. Randy tells Johnny to go out and save Valentine's life.

Johnny thinks that all Randy has to do is call the Oklahoma City police and have them pick up Valentine; that is if he stays on in Oklahoma City. If Tony has gone to Overton and Thomasson finds him, no one will ever see Valentine again. Johnny cabs to the airport and flies to Oklahoma City, Oklahoma. Johnny recounts how Oklahoma City had been the center of the rush for free prairie land, but which has now grown to a city of over 300,000 people and is filled with sky scrapers and business. Johnny rents a car and drives to the police, and talks to a police captain, but they have not seen Valentine. They did talk to Randy and they know about Thomasson, who has searched the city for two days but found nothing in his unofficial investigation. Thomasson had come in and told the police he had some other leads he was following out of town. Johnny asks for directions to Overton and the captain tells Johnny that there is not much in Overton except for an old abandoned oil well called

"Bleeding Heart #1." Johnny is sure that the bleeding heart refers to Tony Valentine, and that he has stashed some of his loot there. Johnny leaves and drives north to Overton. After crossing the empty prairie, Johnny spots a railroad shack. Inside the shack, an old man is sleeping. Johnny goes in, wakes up the man, and shows him the picture of Tony Valentine. The man saw Tony around sundown going to the old oil well. The man has not seen anyone else. Johnny tells the man to watch out for anyone else who might come asking questions, for he is a killer. He might have credentials for the New York police, but do not believe him. Johnny starts to leave but a man blocks his way.

Johnny is sure that the man is Mike Thomasson, who does not know who Johnny is. Johnny notices a bad, mad look on his face. Johnny edges towards the desk, which has a lamp on it, but Thomasson comes in and recognizes that Johnny is not Valentine. He shows the old man the picture and the man tells Thomasson that he is a killer. Johnny calls him by name and he gets edgy allowing Johnny to knock over the lamp and dive for him. Thomasson fires and Johnny fights with him and overpowers him. Johnny drives to the oil well and parks his car. Johnny walks to the oil well and Johnny can see Valentine inside a shack collecting money from under the floor. Johnny kicks in the door and Valentine recognizes him. Johnny tells Tony that he knows that Rhinehart killed Osborne. Tony is relieved, but wants to take his money and skip the country. Johnny tells him he can go back with Johnny, or he can leave him for Thomasson, who thinks that Tony killed his uncle. Thomasson's car drives up and Tony wants Johnny to shoot him, but Johnny does not want to be a cop killer. Thomasson calls for Tony to come out and Johnny breaks a lantern and sets the shack on fire. Johnny tells Tony to show himself in the door as Johnny goes out the back. Johnny dives out the window and circles around to tackle Thomasson and knock him out. Tony gives Johnny a gun, and thinks they better head back to New York before Thomasson wakes up.

"Funny, I never did think to find out if Mike Thomasson kept his job on the force after that little episode. Tony of course is back in the pen finishing out a somewhat extended term."

NOTES:

- THE FIRST COMMERCIAL BREAK IS DENNIS JAMES FOR KELLOGG'S ALL-BRAN CEREAL.
- THE SECOND COMMERCIAL BREAK IS FOR COMMANDER CIGARETTES.
- BILL LIPTON IS TONY, LARRY HAINES IS RANDY, ROGER DE KOVEN IS MIKE, ROBERT COLE IS THE OLD MAN, MANDEL KRAMER IS THE POLICE CAPTAIN, JOSEPH JULIEN IS PAUL.
- ART HANNES IS THE ANNOUNCER.
- MUSICAL SUPERVISION IS BY ETHEL HUBER

Producer: Bruno Zirato, Jr.   **Writers:** Jack Johnstone

Cast: **Bill Lipton, Larry Haines, Roger De Koven, Robert Cole, Mandel Kramer, Joseph Julian**

◆   ❖   ◆

SHOW: THE WRONG SIGN MATTER
SHOW DATE: 4/2/1961
COMPANY: TRI-MUTUAL INSURANCE COMPANY
AGENT: HARLEY TILSON
EXP. ACCT: $129.30

SYNOPSIS: Harvey Tilson calls Johnny from Uniontown, Pennsylvania. He wants to make sure that a policy for $1.2 million is not paid to the wrong person. Can Johnny take the case? "Sure can."

Johnny flies to Pittsburgh and rents a car to drive to Uniontown, where Harvey's office is in the same building as CBS station WNBS. Johnny talks to the staff and Bill Freese tells Johnny that Mrs. John Stacy Minot's death might not have been from natural causes. Bill tells Johnny that the new secretary Danny Pringle was the only person who could have known about Mrs. Minot's affairs. Bill is sure that Pringle forced Mrs. Minot to change her will and leave everything to him, or he will eat his shirt. Bill has no proof, but why else would a young man tie up with an old skinflint like her. And Pringle is not one of those "lah-de-dah" types either, if you know what I mean. She was so tight fisted that her niece Dora Minot had to play housekeeper and nurse for her for no pay so Mrs. Minot could save a few dollars. In the new will, everything goes to Danny rather than Dora and Bill thinks Danny killed Mrs. Minot for the money. Bill has nothing against Danny, it is just wrong for Danny to get away with it. Johnny meets with Harvey and he tells Johnny that Pringle had plenty of reasons for Mrs. Minot to die, and made no bones about it. Dr. Hugo Bessum examined the body, and said that Mrs. Minot died of natural causes and Bill knows about the doctor's report. But Bill is in love with Dora Minot in spite of the fact she was going to inherit a million bucks or so, or because of it. Harvey wonders if Johnny thinks that Bill killed Mrs. Minot to marry Dora and get the money. However, the doctor had said death was by natural causes. Johnny tells Harvey that Bill had just as much reason to want Mrs. Minot out of the way as Danny did, unless he knew that she had changed the beneficiary. Harvey tells Johnny that no one knew about the change until she died. The policy states that the beneficiary is the heir of her estate as specified in the will, and Mrs. Minor typed the will herself. Harvey had the will checked out with the company attorneys, and it was legal, but this new will does not make sense. Dora had found the new will in a safety deposit box after her aunt died. Dora was so upset that she brought it to Harvey, who wanted to tell her to burn it up. No, Danny will get the money that should go to Dora. Harvey has a photostat of both wills, and the typing is pretty bad on both, including a number of repeated errors. Johnny wonders why Pringle had not typed the will for her since she was leaving everything to him.

Harvey shows Johnny that the signature of the witnesses, Marjorie and John Durkin, match exactly on both copies of the will. Marjorie did some cleaning for Mrs. Minot, and both of the Durkins died a month or so ago in a hit-and-run accident. Johnny notes that they died only a few days after the new will was made. Hit-and-run huh? Johnny starts to wonder about the typing. Johnny wonders if Dora liked Danny, but Harvey tells him that she hates Danny. Also, Dora is not upset about her aunt's death as her aunt had worked Dora too hard. Johnny is sure that there is something fishy going on, so Johnny has three people to work on.

Johnny talks to the police who tell Johnny to talk to Dr. Bessum. The doctor tells Johnny that his autopsy was far from routine after he heard about the new will, but the result was the same, natural causes. Johnny drives to the Minot house on Bailey Avenue and Dora, a tall good-looking blonde, is there. She tells Johnny that she is cleaning up the house and looking into rooms she had never been in before, including Danny's room. Dora had hoped that there would be some recompense for all her hard work. Danny is out for the moment, but he will be back to make sure that Dora does not take anything of his. Dora shows Johnny a key ring with keys to every room in the house. Mrs. Minot kept it tied to her. Dora tells Johnny that she had a key to the safety deposit box because Mrs. Minor did not trust Danny. Dora had to go into the box to get the stock certificates and other papers, and that is where she found the new will. The old will was kept in the house in a file, and Pringle got it out to show the police. Johnny notices a typewriter, but it is Danny's. Dora wants to leave Danny's room before he comes in and finds her there. Dora wonders why her aunt wrote a new will when she found out she was going to die. Danny comes in to tell her that she has no business in his room. Danny demands that Johnny to leave until Johnny shows him his credentials. Suddenly Danny is most hospitable. Danny tells Johnny that Mrs. Minor decided to leave everything to him because he had a lot of charm. He had originally come to work for her because he thought she was richer than she was, and he wanted her money. He was going to leave but during her last illness he relented and repented, and Mrs. Minot appreciated the change. Johnny asks if anyone else could have used the typewriter, and Danny tells Johnny that Mrs. Minot used it, but no one else. Johnny points out the similarities between the two wills, including the signatures that match exactly. Johnny tells him that it is impossible to anyone to sign his or her name exactly the same way twice, and gives Danny a piece of paper for him to sign. Johnny tells Danny that he made the new will, traced the signatures and then killed the Durkins so they would not talk. Danny admits everything that Johnny has accused him of with a gun in his hand. Johnny tells Danny he did not come alone, and tells Danny that the police came with him. Danny turns to look and Johnny slugs him. When Dora asks where the police are, Johnny tells her "it's the oldest gag in the world, but amateurs still fall for it."

"On the strength of his statement to us, well, I hope they do pin the murders of the Durkins on him. As for that second will, it can't be genuine simply because of those two sets of absolutely identical signatures."

NOTES:
- THERE IS A COMMERCIAL AFTER THE PROGRAM FOR COMMANDER CIGARETTES
- BOB READICK WELCOMES WKAT IN MIAMI TO THE NETWORK
- LAWSON ZERBE IS HARVEY, ROBERT DRYDEN IS PRINGLE, JOAN LORRING IS DORA, LARRY HAINES IS BILL.
- ART HANNES IS THE ANNOUNCER.
- MUSICAL SUPERVISION IS BY ETHEL HUBER

Producer: Bruno Zirato, Jr.   Writers: Jack Johnstone
Cast: Lawson Zerbe, Robert Dryden, Joan Lorring, Larry Haines

SHOW: THE CAPTAIN'S TABLE MATTER
SHOW DATE: 4/9/1961
COMPANY: GREATER SOUTHWEST INSURANCE COMPANY
AGENT: BARTON H.B. HOLLISTER
EXP. ACCT: $438.00

SYNOPSIS: Barton H.B. Hollister calls (Oh no! Not Hollister in Phoenix, Arizona.) That's' right. (Oh, here we go again.) What was that? (Nothing, just go right ahead.). Hollister wants Johnny to come to Phoenix to defend the life of a client, Henry Kirkum. Johnny tells Hollister that he has never liked, does not now like, and never will like these bodyguard assignments. Johnny tells Hollister to call the Phoenix police. Hollister tells Johnny that the client does not live in Phoenix, and that Johnny will be paid handsomely for his efforts. Suddenly Johnny is interested. Johnny wants to talk about how much he will be paid, but Hollister hangs up. "Ok, friend, just wait until you see my expense account."

Johnny recounts how he had so far avoided assignments from Hollister, who is an egotistical, finicky, penny pinching, stuffed shirt who always commanded rather than asking. Johnny notes $4.00 for a cab; no lets start this off right, $6.00 for a cab to the airport and plane fare to Phoenix, Arizona. Johnny cabs to Hollister's office where he yells at Johnny for not being there earlier. Johnny is too late, as Kirkum has been found dead. Kirkum, who was insured for $70,000, has been murdered, or committed suicide. The police think it was murder. The only suspect they are holding is the beneficiary, Walter Pinkley. Walter is also a policyholder, so if he did commit the murder, Hollister is stuck with two policies. Hollister wants Johnny to rent a car and drive to Tuttle, a small town northeast of here. The police force in Tuttle is Alfred Appleby. Then go to the Yucca Flower Rest Home, where Pinkley and Kirkum lived. The rest home is for people with lung problems. Johnny insists on talking about the fees in the case, and Hollister tells Johnny that if he can prove suicide, Johnny will get $1,000, oh, ok $1,500. But will get nothing if it was murder. Johnny insists on $2,000 in either case and wins the argument. Johnny rents a car and drives to Tuttle, Arizona and stops at the city hall. In the jail he meets Walter Pinkley who thinks the murder of Henry was awful. The chief picked on Walter because he had told everyone at the captain's table that he was going to visit with Henry because he was his friend. Henry appreciated Walter's abilities as a composer and shows Johnny a musical score for a concerto. Walter tells Johnny that it was nice of Henry to leave him the money so that he now can buy a piano and compose. Walter tells Johnny that Henry had been worried about something lately. He and Henry had talked for hours, but Henry seemed depressed. Walter left around ten when Henry told him he had to write an important letter for someone who was coming to visit. Walter tells Johnny that they found Henry on the floor with a pistol the next morning, but Henry would never commit suicide. Walter is happy that the jail is so quiet, so he can work on his music. Johnny is sure that Walter is not a killer in his book. Johnny drives to the rest home, which has an office and a number of cabins. Chief Appleby meets Johnny at the door and tells Johnny that he has the case all sewed up. The chief thinks it was Pinkley because he has proof. The scene was made to look like suicide, and the gun had no prints on it, but only Pinkley was in to see Kirkum. What Pinkley did not know is that Kirkum had written a letter to Johnny. Appleby gives Johnny the letter that says "Dear Mr. Johnny Dollar, honored sir. There is within this place one who would avenge himself upon my life. Nor have I been remiss in my endeavor to assuage the passion that manifestly provoked his wish for my demise. But alas, I had made it only too clear I could no longer abide his ridiculous concettos. And so because of my resentment over his concettos he seeks revenge. And lest he seek to destroy me ere you come to afford me protection, I tell you know his name is, but hark there is a knock upon my door. I shall finish this anon." Johnny learns that Kirkum was an old ham actor but he and Appleby disagree over the word "concetto," with the chief thinking it referred to Pinkley's concertos. This is all the proof that Appleby needs and is sure that Kirkum wrote it before Pinkley came in. Johnny remembers the reference to the others at the captain's table. Johnny is told that they all eat their meals together every day, and have for years. The other members of the group are an old lady named Sarah Sanderson, a man who calls himself "Captain" Howard, and an old man named David Hesher. Johnny asks the chief to get them together so he can talk to them. Johnny gets a dictionary and looks up a word and then goes to meet the others. Mrs. Sanderson just cried, and Hesher's mind was going and he was no help at all. But Captain Eustus Howard tells Johnny that he has used his mind to solve more complicated cases than this. Howard is convinced that Pinkley is the killer, and that he could have written the so-called music Pinkley wrote in a week. Johnny reminds the chief that Kirkum had changed the beneficiary of the policy recently. Appleby tells Johnny that the previous beneficiary had been the whole group. Johnny notes that the others were cut off in the change, and the letter that was left on the desk, where Pinkley could have seen it. Johnny is convinced that the killer misread the letter the same way he and the chief did, and left it there, thinking it blamed Pinkley. Johnny shows the chief that the dictionary defines "concetto" as an old Italian word for conceit. Add them up and the old conceited Captain was cut off along with a couple of others who did not care. He did not like the snub it implied any more than being turned down by Pinkley over the music. He made the killing look like a suicide so no one would get the money. When he found the letter he was sure he could get both Kirkum and Pinkley, so he wiped the prints off the gun. Howard admits he killed Kirkum, but is surprised that the chief would take him in like some common person, and for a very small mistake.

"So, Mr. Barton H. B. Hollister, you better shed a bit of your conceit and pay me not only the fee you promised, but an expense account total, including the trip back to Hartford, and believe me all the incidentals I could possibly cook up, a total of $438 even."

NOTES:
- EDGAR STEHLI IS WALTER, RICHARD DENDRICK AS BARTON, JOHN GRIGGS, AS EUSTUS, JIM BOLES AS THE CHIEF.
- ART HANNES IS THE ANNOUNCER.
- MUSICAL SUPERVISION IS BY ETHEL HUBER

Producer: Bruno Zirato, Jr.   **Writers:** Jack Johnstone
Cast: Edgar Stehli, Richard Dendrick, John Griggs, Jim Boles

SHOW: THE LATRODECTUS MATTER
SHOW DATE: 4/16/1961
COMPANY: PHILADELPHIA MUTUAL LIABILITY & CASUALTY INSURANCE
AGENT: HARRY BRANSON
EXP. ACCT: $111.35

SYNOPSIS: Harry Branson calls John and is as addled as usual. Harry has a client, Eustus Royal Pennybank. Johnny recognizes the name as that of a bug chaser or butterfly collector who made the magazines a few years or so back. Harry corrects Johnny in that Pennybank is one of the greatest entomological researchers in the country today. Pennybank has told Harry that he is being threatened. Harry wants Johnny to fly down so he can meet Pennybank in his office.

Johnny flies to Philadelphia, Pennsylvania and cabs to Harry's office where he meets Dr. Pennybank, an old man with sharp piercing green eyes. Pennybank tells Johnny that his work has always been of value to the scientific world. In his home are priceless records from his research in toxicology. He alone had determined that the south Jersey cattle killing a few years ago was done with the venom of the agkistrodon muccasin; he proved that the killers used the deadly venom of the copperhead snake to kill the cattle. Only he was able to differentiate it from the venom of the agkistrodon piscivorus, the water moccasin. He has decided to study and classify the various arachnida, a profuse class of the order araneae, a small part of the insect world. He has records in his home that are of international importance in these troubled times, but someone has tried to steal them from him, usually at night. He will turn the records over to the authorities only after he has finished his research. He cannot have copies made, as that would run the risk that they would be leaked out, and he needs the papers for his research. Pennybank has, for his protection, isolated a group of the genus latrodectus. Pennybank tells Johnny to come to his home in Kenwood tonight, and leaves to make a speech to the Academy of Science whether they like it or not. He is in danger and must see Johnny tonight. Johnny wonders if Pennybank is an old crackpot, but Harry tells Johnny that there is a $50,000 policy with several scientific organizations and niece, Clara Benson, as the beneficiaries. Johnny parks his bags at the Belleview Stratford and rents a car. Johnny drives to Dr. Pennyback's around three PM and hears a door slam in the back. As Johnny knocks he hears a car pull away and finds the door unlocked. Johnny goes in and finds Pennybank dead on the floor.

Pennybank is dead with two bullets in the chest, and the car Johnny had seen was a dark green compact model. Johnny looks at the laboratory, which is full of all sorts of live insects, complete with their food in a refrigerator. On an empty cage Johnny spots the words latrodectus, Black Widow. Johnny hears footsteps approaching and Johnny jumps the man as he enters the door. Johnny realizes the man is a police officer and shows him his ID. Johnny then shows him the body of Pennybank. The officer tells Johnny his work is done and slugs Johnny and takes him into town, where Johnny's ID is checked and officer Fallon apologizes. The lab crew examines the house and takes the body for an autopsy. The initial report names the cause of death as a .25 Colt. The police could find only a few things belonging to the niece in the house. Johnny notes how a belt loop had been torn, like if a key chain had been torn off, but no keys were found. The cleaning woman has been in the hospital for several weeks, and was fed up with the old man. Johnny thinks about the term latrodectus and gets a hunch.

Johnny visits the beautiful niece, Clara Benson in her apartment, and she is upset about her uncle and has no idea who could have killed him. He was peculiar, but he was doing no harm. Clara tells Johnny that men had come and offered money for his reports, but Clara does not know who they were. Johnny asks about her car, which is an old beat-up model, and she is upset that Johnny would suspect her. She tells Johnny that her husband had died recently from a hit-and-run driver, and is so alone now. Johnny wonders: cui bono, who benefits? No one but the beautiful black-haired young widow. And what about the papers in the safe? And the missing keys? And what about using latrodectus for protection? Johnny looks for used car dealers in the area and finds the dealer that sold her the old car earlier that day in trade for a new green compact. Johnny drives back to the apartment but Clara is gone. Johnny drives to Pennyback's home and sees a light on inside. Johnny climbs in through a window and looks for the source of a light. In the kitchen Johnny sees a doorway to the cellar and hears keys trying to open a lock. Johnny hears a scream and runs down to find Clara covered with Black Widow spiders.

"But by the time I could reach her side and beat them away she had fallen unconscious. She had been struck by tens, by scores of them. On her hands, on her arms, struck down by the beautiful deadly protectors of that safe, latrodectus,

Black Widows. Clara died within minutes before I could possibly get help. And the papers she had killed her uncle to obtain: nothing. Nothing but the confused scribblings of a demented old man."

NOTES:

- THE FIRST COMMERCIAL BREAK IS DENNIS JAMES FOR KELLOGG'S ALL-BRAN. COMMERCIAL BREAK #3 IS ARTHUR GODFREY FOR A CANCER LIFE SAVINGS FACTS BOOKLET AND THE NEED TO MAKE CONTRIBUTIONS TO THE CANCER FUND
- THE COPPERHEAD (AGKISTRODON CONTORTRIX) IS MISIDENTIFIED AS AGKISTRODON MUCCASIN, BUT THE WATER MOCCASIN IS CORRECTLY IDENTIFIED AS AGKISTRODON PISCIVORUS
- RadioGOLDINDEX LISTS LAWSON ZERBE IN THE CAST, BUT THE OTHER CREDITS ARE NOT LISTED, NOR OR THEY ON MY PROGRAM

Producer: Bruno Zirato, Jr.   **Writers:** Jack Johnstone
Cast: Lawson Zerbe, Unknown

SHOW:	THE RAT PACK MATTER
SHOW DATE:	4/23/1961
COMPANY:	ETERNITY MUTUAL INSURANCE COMPANY
AGENT:	GEORGE FRANKLIN
EXP. ACCT:	$0.00

SYNOPSIS: [Opening Missing] Johnny tells George that only $700 more dollars and Johnny can drive around the countryside in a new sports car, "So if you want me to come to Corpus Christi, you will have to guarantee me that amount." George tells Johnny that his car sounds like what he keeps in his garage, the Franzetti. George loves it, now that he has gotten used to it. Come on down and drive mine, and if you clear up this case, the car is yours for as long as you like, and maybe he can dig up a little extra for Johnny, say $700.

Johnny flies to Corpus Christi and George meets Johnny at the airport, but the Franzetti is safe in his garage until after Johnny cleans up the case. George has rented a new compact car for Johnny to drive to Summit Hill, Texas, a nice well to do residential area inhabited by retired oil people. George has been writing checks to settle claims for malicious mischief to cars. Most have been hot-rodded in the country and abandoned. Johnny tells George that it sounds like the work of kids, and George agrees. It is the work of a rat pack. The police force is only one man and a couple of half-witted deputies. Even the police have had a car stolen. When the State Police come in, everything settles down. That is why Johnny will not get the Franzetti.

Johnny buys a blank book with "Official Business—Federal Population Survey" embossed on it. Johnny drives to Summit Hill and interviews a number of families. At a gas station Johnny is told that the owner has a gun, and would use it. Chief Foster cannot do anything, and the kids always seem to know when the police are around. They hot wire the cars and use Halloween costumes to disguise themselves. The man tells Johnny to not go there tonight, but go in the daylight. Johnny goes to visit the Briarleys and is let in, as Mrs. Briarley knows Johnny is taking a survey, but Mr. Briarley is carrying a shotgun. Their son Frank is out on a date and Mrs. Briarley is unsure about having bought a new car with all those awful things being done. They wish something could be done, and Johnny tells them that there is a local informant in town who tips off the kids. Johnny tells them that there are no places for the kids to get together and blow off steam. Mrs. Briarley tells Johnny that the parents provide for that by giving their children everything they want. Buy they do not give the kids cars, as the do not want to spoil them. Their son Frankie is twenty-two, and does not work because he does not have to. Johnny starts to yell at them but hears a noise outside. Johnny pulls his gun and goes outside and yells at the kids just as they drive off with the new car. Johnny tries to blow out a tire by shooting at the car. After five shots someone puts a switchblade in his back and tells him not to turn around.

The knife is pulled along Johnny's neck and he feels blood. "Jean" is told to take his gun, and Johnny sees heavy gloves, torn jeans and a mask on the figure of a girl. Johnny calls the boy a tough guy, and the boy tells him to turn around to see his face. Johnny turns slowly and knocks the knife from the boy's hand but is knocked out with is own gun. Johnny wakes up on the Briarley's couch with the taste of bourbon in his mouth. They tell Johnny that they had found Johnny after the chief called to tell them that their car had been wrecked. They searched him, and know who he is. Mr. Briarley tells Johnny that he has thought about what Johnny had told him. Frankie comes in and asks about the missing car. Frank is introduced to Johnny, and he knows who Johnny is. He tells Johnny that he and his girl had taken a bus to a dance. Johnny hopes he is not involved with the kids. Frankie plays innocent, but tells Johnny that if he finds out who the gang is, maybe Johnny can help. They cannot leave because their parent will not let them do anything. Mrs. Briarley gets upset but Johnny tells her to let Frankie work things out for himself. Frankie tells Johnny that he knows who the kids are. Johnny wants to know who they are, but Frankie tells Johnny he would not think much of him if he did.

"These cases usually have big fat dramatic endings, and the devil with any kind of a message, well not so this time. I honestly do not know if I did the right thing or not on this one. Too much faith in the younger generation, well maybe I have. But the next evening there at the home of the Briarleys there was a meeting of the parents, of all the wealthy, doting indulgent parents of all the kids in their late teens and early twenties. I tore into those parents, and by the time I finished there were plenty of red faces among them. Incidentally, out of the corner of my eye, I thought I saw the face of a teenager in the shadows outside a window. What I said to those people in laying down the law to them, well I honestly do not remember exactly. But it must have given them a jolt. And if they carry out their plans there won't be a kid in that town with an idle moment on his hands. But their activities, their projects will be their own, with as little parental advice and guidance as possible. Then the following night, thanks to a tip off by young Frank, without the knowledge of his parents, I barged into a meeting of the kids, seven or eight of them. As I might of expected, they were there in their foolish masks and makeup knowing that I would be among them. And if you think I had been rough on their parents, but by the time I had finished with them . . ." Johnny tells the kids that they will go to jail if they continue with their activities. They take off their masks, and one tells Johnny he will get a job to repay the damage he has done.

"Well I sure hope I did the right thing by simply leaving it the way it stood, but what else could I have done, have them all locked up for something that was only partly their doing. Try to make them into criminals, I don't think so. Incidentally because of a call to get right back to Hartford, I never did drive George Franklin's Franzetti. But I did get that $700 fee, and that will help me buy one of my own. Expense account, what am I talking about, this one is on the cuff."

Notes:
- William Redfield is George, Gertrude Warner is Mrs. Briarley, Phil Meader is Frank, Jack Grimes is the kid, Roger De Koven is the gas station attendant, Bob Dryden is Mr. Briarley
- The Franzetti is a fictitious automobile. But the early 1960's was the age of the sports car, with the Corvette, the Jaguar XKE and host of other European imports

Producer: Bruno Zirato, Jr.   Writers: Jack Johnstone
Cast: William Redfield, Gertrude Warner, Phil Meader, Jack Grimes, Roger De Koven, Bob Dryden

◆   ❖   ◆

Show: The Simple Simon Matter
Show Date: 5/14/1961
Company: Tri-Western Life Insurance Company
Agent: Frank Francis
Exp. Acct: $450.00

Synopsis: Frank Francis calls Johnny from Los Angeles, and wants Johnny to get there before noon, or it will be too late. He will meet Johnny at the airport. Johnny has to find out if the recent death of a policyholder was an accident, suicide or murder.

Johnny flies to Los Angeles, California and the flight arrives early. Frank meets Johnny and takes him to his office. He tells Johnny that he will get a phone call at noon for Johnny. On the way in, Frank tells Johnny that Gerald Raymond Hilton is on the books as an accident or suicide. His wife is the beneficiary of the $16,000 policy, with double indemnity for accidental death. The accident happened off a side road near Newhall, where Gerry lost control on a curve and went into a canyon and died. Frank is sure that it was not an accident. The police found that Hilton had stopped, or been stopped. The phone call Frank is expecting makes him feel otherwise. The investigation found that the car had been driven over the edge of the road. Gerry had been having financial troubles, and his wife is sick but working in a factory. Frank thinks that it was suicide made to look like an accident. Hilton had a shady reputation, and only the policy to leave the wife and a three-year-old son who needs an operation. Frank has known the wife for years, and Gerry deserved to have a police record. The caller told Frank to get ready to pay off the policy, and that he would only give his information to Johnny Dollar. In the office the call comes in and Johnny answers. The operator has a person-to-person call from San Diego. A voice tells Johnny that Gerry Hilton was not an accident or a suicide, and the voice knows who did it. Johnny is told to meet him on the Pescadero Pier in San Diego at 11:00 PM, and no tricks. The voice tells Johnny that maybe he will recognize him and hangs up.

Frank wants the money to go to the family, and Johnny thinks he recognizes the voice, so Johnny is going to go. Johnny rents a car and visits Gerry's widow, Marjorie. The apartment is small and Tommy is on a cot, very sick. Johnny learns that a free clinic will do the intestinal operation. She tells Johnny that Gerry would never commit suicide and he had tried to get her out of the shabby apartment. They got married last year, and Tommy is not their child. Gerry was sure that something was going to turn up soon. He was better than Tommy's father, Allie Parson. Johnny recognizes the name as Alfred H. Parson, and the "H" stands for Heroin. The police have been looking for him for five years. He came to see Marjorie a couple weeks ago and Gerry threw him out. Alfred was always good at smooth talk. Johnny gives her $50 in case Tommy needs something. Johnny is puzzled by Marjorie, and the way she talked—like a movie gun moll. Johnny drives to San Diego and finds the Pescadero pier, which has no ships and only an old warehouse. Johnny catches a couple movies and has dinner while he waits. At eleven Johnny goes to the pier, which is shrouded in fog. Johnny is stopped by a voice that tells Johnny to hide behind a box. Johnny recognizes voice as Simon "Simple Simon" Hacker. Johnny had chased him once and had to let him go. Simon knows where Allie Parson is, and knows that Johnny will protect him. He tells Johnny that the police in Newhall know that Gerry was dead before he went over the cliff. Allie killed Gerry so he could get his girl back. Johnny gives Simon $100 and just as he is about to talk, Simon is shot several times. Three shots are aimed at Johnny, so he dives into the water and swims under the pier and back to his car. Johnny goes to the harbor police and tells them about Simon. So maybe Allie is making a play for Marjorie, and she would be a push over for Allie. Johnny drives back to her apartment at 4 AM and there is a light on. Johnny spots her bags packed, and she tells Johnny she is taking Tommy to the hospital. Johnny tells her that she knew where Allie and Gerry got their money, and there were probably three or four husbands before Allie. "There were only two," she blurts out. Johnny tells her that Allie killed Gerry because he was afraid Gerry would tell the police where Allie was, and Allie killed Simon because Marjorie had called and told Allie where Johnny was going. Marjorie calls for Allie, and Parson comes out with a gun. Allie takes Johnny's gun and prepares to shoot him with a silenced gun. Marjorie tries to close the door and the police come in with Simon and shots are fired. The police tell Johnny that Simon had told the police what was happening and brought them to Marjorie's apartment. Johnny talks to Simon who is not doing too well. Simon tells Johnny that he wanted to go straight but waited too long. But he tried. Johnny notes he tried but waited too long, as Simon dies.

"Marjorie and the boy, I don't know. I kind of felt sorry for the poor kid. But her, I can't help wondering if she even deserves a break."

NOTES:
- THE FIRST COMMERCIAL BREAK IS ABOUT THE EISENHOWER COMMISSION ON AMERICAN GOALS. CBS FEELS THAT THIS IS AN IMPORTANT DOCUMENT.
- JACKSON BECK IS FRANK FRANCIS, ELIZABETH LAWRENCE IS MARJORIE, MASON ADAMS IS SIMON, BERNARD GRANT IS ALLIE, MAURICE TARPLIN IS THE POLICE LT.
- ART HANNES IS THE ANNOUNCER.
- MUSICAL SUPERVISION IS BY ETHEL HUBER

Producer: Bruno Zirato, Jr.   Writers: Jack Johnstone
Cast: Jackson Beck, Elizabeth Lawrence, Mason Adams, Bernard
            Grant, Maurice Tarplin

◆   ❖   ◆

SHOW: THE LONE WOLF MATTER
SHOW DATE: 5/21/1961
COMPANY: STATE UNITY LIFE INSURANCE COMPANY
AGENT: HARVEY WAKEMAN
EXP. ACCT: $88.40

SYNOPSIS: Harvey Wakeman calls Johnny from New York, and he has a problem, or rather his client Thomas Rayburn Morgan does. He is a stockbroker over in Newark. Morgan called Harvey and he needs Johnny Dollar, and no one else. Harvey gives Johnny the address and tells Johnny that he will call Morgan and tell him Johnny is on the way over. Harvey has no idea what the problem is, and Johnny wants to beg off a blind assignment. Harvey tells Johnny that he has told Morgan that a man like Johnny comes expensive and will require a big fee. Fee? I'm on my way.

Johnny flies to Newark, New Jersey and cabs to Morgan's office on Commerce Street. Morgan tells Johnny that he is the only one who can help Morgan, especially in the area of confidentiality. Morgan has not talked to the local authorities or the police in Philadelphia, where the letter came from. Morgan tells Johnny the matter could cause complete and utter ruin for him and his family. Morgan makes Johnny promise that he will keep the details quiet. The letter is addressed to "Thomas, or rather Danny Fairland," and continues on how the writer has followed Morgan's business ever since the time they worked together on an investment scheme some years ago. The writer has fallen on hard times and is sure that Morgan would be more than happy to help him out, as he has never revealed the details of their enterprise to anyone. The writer wants Morgan to withdraw $10,000 from the bank and he will contact him later on where to deliver the money. The writer has completely written out the details of their scheme and has given it to a friend. If anything happens, the friend will give it to the newspapers. The signature is "HBW." Morgan tells Johnny that the writer is Henry B. Wolf, and the crime is a stock swindle that Morgan was involved in many years ago. Morgan was young and gullible, and he thought he could get enough money to start his business. Morgan had kept a list of those he had defrauded and has anonymously paid them back with interest. Morgan asks Johnny what he can do, and Johnny tells him, "That is a good question."

Johnny is convinced that Morgan is telling the truth, but how to find Wolf? Morgan has withdrawn the money and is waiting for the call. If it were not for his family, Morgan is not sure what he could do. Johnny tells him that all you can do is pay Wolf off, but he will constantly need money. Johnny asks Morgan to have his secretary buy him some magazines as Johnny is going to stay in the office until Wolf calls. Johnny spends three days reading in Morgan's office, going to lunch with him and spending his nights with Morgan at his home, posing as an old school friend. On the third day the call comes in and Wolf tells Morgan he has no choice but to lend him the money he needs. Wolf tells Morgan that if he calls in the police, Morgan's old transgressions will be released to the papers. Wolf laughs when Morgan asks how he can be sure that Wolf will not come back asking for more money. Wolf has called Morgan's wife and told her that he is going to have dinner with him tonight and then Wolf gives Morgan the instructions. After hearing what Wolf wants, Johnny tells Morgan he is leaving and tells Morgan to meet Wolf in Monroe Park and give him the money. "See you some day," he tells an abashed Morgan. Johnny makes a phone call and then has drinks and dinner with an old friend, retired Judge Amos Ordway, who has been around a long time and has a good memory. The judge remembers the swindle, and was a lawyer at the time and a few of his clients were bilked. Johnny is told that for those who were repaid may not have a claim in the courts. The laws were not as strict then and the operation could have been construed as legal. If the less guilty one of them has lived a good life, there might not be a problem. Johnny tells the judge he knows who Danny Fairland is, but the judge plays ignorant. The judge does tell Johnny that if he needs a good broker to go see Thomas Morgan. Later that night Johnny goes to a local park, roughs up a park guard and takes a key, after making a $5 deposit to his pocket. Johnny waits in the park maintenance shed with the unconscious guard. At eleven Johnny hears footsteps of a man pacing. Johnny opens the shack door as another man walks up. Henry has met Morgan and tells him he had to make sure that Morgan was alone. He laughs and tells Morgan he might just do this again. Morgan is told to leave and Wolf waits for him to go. A man who has overheard the blackmail conversation approaches Wolf. He wants the money and the envelope so he can do the same thing. Wolf tells the man that there is no envelope, and it was only a bluff. Suddenly Johnny tells him who he is. Johnny tells Wolf that he is a lone Wolf. And even if he tries to tell anyone about his past, he would only embarrass himself. No one would believe him if he tried to claim that Danny Fairland was someone else. Johnny tells Wolf that if he tells what he knows, he will go to jail for the blackmail, not for a swindle everyone has forgotten. Any tales of the past would not make the papers, as Johnny knows a judge.

"Turn him in? Take the chance that he might be able to hurt Thomas Morgan? Or let him go with the full knowledge that I could prove a charge of blackmail against him? What would you have done? Oh? Well that's just exactly what I did."

NOTES:

- THE FIRST COMMERCIAL BREAK IS FOR **CBS** NEWS, WHICH GOES ALL OVER THE WORLD TO BRING THE MOST UP TO DATE EVENTS. ALSO, IT IS NATIONAL HOSPITAL WEEK.
- SANTOS ORTEGA IS WOLF, SAM GRAY IS MORGAN, WILLIAM REDFIELDS IS HARVEY, ROBERT DRYDEN IS THE JUDGE.
- ART HANNES IS THE ANNOUNCER.
- MUSICAL SUPERVISION IS BY ETHEL HUBER

Producer: Bruno Zirato, Jr.   **Writers:** Jack Johnstone
Cast: Santos Ortega, Sam Gray, William Redfield, Robert Dryden

SHOW: THE YAAK MYSTERY MATTER
SHOW DATE: 5/28/1961
COMPANY: FOUR STATE MUTUAL INSURANCE COMPANY
AGENT: STEVE YOKUM
EXP. ACCT: $207.75

SYNOPSIS: Steve Yokum calls Johnny from Kalispell, Montana. Steve wants Johnny to fly out about his client John Turner Whiticum, who is insured for $500,000 double indemnity. It looks like the company will be out a million, if it has happened. Steve does not know if Whiticum is dead or not, but Johnny has to find out.

Johnny buys the paper and checks the weather for Montana and flies to Kalispell, Montana where Steve meets him with a jeep. Steve tells Johnny that he is going up to the town of Yaak, Montana, up in the real snow country. Steve tells Johnny that Whiticum made his money in lumber and retired after his wife died.

He and his and daughter Valerie and her husband Lou Larson have gone up to Shorty Bessum's camp to do some hunting. Steve has heard from Shorty, and Whiticum the kids are out in the woods hunting. After lunch Johnny and Steve drive through a wet snowfall on the way to Yaak. Steve tells Johnny that the hunting is good in that area. After buying gas in Yaak, they drive on to Shorty's camp. In the cabin, Kate Bessum gives them coffee with rum to warm them up. Shorty tells Johnny that he told them not to go out, but Whiticum did not listen. Shorty thinks Whiticum was trying to make his son-in-law into a real man. After the snow, Shorty and others started looking for them, but could not find anything. Shorty hears a horse and they go outside.

Lou Larson is on the horse and they take him off and into the cabin. Larson is still alive and Johnny wonders how he survived. Later that night Larson tells Johnny that the others are dead. It was somewhere on the south side of Lost Horse Mountain. They made camp when the snow started. It was in an area near a deep crevice. Kate calls the area Dead Man's Hole, a death trap. Lou was sent to find wood, and his horse followed him. He heard a loud sound and looked back to see snow and rocks falling down. It was an avalanche. Johnny tells them to put Lou to bed, and Johnny asks Shorty how far it is to the area. Shorty tells Johnny it is only a couple hours if you know where to go. Shorty tells Johnny that no one has ever come out of the chasm and that it does not take much the start an avalanche in that area.

Johnny looks through Lou's room and in a suitcase he finds a topographic map of the area around Lost Horse Mountain, and a book about the legends of the area. Next morning Johnny wants to look at Dead Man's Hole before it washes out in the spring floods. Shorty and Johnny leave and head into the woods as a storm starts to blow in. Johnny wants to get into the chasm before the storm hits, but it breaks before he gets there. While waiting for the storm to ease, Johnny uses binoculars and spots the bodies on the side of the chasm. Johnny rigs a line to go down and get the bodies, because Johnny saw bullet holes in their heads through the binoculars. While Johnny is trying to get a line on the bodies bullets start to hit the area and trigger another avalanche. Shorty pulls Johnny up and tells him that he saw the rocks shot away. Johnny tells Shorty about the book that Lou had brought, and that Lou had killed Whiticum and his daughter for the money. Whiticum did not like Lou, so by killing them he would get all the money. Larson only married the daughter to get at the money. While Johnny is wondering if Lou is around, Lou comes up with the rifle to kill them. Lou tells them that he will tell them that he was just wandering around, and that he really had spent the previous night in the hay shed with his horse. Lou tells Shorty and Johnny to back up into the chasm, and Johnny tells Lou to look behind him, but he does not take the bait. Just as Lou is going to shoot, Steve shoots him. Steve had decided to follow Lou and almost lost him.

"So the laws of succession take over, and somebody else gets the insurance, and the old man's estate. And as for Lou Larson, well even hanging is too good for that kind."

NOTES:
- BOB READICK MAKES AN ANNOUNCEMENT FOR NATIONAL RADIO MONTH: "THE CBS RADIO NETWORK AND THIS STATION ARE BOTH VERY MUCH A PART OF NATIONAL RADIO MONTH. BUT THE FIGURES SHOW THAT YOU THE LISTENER ARE JUST AS MUCH A PART OF THE CELEBRATION. YOU TAKE PART EVERY MONTH OF EVERY YEAR WITH YOUR PURCHASES OF NEW RADIO SETS. TODAY THERE IS AN ALL TIME RECORD NUMBER OF RADIO SETS IN USE. TODAY THERE ARE MORE LISTENERS THAN EVER. AND THE NUMBER ONE NETWORK FOR THE BEST SOUND AROUND IS OF COURSE, CBS RADIO."
- ROBERT DRYDEN IS SHORTY, BILL LIPTON IS STEVE, ATHENA LORDE IS KATE, ALLAN MANSON IS LOU.
- KALISPELL IS IN THE NORTHWEST CORNER OF MONTANA, AND YAAK IS ALMOST ON THE CANADIAN AND IDAHO BORDERS
- I HAVE CHANGED THE NAME OF THIS EPISODE TO CORRESPOND TO THE ACTUAL NAME OF THE LOCATION
- ART HANNES IS THE ANNOUNCER.
- MUSICAL SUPERVISION IS BY ETHEL HUBER

Producer: Bruno Zirato, Jr.   **Writers:** Jack Johnstone
Cast: Robert Dryden, Bill Lipton, Athena Lorde, Allan Manson

SHOW: THE STOCK-IN-TRADE MATTER
SHOW DATE: 6/4/1961
COMPANY: WORLDWIDE MUTUAL INSURANCE COMPANY
AGENT: RIP TEETER
EXP. ACCT: $325.00

SYNOPSIS: Rip Teeter calls from Memphis, the finest town on earth. Rip has trouble in Summerville. The trouble is murder.

Johnny flies to Memphis, Tennessee and meets with Rip who tells the secretary Mary Belle to get a rental car for Johnny. Rip tells Johnny that the deceased is Valney Beauregard Exum. Early this morning his housekeep found him with his head broken in, and there were no prints on the heavy poker that was used. That is why Johnny was called. The area is rich in plantations and the Exum money came from cotton. He is living in the plantation house, but the land has all been sold off. Valney somehow managed to keep up the payments on his insurance policy for $35,000, but Rip does not know where his money came from. After the war a lot of the families had to sell of heir land and made investments. "You mean the Civil War, Rip?" asks Johnny. "I said THE WAR, didn't I?" Rip laughs. Rip thinks that Valney got his money from his kinfolk, a niece and a couple of nephews who are also the beneficiaries. There is Clara Belle Otway Exum who lives in town. A nephew also named Valney Beauregard Exum lives in Corpus Christi, Texas. The other nephew is Culpepper Van Buren Oglethorpe who lives in Summerville and works in a real estate office. Rip is sure that neither of them would kill Exum, as they are a fine old southern family. Valney had no enemies and no real friends. Dolly Cato did the day work cleaning for Valney. The insurance is only $10,000 apiece and the plantation is only worth $10,000. Johnny thinks he better go see the place. Johnny drives to Summerville, Tennessee and goes to meet Clara Belle Exum in the five and dime where she works. Clara is glad that her uncle is dead. With the money from the insurance she can pay her bills and buy some new things. She tells Johnny that Mrs. Cato probably has more money than Valney did. She worked for Valney out of pity. Clara tells Johnny that she does not know where Valney's money came from. Clara Belle did not know anything. Johnny drives to the Exum home, which is a wreck with missing columns, broken windows and peeling paint. Johnny meets Sgt. Aiken at the door and gets a look at the crime scene. Valney was found sprawled on the desk with a tin box in front of him. Johnny is told there were no prints on the box. Sgt. Aiken thinks that Valney let someone in and was killed late last night. Anyone he would let in at night must have been a friend. Sgt. Aiken does not know where Valney got his money, but he would cash a check once in a while. Johnny finds a piece of paper in the hinge and it looks like parchment used for insurance policies, and Johnny wonders if that is where his money came from. Sgt. Aiken tells Johnny that Culpepper Oglethorpe is not doing anything and is stupid enough to kill his kinfolk for money. Sgt. Aiken tells Johnny that Culpepper did not kill Valney, because he is in jail.

Johnny has no clues he could put his fingers on. Sgt. Aiken tells Johnny that the other nephew lives in Texas. Sgt. Aiken had called and he told Sgt. Aiken that he could not make it back and would pay for a funeral. Johnny thinks that the other Valney is his only hope and is ready to fly to Corpus Christi. Johnny has to admit that sheer luck helped him solve this case. It came in the form of a stack of letters in the mailbox, one with a well-known name, Intrastate Telephone Company. Johnny rips the letter open before Sgt. Aiken can stop him, and it contains a dividend check for $250, dividends on 500 shares worth $40,000. Johnny knows because he owns some of the stock. Johnny flies to Corpus Christi, Texas and gets a room at the Robert Driscol. The next day Johnny talks to his friend Wayne Stockfort who tells Johnny that he does have a client named Exum who has a small account. Valney had called Wayne to tell him he had some Intrastate Telephone shares to sell. Just then Valney walks in and sits at Wayne's desk with Johnny watching from the next desk. As Valney signs the certificates he tells Wayne he wants cash, as he has to take a business trip. Johnny tells Wayne to call the police, as the signatures are forgeries. He is Valney Beauregard Exum, but the certificates were stolen from his uncle, who has the same name, when he was murdered. Johnny is sure he can prove it with the pieces of paper that were left in the tin box. Valney tries to run, but Johnny stops him.

"What Exum didn't know of course, was that Wayne, who had done a lot of investigating before handing over all that money, in spite of the way he had carried a small account with firm, set things up for the murder and robbery."

NOTES:
- CAST INFORMATION IS FROM RadioGOLDINDEX.
- ART HANNES IS THE ANNOUNCER.
- MUSICAL SUPERVISION IS BY ETHEL HUBER

Producer: Bruno Zirato, Jr.   **Writers:** Jack Johnstone
Cast: Joan Lorring, Mandel Kramer, Ralph Bell, Robert Dryden, Robert Readick, Wendell Holmes

◆   ❖   ◆

SHOW: THE BIG DATE MATTER
SHOW DATE:
COMPANY: TRI-STATE LIFE & CASUALTY INSURANCE COMPANY
AGENT: DON BOOMHAUER
EXP. ACCT: $20.00

SYNOPSIS: Don Boomhauer calls Johnny, but Johnny wants to duck whatever Don has for him. Don pleads for only five minutes with Johnny. Don does not want Johnny to take on a case, but if Johnny will come down he can keep Don from getting involved in something serious, like spending a few years in a federal prison. Don tells Johnny to come down to Sarasota, and Johnny relents. But he is sure is it a gag, it has to be. And yet, coming from Don Boomhauer . . .

Johnny flies from Miami to Sarasota, Florida and goes to Don's office. Johnny tells Don he only came to Sarasota to delay his return to snowy Hartford. Don mentions the jewelry robbery Johnny had just been working on, and Johnny tells him he almost got his head shot off and wants to relax. Don tells Johnny that all he wants Johnny to do is to verify some figures, and Johnny notes he only likes to verify one type of figures, those on a pretty girl. Don gives Johnny a list of the money he has been paid, and Don tells him to sign it so that the IRS will not send him up the river. His accounts had been messed up and the IRS wants proof that Don actually paid Johnny the money. Johnny is about to sign the paper when shots ring out, but Johnny looks out the window and goes outside to investigate. Johnny notices a backfiring car with a pretty blond sitting in it. As a crowd gathers Don tells Johnny that she might be a good date for a wing-ding Johnny is going to be taken to that night out on Bird Key.

As Johnny gets to the car, all the merchants on Main Street are on the sidewalk watching the car to see what will happen. The girl cannot get the car to stop so Johnny gets her to pull the hood release so he can open the hood, but it is stuck. A police sergeant arrives and asks what is going on. Johnny explains what is going on, and the sergeant tells Johnny to stop all the noise. Finally the car stops backfiring and the girl thanks Johnny and drives away. The sergeant accuses Johnny of causing the car to make the noise and threatens to arrest him for disturbing the peace. Johnny goes in to talk to Don and tells him that the girl is a living doll. Johnny is thinking and bets Don that the girl dances like a dream. Johnny signs the statement (legibly too, Don notes) and wishes he had noted the license on the car, and is sure that no one knows who the girls is, but Johnny will find her. Johnny has an idea and asks to borrow Don's car. The police arrive at a jewelry store across the street and the sergeant comes in to arrest Johnny. He tells Johnny that he knows that Johnny and the girl were causing a disturbance so that his confederate could rob the jewelry store across the street. Don is told that $60-70,000 was stolen, and Don realizes that he insures most of it. The sergeant is ready to take Johnny downtown until Don tells him who Johnny is: Johnny Dollar, the insurance investigator and friend of the Lieutenant who comes down there now and then. Johnny shows him his ID and Johnny asks Don if he is on expense account. As Johnny leaves the sergeant tells him that Lt. Phillips will have to identify him, as Johnny is his only suspect.

Johnny takes Don's car and goes to the agency that sells the type car the girl was driving, but she had not been there. Johnny checks every car agency in town and finds nothing. Johnny drives aimlessly and hopes Don can explain to the police so that they will not follow him and cramp his style. Johnny finds himself way out on Bee Ridge Road and turns around on a dirt road, only to see the car he had been looking for stalled up ahead. Johnny drives to the car and the girl recognizes Johnny. She tells Johnny that the car just stopped and she needs somebody to fix it. The hood is open and Johnny looks into the car as he tells the girl that he was out looking for her. Johnny tells her his name and she acts as if she recognizes his name. Johnny replaces an ignition wire and spots a device used to make the car backfire, just like the Chicago gangsters used to do to hide gunshots. Johnny hears a noise in the car and goes to investigate and finds a man named Jim with a .38 in the back seat. Johnny spots the loot in a bag and Jim tells Johnny to turn around so he can be nice to him and shoot him in the back of the head. A car drives up the road and the girl, Sally, recognizes it as a police car. Jim is distracted and Johnny slugs him just as the police sergeant walks up and asks the girl if she is ok. Johnny thanks him for tailing him and Johnny tells the officer he had asked Sally for a date, but suggests that she have a date with him instead, say at headquarters.

"So thanks to shear luck, and clean living of course, I'll pick up a commission on the recovery of all that jewelry."

NOTES:

- UNDATED PROGRAM FROM RadioGOLDINdex. BASED ON THE PREVIEW OF THE NEXT CASE, IT LOGICALLY SHOULD HAVE BEEN BROADCAST JUST PRIOR TO THE VERY FISHY MATTER. SINCE THIS PROGRAM IS UNDATED, IT COULD BE ANY ONE OF FOUR READICK PROGRAMS WITH NO TITLE.
- NEXT WEEK, A FISHING TIP WITH A REAL FRIENDLY CROWD OF PEOPLE, ONE OF WHOM IS A KILLER.
- MADELINE SHERWOOD IS SALLY, ROBERT DRYDEN IS THE SERGEANT, CARL FRANK IS DON, LARRY HAINES IS JIM, LARRY ROBINSON IS THE CAR DEALER

- ART HANNES IS THE ANNOUNCER.
- MUSICAL SUPERVISION IS BY ETHEL HUBER
- THERE IS A PUBLIC SERVICE ANNOUNCEMENT FOR MENTAL HEALTH THAT OFFERS THE PUBLICATION "HOW TO DEAL WITH MENTAL PROBLEMS.
- DALLAS TOWNSEND GIVES A PROMO FOR HIS NEW CBS PROGRAM "THE SOUND STORY"

Producer: Bruno Zirato, Jr.   Writers: Jack Johnstone
Cast: Madeline Sherwood, Robert Dryden, Carl Frank, Larry Haines, Larry Robinson

Section 6: Mandel Kramer

M andel Kramer became the sixth and final actor to play Johnny Dollar.

Mandel Kramer was an established New York actor with a long radio and television record. Mandel was a very personable Johnny. As the program tried to adapt to the hip nature of the 1960's, Johnny tried to move with it. The Johnny Dollar of Mandel Kramer was a personable ladies man who was also able to get the job done.

Mandel continued as Johnny until September 1962, when radio drama disappeared.

The following are the Mandel Kramer Johnny Dollar programs.

SHOW:	THE LOW TIDE MATTER
SHOW DATE:	6/18/1961
COMPANY:	TRI-MUTUAL INSURANCE COMPANY
AGENT:	FREDERICK BENNOM
EXP. ACCT:	$0.00

SYNOPSIS: Frederick Bennom calls Johnny and has an important matter for him. Bennom usually uses investigators from his own company, but none of them is a fisherman. Bennom understands from the radio broadcasts that Johnny is a very good fisherman. Bennom wants Johnny to meet him at 3:30 to discuss the case.

Johnny notes he would not select Tri-Mutual as a company to work for, as they are notoriously stingy. But mention fishing and Johnny is gone. At 3:30 exactly Johnny is brought into the office and tells Bennom that he will have to pay Johnny's expenses, and a fee or a commission on the amount of the insurance involved. Bennom corrects Johnny and tells him that the commission will be on the amount of money saved. Bennom finally agrees to the larger of the fee or the commission. Bennom tells Johnny that the Foster Machine Tool Company has a partnership policy for $500,000. He is worried about Charles Foster, who asked if the policy could be cancelled. Business has not been good, and Foster suspects his partner, Michael Brady, of being responsible for the down turn. Brady would not cancel the policy and told Foster that he needed a vacation. Bennom has tried to contact them, but they have gone fishing. Bennom wonders if Brady is right, and that Brady knows that the only way to get the business is to get Foster out of the way. Brady has refused to tell anyone, including their wives, where he has gone fishing with Foster. Johnny has no idea what his first move will be.

Johnny calls on Mrs. Foster who is worried sick about her husband. After talking, Johnny suspects that Bennom might be right. Johnny calls on Mrs. Kathy Brady, who is a living doll, and is not worried about her husband. They are living high on the hog, and she has been partying while Mike is away. Mike will come back, he always does. He has gone fishing at Lake Mead, Lake Mojave and in Maine too. She senses that Johnny is worried about Mr. Foster, and assures Johnny that that sort of thing could not happen again. Johnny asks what she means, and she tells Johnny that Mike had another partner a couple years ago. They went hunting in Canada, and some fool shot his partner and almost killed Mike. He was so upset he sold the business. Kathy really wants Johnny to come to one of her parties, but Johnny tells her he has to go a long, long way away. Johnny realizes how well Mike could use the money and how much of a gold mine the machine tool company is. And what about that hunting accident? Johnny is ready to have a drink and cook a steak when he has a brainstorm and calls Ham Pratt at Lake Mojave Resort. Johnny asks Ham if he has seen Charles Foster, and Ham tells Johnny that the police, the sheriff and the coroner seem to think that Charles Foster has been in some sort of accident. Johnny grabs a flight to Las Vegas and rents a car for the drive to Lake Mojave. At the resort Ham tells

Johnny that the authorities have asked Brady to hang around. Ham tells Johnny that Foster and Brady had not been getting along, and they went fishing separately on Monday. Foster went up to the Big Basin and Brady went down by the dam. The wind came up and everyone came in but Foster. After the wind died down, they went looking for Foster but all they found was the boat, beached up by the big island, and the body has not been found. The sheriff calls and tells Ham that Brady can leave, but Johnny tells him not to relay the message. Johnny asks for a boat and makes a phone call to the weather bureau to get the direction of the winds during the storm. Johnny explores the shoreline along the Arizona side of the lake north and east of the island. In a cove called the "rock pile" Johnny finds a body in fifteen feet of water, with a foot tangled in an anchor line. Johnny dives for the body and, after dark Johnny brings the body of Charles Foster back to the dock.

Johnny does not want Ham to call the police yet, as they have no proof that Foster was killed. Johnny wants a way to get Brady to show his hand, and gets an idea. The next morning Ham eats breakfast with Brady, and tells him it is the least he can do, what with all he has gone through. Ham tells Brady that he had been expecting someone else to join him when Johnny comes in and is introduced as Johnny Harris. Brady thinks he recognizes Johnny's voice, but Ham tells him that "Mr. Dollar" is one of their best fishermen. Johnny tells Brady that he is going to go to the rock pile today and invites him to come along. Brady asks Ham why he introduced Johnny as "Mr. Harris" and then called him "Mr. Dollar," but Ham nervously tells Johnny that the dam level is going to be lowered today, so the rock pile will be exposed. Ham tells Brady that the water might go down by twenty feet, and Brady tells them he is going out to do some things. Johnny tells him that he wants to go to the rock pile and move the body of the man he murdered and hide it somewhere else. Brady tells "Mr. Johnny Dollar" that he cannot deny that, nor can Johnny deny who he is. Brady pulls a gun and tells Johnny it is too bad Johnny caught up with him. Johnny tells Brady that there is no way he can get off a shot before Johnny draws his gun. Johnny outdraws Brady and shoots him. Ham tells Johnny that he had a lot of nerve, but Johnny tells Ham he was scared to death. "I guess I'll never qualify for a part on Gunsmoke."

"Needless to say, Ham's talk about dropping the level of Lave Mojave by a full twenty feet was all a bluff, but it worked. Expense account total, including the trip on back to Hartford, well Mr. Bennom, I'll just forget that, in view of my nice fat commission on that half million dollar policy."

NOTES:

- THE FIRST COMMERCIAL BREAK IS FOR MENTHOLATUM DEEP HEAT RUB.
- THE SECOND COMMERCIAL BREAK IS FOR ALPINE CIGARETTES.
- SANTOS OTEGA IS BENNOM, TERRI KEANE IS KATHY, BERNARD GRANT IS BRADY, BOB DRYDEN IS HAM.
- THIS IS THE FIRST PROGRAM WITH MANDEL KRAMER AS JOHNNY DOLLAR.

- ART HANNES IS THE ANNOUNCER.
- MUSICAL SUPERVISION IS BY ETHEL HUBER

Producer: Bruno Zirato, Jr.   **Writers:**   Jack Johnstone
Cast: Santos Ortega, Terri Keane, Bernard Grant, Bob Dryden

◆ ❖ ◆

SHOW: THE IMPERFECT CRIME MATTER
SHOW DATE: 6/25/1961
COMPANY: STATE UNITY LIFE INSURANCE COMPANY
AGENT: LOU LITTLE
EXP. ACCT: $0.00

SYNOPSIS: Lou Little calls, and Johnny is glad to hear from him. Lou tells Johnny that his wealthy clientele have not been cooperating to give Johnny some business. He has a crazy writer on his hands right now. Johnny tells him that the only writer he knows is Johnstone, the man who puts his stories on the air. "Is he Normal?" asks Lou. Johnny replies, "He is a bit of a nut about fishing." Lou tells Johnny that all writers are crazy about something, and this author is a nut on murder, and writes nothing else. Can you think of anyone better qualified to plan a perfect crime? Lou thinks that Johnny better come over so they can talk about it. Johnny agrees.

Johnny drives to Lou's Hartford, Connecticut office where Lou tells Johnny that he should really want to be a bodyguard to Mrs. Porter, the wife of G. Stanley Porter. Johnny recognizes the name and really likes Porter's books and the way he can take a simple plot and develop it into a real story. Mrs. Porter is coming over to talk to Johnny about her problem. Lou had sold them each a $750,000 policy with double indemnity, and now they are not getting along. Mrs. Porter arrives and Johnny's eyes light up at Denise Porter, about 26 with a figure to die for, and an apprehensive look in her eyes. Denise tells Johnny that her husband has been really good to her, but it seems insincere lately. "Like a last meal," suggests Lou. Denise tells Johnny that her husband has been married four other times, and she just found out about them. Each of the other wives had died. All he thinks about is planning the perfect crime, and after each of the wives died he wrote a book about the murder of a woman. Johnny thinks it would be ridiculous to write about killing a wife, and then collecting the insurance. She wants to know what her husband is writing, but he keeps himself locked up at night while he writes. Denise asks Johnny to protect her, and Johnny tells Denies he will get back to her in a couple days.

Johnny goes home to think this case over, and wonders about an author who writes crimes, and who thinks he could get away with it. Johnny decides to take the case, but not to tell Denise, primarily because of the plane ticket to New York that had fallen from Denise's purse in Lou's office. Johnny calls Randy Singer in New York and then drives to the Porter home. Inside Johnny sees an impressive house after being met at the door by Mr. Porter. He follows Johnny's radio shows and describes Johnny as six feet, 160 pounds (on the nose, Johnny notes), with dark hair and gray eyes and built like a steel spring. Johnny asks for his wife, and Porter tells Johnny that his wife has probably been talking to the insurance company, but he has all the insurance he can use. Johnny tells him that for policies like theirs, they like to keep in touch. Porter tells Johnny that he likes to surround him self with beautiful things, like Denise. But writing is his life, and he gets ideas from everyone he meets. Even his former wives, whom he loved dearly, gave him ideas that he wrote down so he will not forget. Denise had nursed him back from an illness, and cannot think of loosing her. Denise is in New York with friends, at the theater. Porter asks Johnny to come upstairs so he can talk. Johnny is surprised when Porter walks up the stairs with a cane, as he is totally blind.

In the study Johnny finds a complete apartment, but all Porter can talk about is plots for his books. After drinks Porter fixes a steak dinner for them. Porter washes the dishes, and tells Johnny that he always eats upstairs when Denise is away. But late at night he loves to go down stairs to raid the big refrigerator after he puts his typewriter away. Johnny tells him that he would love to raid it with him for two or three nights, but only if no one knows that he is there. Johnny goes to move his car, and thinks from experiences that he might have a hunch. Johnny calls Randy and he tells Johnny that a man met Denise at the plane, and they made a stop at a machine tool supplier before going to some clubs. Johnny is sure that he was called in as a cover-up for the police, to convince Johnny to convince the police that, when it was all over, Mr. G. Stanley Porter had slipped up. That he had forgotten the trap he had set and that he had fallen into it himself. That's what it would look like, all right. Back with Porter, they are talking, and there is noise at the front door. Porter tells Johnny that it is Denise coming in. Johnny hides in the kitchenette when Denise comes in. She tells Porter that she and the girls liked the play, and that she has left some milk and chocolate cake in the refrigerator for his late night snack. Johnny comes out and tells Porter that it was a silly little game he had played with his wife. Porter tells Johnny that he will show him his latest manuscript later, but he has not written the ending yet. Johnny asks if there is a character like Porter in it, but he will not tell Johnny. Porter suggests going down for the cake, but Johnny tells him a snooze would be better. After Porter falls asleep, Johnny goes down stairs slowly and finds several dozen ball bearings that Denise and her boyfriend had bought. Had Porter stepped on them, he would have crashed to the bottom. Denise could then have collected the ball bearings and no one would have thought anything except that a blind man had missed a step and fallen. There would be no marks or signs of being pushed. Johnny collects the ball bearings and is met on the top step by Porter, whose ears have told him everything. Porter tells Johnny that he has provided an ending to the book, and that he has known all about Denise and her boyfriend for a long time. Johnny tells him that he knew Porter would not be the one to do the plotting. Porter asks for the balls, so he can give them to Denise. His will be a lonely life after that.

"I left him then, and walked out to my car, drove home to my apartment, poured myself a good stiff drink, and have been quietly sitting here writing out this report. What ever may have happened when he faced her with the evidence of her attempt to murder him is none of my affair. The expense account, forget it."

NOTES:
- THE FIRST COMMERCIAL BREAK IS FOR MENTHOLATUM DEEP HEAT RUB
- ALLAN MANSON IS LOU, EVIE JUSTER IS DENISE, RAYMOND EDWARD JOHNSON IS PORTER, EUGENE FRANCIS IS RANDY
- ART HANNES IS THE ANNOUNCER
- MUSICAL SUPERVISION IS BY ETHEL HUBER

Producer: Bruno Zirato, Jr.   Writers: Jack Johnstone
Cast: Allan Manson, Evie Juster, Raymond Edward Johnson,
            Eugene Francis

SHOW: THE WELL OF TROUBLE MATTER
SHOW DATE: 7/2/1961
COMPANY: STATE UNITY LIFE INSURANCE COMPANY
AGENT: LOU LITTLE
EXP. ACCT: $0.00

SYNOPSIS: Lou Little calls, and Johnny tells him it must be a mistake. He had to wait for two years to get an assignment from Lou, now it's two in two weeks! Lou has a problem getting rid of $1,000 and tells Johnny to come over and get it.

Johnny cabs to Lou's office where Lou gives Johnny a check for $1,000. The check is from G. Stanley Porter, who insisted that Johnny take the money for his last case. Johnny notices a big stack of money on Lou's desk, and Lou tells Johnny it totals $2,388.24. Lou got it from Jeremy L. Withers, who mails him the cash for his insurance premiums every year. Johnny tells Lou about Durango Laramie Dalhart, who lived in Bum Spung, Oklahoma, and would bring in the premiums cash, in person, totaling nearly $4,000 a year. Johnny recounts to Lou how Durango had once washed his money and looks at a bill in the stack, and asks for the location of Mr. Withers. Johnny calls the police and gets some interesting information. Johnny buys gas and drives to Granby and then to Millbury Corners. Johnny finds the shabby Withers place in a weed-grown lot. Johnny knocks on the door and introduces himself. Withers unchains and unbolts the door and Johnny tells him he wants to talk about his insurance premiums. Johnny tells Withers that some of the new $20's are hot and wants to know where he got the money.

Johnny asks Withers about the money and tells him that it is not counterfeit, but it is plenty hot. Johnny asks why Withers locks himself in and he tells Johnny it is to protect himself from nosy people like Johnny. Johnny tells Withers that the money is from a bank robbery over in Millville where over $20,000 in new twenties was taken. Johnny remembers the serial numbers because he had worked on the case and had to memorize a series of sequential serial numbers. Withers tells Johnny that it was just part of his money he gets from a pension. Johnny asks how he can pay the insurance premium on a pension. Withers tells Johnny that he had saved his money and bought insurance. After his wife died and he retired, he continued to buy insurance for his daughter to get when she dies. He tells Johnny that he was a flagman for the railroad. Johnny asks if Withers would like to talk to a judge and he tells Johnny that he had a stepson named Bernard. Johnny recognizes him as Barney the Bum who was killed in a failed bank robbery after the Millville job. Withers tells Johnny that Bernard was no good and deserved what he got. Withers tells Johnny that he kept his money out of the bank, and under the floor but he has used up all his money, now he is using Bernard's money. He did not turn Barney in because he was looking out for himself. Withers tells Johnny that Bernard's partner had killed the bank guard, and that is why he locks himself in. The killer is Jerry McNear, and he had not told the police because the police would want to know where the money is. McNear has not killed him, because if he does, he will not get the money. There is a noise outside, but Withers tells Johnny that it is only a shutter. Withers tries to work a deal with Johnny for lenience with the police and finally tells him about the Hacker Farm up the road. At the back of the house is a well, and in the shaft is a shelf, and that is where the money is. Jerry McNear comes in and thanks Withers for telling him where the money is and shoots him. Johnny knocks out a lamp, but McNear laughs and shoots at Johnny three times.

Johnny realizes that he does not have his gun. The first shot puts a crease in Johnny's hair and the others miss when he rolls under the table. After McNear leaves Johnny goes to his car and drives up the road to find the Hacker farm while following McNear with his lights out. McNear turns into a farm where the lights are on in the house, but Johnny continues up the road to the real farm. Johnny parks and locates the well. Johnny secures the rope and bucket, and climbs down the well. Johnny finds a hole big enough to crawl into and finds two suitcases with the bank money in them. Johnny then hears McNear, who tells Johnny that he stopped so he could follow Johnny. Johnny tries to bluff about a gun and puts his jacket and hat on a suitcase. McNear lights a match and shoots the suitcase. Johnny cries out and drops the suitcase into the well. McNear climbs down the well and when he comes along side of the shelf, Johnny slugs him and he falls into the water.

"All he could do when he recovered from the shock of his fall, was stand there in the water at the bottom of the well, knee-deep in the money from the suitcase I'd thrown down there, cursing me as I climbed out and pulled the bucket out of his reach. He was still there when I brought back a couple of the state police. Expense Account total, why bother with it when I'll collect such a nice commission on the loot I recovered. Not bad, you know. I mean for one night's work"

NOTES:

- THE FIRST COMMERCIAL BREAK IS FOR MENTHOLATUM DEEP HEAT RUB.
- THE SECOND COMMERCIAL BREAK IS FOR 7-UP.
- THE THIRD COMMERCIAL BREAK IS FOR TENDER LEAF ICED TEA.
- THE FOURTH COMMERCIAL BREAK IS FOR ALPINE CIGARETTES.
- PARKER FENNELLY IS WITHERS, LEON JANNEY IS MCNEAR, ALLAN MANSON IS LOU.
- JOHNNY IS SHOT FOR THE 12TH TIME.
- ART HANNES IS THE ANNOUNCER
- MUSICAL SUPERVISION IS BY ETHEL HUBER

Producer:	Bruno Zirato, Jr.	Writers:	Jack Johnstone
Cast:	Parker Fennelly, Leon Janney, Allan Manson		

SHOW:	THE FIDDLE FADDLE MATTER
SHOW DATE:	7/9/1961
COMPANY:	TRI-STATE LIFE & CASUALTY INSURANCE COMPANY
AGENT:	EARLE POORMAN
EXP. ACCT:	$681.80

SYNOPSIS: Earle Poorman calls Johnny, but this time from Florida. Earle and Mike have moved back to Sarasota and have taken over the Tri-State office again. Earle asks Johnny how his musical ear is, and Johnny tells Earle he can tell the difference between a fiddle and a bass drum. Earle tells Johnny that that may be good enough, so come on down.

Johnny flies down to Earle's office and greets Don Boomhauer who tells Johnny that Earle probably wanted Johnny to come down just to go fishing or convince him to move to Florida. Don tells Johnny that this is really an unimportant case. Joseph R. Tetrick retired from the oil and Gas business and has an air-conditioned vault built into his house to keep his collection of fiddles in, but he does not know a hemisemidemiquaver from a d-string. The collection has a couple of Strads and an Amati and a Guarneri. It seems a Mr. Bisiach in Italy has made a collection of musical instruments, and one in particular is called the Canary, and it is insured for $10,000. The Bisiach was taken to a fiddle maker, Antonio Depolito, for a check up and this morning the place was broken into and the fiddle is gone. Two hours ago Tetrick called and told Earle that he had the answer to the whole thing. Johnny is about to call Earle when he comes into the office. Earle is very glum, and tells Johnny that Tetrick must have known who took the fiddle, as he was dead when Earle got there.

So far the investigation has showed nothing to tell who killed Tetrick. Johnny borrows a car from Don and goes to the shop of Depolito. There were some cheap violins in the window and Depolito was working on a re-varnishing job on a violin. Johnny tells Depolito who he is, and Depolito tells him it was awful what had happened. The violin was beautiful and sang like a bird. Oh, if only his son . . . Depolito was working on the Bisiach last night and had locked the shop and drawn the shades. He fell asleep and woke up when someone was in the shop. The man hit him, and he was out until morning when the police came. Johnny looks at a window with the glass cut, but it is an amateur job. Johnny asks where a Bisiach could be purchased, and Johnny is told that a fine violin is like a fine jewel. Earle come in and tells Johnny that the only place where a Bisiach could be purchased is from the Wurlitzer Collection in Chicago. Johnny thinks that the violin is the key to Tetrick's murder, and asks Earle to drive him to the airport. Johnny flies to Chicago and spends the night in the Blackstone Hotel. The next morning Johnny talks to an expert at the collection, and they will put out an alert. Johnny is told that no artist will use it, because of its unique color. Johnny is told that Emil Victor, the previous owner, will be heartbroken. Victor sold it because of an accident that injured his hand and left him blind. Johnny suddenly remembers a name has a hunch, and asks for the address of Emil Victor, and a list of concert bookings for the whole country.

Johnny makes several calls to Earle and learns that the man Johnny is looking for had been in Sarasota on the night in question, and where he will be playing next. Johnny cabs to the flat of Emil Victor and tells him of his suspicions and what he plans to do with his help. Victor cannot believe that the young musician could do that to his own father. Johnny tells him that Depolito had told Johnny that the shades were drawn when he was working, but he could see the police in the window the next morning. Johnny remembers that the scratches on the glass in the window were on the inside. Also, Johnny remembers that Depolito was a master at refinishing violins and remembers that Depolito had mentioned that his own boy would never have a violin like that. Johnny tells Emil that he is going to help find the violin, and they hurry to catch a plane to El Paso, Texas. Johnny and Emil get into the concert for Antonio Depolito, who was playing a reddish brown violin. Emil is sure that the violin is the Canary by it's sound, like a father knows his son. The varnish had changed the tone, but it is still the Bisiach. Johnny gets the police and goes to the dressing room. Johnny faces Antonio with the facts he knows, and he reacts violently. After Emil tells him what he knows, Antonio confesses to stealing the violin with his father's help, and to the murder of Tetrick. Tetrick had called Antonio is to tell him of his suspicions, and when Tetrick started to call Earle, Antonio killed him. Antonio tells Johnny that Tetrick deserved to die for keeping the Canary in a vault, but knows his talents are wasted, as an audience will never hear his skills again. Johnny reassures Antonio that where he is going, he will have a captive audience.

"So, from here on out it is up to the courts. And that means for his father too. You know, I wonder if the Tetrick estate will put those priceless fiddles in that collection into the hands of musicians where they could be used and appreciated. I hope so." The expense account includes a couple of days fishing with Earle Poorman.

NOTES:

- THE FIRST COMMERCIAL BREAK IS THE KINGSTON TRIO FOR SEVEN-UP.
- THE SECOND COMMERCIAL BREAK IS FOR ALPINE CIGARETTES.
- THE THIRD COMMERCIAL BREAK IS FOR MENTHOLATUM DEEP HEAT RUB.
- SANTOS ORTEGA IS DEPOLITO, LEON JANNEY IS EMILE, RICHARD HOLLAND IS TONY, FRANK BEHRENS IS DON, SAM GRAY IS EARL, BILL LIPTON IS THE VIOLINIST.
- A HEMISEMIDEMIQUAVER IS A 64TH NOTE.
- LEANDRO BISIACH MADE MUSICAL INSTRUMENTS IN THE LATE 19TH EARLY 20TH CENTURY
- ANTONIO STRADIVARI WAS BORN IN 1644, WORKED IN CREMONA, ITALY UNTIL HIS DEATH IN 1737
- ANDREA AMATI (1525-1611) IS KNOWN AS THE FOUNDER OF THE GREAT CREMONESE SCHOOL OF VIOLIN MAKING.
- ART HANNES IS THE ANNOUNCER
- MUSICAL SUPERVISION IS BY ETHEL HUBER

Producer: Bruno Zirato, Jr.   **Writers:**   Jack Johnstone
Cast: Santos Ortega, Leon Janney, Richard Holland, Frank Behrens, Sam Gray, Bill Lipton

◆   ❖   ◆

SHOW:	THE CHUCKANUT MATTER
SHOW DATE:	7/23/1961
COMPANY:	WESTERN MARITIME & LIFE INSURANCE COMPANY
AGENT:	LUCIEN PETERSON
EXP. ACCT:	$351.18

SYNOPSIS: Lucien Peterson calls Johnny from Seattle. He is doing fine, but has had to settle a number of large claims lately, and the home office does not like him. Right now Luke does not want to pay off on Mrs. Myra Britingham. She is not dead, yet. Luke has a hunch and thinks that if he told the police, they would laugh at him. Luke wants Johnny to come out and see if her husband Mark would try it.

Johnny flies to Seattle and arrives late at night and stays at the Benjamin Franklin Hotel. The next morning Johnny goes to visit Lucien who tells Johnny he will get him a rental car so he can drive to Chuckanut, Washington, just this side of Bellingham. The Britinghams live on Pallioop Lane, a rugged road that winds up the mountain and is treacherous if the road is wet. Both of the Britinghams are insured for $500,000 and each is the beneficiary of the other. Mark is about thirty-five and a playboy and sportsman living first on money his father gave him, and now on the insurance left him by his last wife. Myra is wife number four. Luke is sure that Mark married her because she had an incurable disease, but modern science found a cure for it. Johnny asks if the former wife died from an incurable disease, and is told that that is what the police and the courts decided, but Luke is sure Mark helped the old biddy on her way. Luke has no evidence, and they have not been getting along lately. Myra is older than Mark, and loves to spend his money before he can. Johnny is supposed to scare the truth out of Mark. Luke tells Johnny to go on the pretense of buying the property, and then let it slip out who he is. Johnny drives up to Chuckanut and the road up the mountain was anything but a road. On a tight turn Johnny almost hits a police car, and a new compact car crashed on the road. Johnny stops and meets Sgt. Bill Foreman who knows who Johnny is, and wonders how he found out so quickly and that one of the Britinghams is in the car. Johnny looks into the car to see Mark Britingham. Sgt. Foreman tells Johnny that Myra had called the police. She was alone, and while sitting on the porch she saw a car coming up the road. She did not want any prowlers and called the police. She screamed over the phone that there had been an explosion and Sgt. Foreman came right over. Johnny asks Sgt. Foreman if she had recognized the car, and is told that the sun would have been in Myra's eyes and to Mark's back. Sgt. Foreman had warned Mark about how he drove up the road, but he had been a racing driver and took Sgt. Foreman up one day, and Mark could handle a car. Sgt. Foreman mentions Hartford Homer Ransom, the sudden death detective. He reconstructs traffic accidents and lives near there. Johnny asks Sgt. Foreman to call Ransom and suddenly Johnny notices that Mark looks like he had thrown his arm up in front of him. Sgt. Foreman thinks it was a reflex, but Johnny thinks a professional driver would have slumped down. He must have put his arm up while he was in the curve. Johnny tells Sgt. Foreman to get an autopsy started and then goes to see Myra. The home on the mountain is new, modern and expensive. Mrs. Britingham is forty, but does not look it. Johnny introduces himself, and tells her who he is. On the porch Myra asks if it was Mark, and tells Johnny that she had warned him and knew he would kill himself. She is not sad, as it settles things. She tells Johnny that she married Mark for his money, while he had it. She hates the small house and fought with Mark over money. Mark should have gotten a job, but he just sulked. One night he was laughing to himself and told her that it would be nice for her if he would die. He had been taking long trips lately and left her alone. Myra tells Johnny that she wants to get as far away as possible. J   o   h   n   n   y wonders why she painted herself so darkly, and what about the alarm when she saw the car?

The next morning Johnny meets with Sgt. Foreman, Dr. Bascum the coroner, and Mr. Ransom, who knows more about inertia, matter and motion and reaction times than anyone Johnny knows. Ransom does not understand why the right arm was up, and is sure Mark must have done it while on the curve. Johnny wonders about a bird or animal in the road, but that is discounted. The car was ok, and there was nothing wrong found in Mark's autopsy. Dr. Bascum had given Mark a physical only two weeks ago. The only conclusion is suicide, but Ransom cannot agree because the tire tracks were erratic and the right arm shielding his eyes from the sun. Johnny has and idea that it was the sun and asks for time to play a hunch that Mark was murdered. Johnny asks Sgt. Foreman to bring Myra to the office on some pretext. When Johnny calls, Sgt. Foreman is to drive her home. Johnny tells Sgt. Foreman that when he is on the curve where Mark died, take it very slowly with one foot on the brake. Johnny goes to the house and searches it, and finds a lot of mirrors. Johnny is looking for a signaling mirror with a whole in the middle and finds it hidden in a book on the porch. Johnny calls Sgt. Foreman and Johnny aims the mirror at the car while it is on the curve. Sgt. Foreman is able to stop the car and waits for Johnny to come down. Sgt. Foreman tells Johnny that Myra has not said a word since he raised his arm and stopped the car. Myra asks Johnny how he knew she killed Mark? Johnny tells her didn't. He had a hunch, and it seems to have paid off.

"$500,000? That's a nice round figure, a lot of money. Don't they ever learn that millions aren't enough to murder for? Expense account total, call it a nice round figure, like uh, say $351.18."

NOTES:
- THERE IS A COMMERCIAL BREAK FOR BIG BROTHERS AND BIG BROTHER WEEK.
- CAST IS UNAVAILABLE ON THIS RECORDING, WHICH IS ALSO VERY NOISY.
- THERE IS A TOWN CALLED CHUCKANUT, JUST SOUTH OF BELLINGHAM, WASHINGTON.

Producer:	Bruno Zirato, Jr.	Writers:	Jack Johnstone
Cast:	Unknown		

◆   ❖   ◆

SHOW:	THE PHILADELPHIA MISS MATTER
SHOW DATE:	7/30/1961
COMPANY:	AMALGAMATED LIFE ASSOCIATION
AGENT:	GEORGE CALDWELL
EXP. ACCT:	$485.75

SYNOPSIS: George Caldwell calls Johnny from Meridian, Mississippi. George understands that Johnny has a top security clearance, and Johnny confirms that. George has a client who has asked for Johnny to be brought in. The client is Dr. Emit Melcher, who owns the Melcher Labs, and does a lot of work for the government. George does not know what the problem is, but it is top secret.

Johnny flies to Meridian with two stopovers and arrives around seven PM. Johnny takes a cab to the Amalgamated office, and the cabby asks Johnny to repeat his destination, and then tells him that he drove Johnny around New York City once. The driver is Bernie Yorkin, and he remembers the tip that Johnny gave him. Bernie asks what the case is, and Johnny tells him he does not know. Bernie promises to keep an eye on Johnny. George Caldwell is in the office and he tells Johnny that he had called the labs, and Mr. Melcher is out of town. But his secretary, Miss Mona Little Wolf is waiting for Johnny. Mona is a Philadelphia girl, and part Indian. Johnny cabs to the lab with Bernie again. Bernie tells Johnny that there are a lot of government secrets at the lab, so call Bernie if you need him. Johnny meets Mona, and the trip was worth it. Johnny and Mona hit it off immediately, and Johnny learns that she is part Indian, and Mona asks if Johnny's last name isn't Big Wolf? Mona tells Johnny that she is the secretary, but knows nothing about what Melcher is working on. Mona tells Johnny that she is going on vacation tomorrow, and with Melcher out of town, they decide to spend a pleasant evening in Meridian. Bernie is still waiting and takes Johnny and Mona into town. At 3:00 AM Johnny and Mona close down the last club and look for a cab. Mona tells Johnny that she better get away on her vacation when a car drives up. The driver forces Mona into the cab and hits Johnny.

Johnny wakes up in his hotel with Bernie pouring bourbon into him. Bernie tells Johnny that he found him passed out on the sidewalk while he was driving. Johnny grabs the phone and makes a call to Mona's apartment, but there is no answer. Bernie remembers seeing a car drive away, not a cab. There is a knock at the door and Bernie opens it and a man forces his way into Johnny's room. The man is Dr. Melcher. Johnny asks Bernie to look around for Mona with his buddies, and he leaves. Dr. Melcher tells Johnny that it is too late, that the classified materials have been stolen. Melcher tells Johnny that he has found that the vault where a formula has been stored has been broken into and the product has been stolen. Unless it is found within two days it will be too late. What Dr. Melcher tells Johnny is classified, but it concerns an experimental fuel. The fuel Melcher is working on is very powerful and very unstable. If it is not cared for carefully, it could explode, and knowledge of it would be worth millions. The sample that was stolen is incomplete and must be handled carefully. Johnny is told that only Caldwell knew Johnny was coming, but Johnny remembers that Caldwell had phoned Mona, and since she knew what was happening, she had to act fast. The club last night was really a rendezvous with the goon that hit Johnny. Bernie calls and tells Johnny that Mona took a bus to Philadelphia, and Johnny hangs up and heads for the airport.

Johnny flies to Philadelphia, Pennsylvania. Johnny calls the bus line and asks them to check on all passengers coming there. Johnny meets with Lt. Harry Langley of the police, but a day later the police have found nothing. Harry tells Johnny that the bus line has no record of a woman buying a ticket to Philadelphia. Harry tells Johnny that Philadelphia only had 200 people in it when he was born, but that was in Indiana. Johnny realizes that he has the wrong city and asks for an atlas. Johnny finds a third Philadelphia just north of Meridian. Johnny flies back to Meridian, rents a car and drives north to Neshova County, the heart of the Indian country where Mona could hide easily. At an old farmhouse out side of Philadelphia Johnny finds Bernie asleep in his cab. Johnny wakes Bernie and he tells Johnny that he had found out that Mona and Willie Picktooth are inside the house. Bernie has been waiting for a day, and that has been too long, what with them shooting at Bernie. Mona starts shooting and Johnny warns her about the danger of the fuel. She tells Johnny that it is worth a fortune, and they will be able to get out after dark, after all, they are Indians. Suddenly the house explodes several times.

"Any comments on this case? Why bother." notes a saddened Johnny.

NOTES:
- THE FIRST COMMERCIAL BREAK IS AND **AFRS** STORY ABOUT THE ACTIVITIES OF DR. EUGENE WOOD.
- THE SECOND COMMERCIAL BREAK IS AND **AFRS** STORY ON DEMOCRACY AND OPPORTUNITY.
- MASON ADAMS IS BERNIE, ARTHUR KOHL IS MELCHER, RITA LLOYD IS MONA, MARTIN BLAINE IS HARRY.
- STUART METZ IS THE ANNOUNCER
- MUSICAL SUPERVISION IS BY ETHEL HUBER

Producer: Bruno Zirato, Jr.   **Writers:** Jack Johnstone
Cast: Mason Adams, Arthur Kohl, Rita Lloyd, Martin Blaine

SHOW: THE PERILOUS PADRE MATTER
SHOW DATE: 8/6/1961
COMPANY: TRI-WESTERN LIFE INSURANCE COMPANY
AGENT: JACK PRICE
EXP. ACCT: $485.00

SYNOPSIS: Jack Price calls Johnny, but he does not have an insurance problem. He asks if Johnny has heard of the Padre Island treasure, and Johnny has not, but he knows of the island. Jack tells Johnny that the island is over 115 miles long, so it will be hard to find the old Spanish ship, and all the doubloons. Jack wants Johnny to come down and hunt for treasure, among other things

Johnny flies to Corpus Christi, Texas and cabs to the Robert Driscol hotel and gets a room. Johnny walks to Jack's office and feels a gun in his back and is told to walk straight ahead or he will get shot. Johnny tells the man to consider his wife and thirteen children, but is told his sob story will get him nowhere. The man tells Johnny that they do not like the eastern hoods coming into town. Try anything in Corpus, and you will become the corpus. Johnny laughs at the joke that Doug Johnstone was playing on him, and tells Doug that his brother Jack will never put it in the script. Doug asks Johnny how he found out so soon and Johnny asks about what. Doug tells Johnny that Jack Price is a good friend, and his wife had called this morning to find out what had happened to Jack. Doug was told that Johnny had been called, so he wondered if Jack and Johnny had gone out there last night, but that did not make sense. Doug takes Johnny to get some equipment and get out to Padre Island.

Doug takes Johnny to get a beach buggy, an old jeep with huge tires on it, from Obie O'Brien. Doug tells a curious Obie that Johnny is wild about fishing, and they will pick up the fishing tackle later. At Doug's house they get some extra gas, some shovels and an old Winchester 30/30. On the way to the island Doug tells Johnny about the history of the Spanish treasure fleet of 1553. They left from Vera Cruz, Mexico with a cargo of gold. Three ships were lost in a storm, and some got through to the east. Several ships tried for Tampico, south of there, but thirteen ships came aground on Padre Island. A salvage fleet recovered most of the wrecks and took the gold away. A client of Jack's, Jose Pinetta, found a chart in an old chest that shows the location of a ship. Doug notices a car abandoned on the road, but continues driving. The chart gave locations for finding the ship, but the markers are hard to find now. Before the Civil War a man found a chest full of jewels and buried it, and then lost the location. Jose has only told Jack about the chart. Jose has bought a lot of sophisticated search gear, and had agreed to pick up Jack yesterday. Jose was unsure of one of his suppliers, Tony Larker. When Jose did not show up, Jack got worried and looked for Tony and could not find him. Jack then told Doug and went looking for Jose. Johnny spots Jack's Model A Ford beach buggy in the dunes and they head for it. Suddenly there are shots and they hide behind the jeep. Johnny is sure that Jack and Jose are not shooting at them, so it must be Larker.

Bullets hit the tires and Johnny gets a shovel to dig in and wait for dark, and to make a plan of action for nightfall. A thunderstorm blows in and they separate and head for Larker. Johnny is about to reach the car, when it drives off. Doug spots Jack and Jose in the dunes. Jack has a head wound and Jose is dead. Jack tells Johnny that Jose had found the treasure and was going to get Jack when his car broke down. Larker followed them, so Jack and Jose decided to dig in the dunes to distract him. Larker came up on them and shot both of them. Suddenly Larker is back and tells them to drop their guns. Larker tells Johnny that he will shoot them and force Jack to tell him where the treasure is. Larker starts to fire when Johnny calls "Obie." Obie O'Brien hits Larker and Johnny gets his gun. Obie tells them they should have let him come with them, and that he had a hard time following them. Now the only thing he has to show for it is soaked clothes and sore knuckles.

"Treasure? I am afraid the secret of its location there on Padre Island died with Jose Pinetta. Unless, of course, someone happens to find out where Jose hid the chart. But you can bet you bottom dollar that here will be plenty of people looking for it. Maybe even Jack Price and Obie O'Brien. As for Doug, he says he has had enough of it."

NOTES:

- THE FIRST COMMERCIAL BREAK IS THE KINGSTON TRIO FOR SEVEN-UP
- THE SECOND COMMERCIAL BREAK IS FOR IPANA TOOTHPASTE
- THE THIRD COMMERCIAL BREAK IS FOR INSTANT TENDER LEAF ICED TEA
- THE FOURTH COMMERCIAL BREAK IS FOR MENTHOLATUM DEEP HEAT RUB
- LUIS VAN ROOTEN IS DOUG, LARRY HAINES IS TONY, MAURICE TARPLIN IS PRICE, LAWSON ZERBE IS OBIE.
- THE ANNOUNCER IS STUART METZ

- MUSICAL SUPERVISION IS BY ETHEL HUBER

Producer: Bruno Zirato, Jr.   **Writers:**   Jack Johnstone
Cast: Luis Van Rooten, Larry Haines, Maurice Tarplin,
               Lawson Zerbe

◆   ❖   ◆

SHOW: THE WRONG DOCTOR MATTER
SHOW DATE: 8/13/1961
COMPANY: TRI-WESTERN LIFE INSURANCE COMPANY
AGENT: JACK PRICE
EXP. ACCT: $532.40

SYNOPSIS: Jack Price calls Johnny and tells him to come on back to Corpus Christi. Jack tells Johnny their adventure on Padre Islands had taught them all a lesson. Jack asks Johnny if he would like to take on another case? Johnny says sure, as long as the fees are big and Jack does not check the expense account too carefully. Jack thought he was talking to that fine, generous, self-sacrificing, do-it-for-nothing gentleman named Johnny Dollar. Seriously, Jack wants Johnny to come down on an international incident. A client is involved with narcotics, and the case could be dangerous. Johnny tells Jack, that whenever he is called in on a case that is a lead pipe synch, he usually gets shot at. So this one that looks big and dangerous, maybe this one will be a lead pipe synch. Johnny will come down first thing tomorrow.

Johnny takes a midnight flight to Corpus Christi, Texas and cabs to the Robert Driscol for breakfast and a shower. Jack calls and tells Johnny that he is at the office and the case is hotter than he thought. The client, Julio Olivera had worked on the shrimp boats. One of them started carrying heroin, and the judge gave Julio three years for just being on board. He is out of jail now and is clean. Consuelo Diaz, his girlfriend, tells Jack that, well come on to the office. Johnny picks up his .38 lemon squeezer and his hat to take with him. There is a knock at the door and a voice tells Johnny that it is room service. Johnny opens the door and a man enters with a silenced gun. Johnny is on the floor when the maid walks in. The man tells the maid that his friend hurt himself and tells her to get the doctor. The man tells an unconscious Johnny that when the doctor gets there he will be dead.

Johnny plays it smart and goes to the floor. When the maid leaves Johnny kicks the man and knocks his gun away. Johnny gets into a real fight and takes a number of hits. The man puts Johnny in a squeeze-hold and there is a knock on the door. Johnny yells to break down the door and the maid enters with the hotel detective. The man is hiding behind the door. He shoots the detective and leaves. Johnny wakes up to Jack Price with a bottle of brandy. Jack tells Johnny that the welcoming committee was Diego Hernandez. Jack did not think that Hernandez would find out about Johnny. Hernandez was the skipper on the boat Julio was on, and was never caught. Consuelo had called Jack because she found out the

Hernandez was in town, and the police know it now. Hernandez had come to town to get Julio, whose testimony put the finger on the drug racket. Hernandez had visited Consuelo trying to get information. Jack realizes that she probably told Hernandez that Johnny was coming. Julio is out of town and does not know about Hernandez. Johnny tries to get dressed and tells Jack to leave a note for the police. Johnny and Jack go to Consuelo's house in the country and the front door is wide open and the house smells of cordite. Hernandez had gotten there and done his job too well. Julio was dead and Consuelo was barely alive. Jack calls the police and Johnny tries to help Consuelo. She finally tells Johnny that it is no use now with Julio gone. Consuelo tells Johnny that Hernandez did the shooting. Hernandez wanted Julio to go back into business again. Johnny asks Consuelo to tell him where Hernandez went and she says "Doctor" and then "Doctor Velasquez" and dies. Johnny tells Jack that she did not make much sense, but then again, maybe she did.

Johnny spends the next 15 hours working with Sgt. Ortez to find a doctor named Velasquez in any city in Texas. Johnny is frustrated at not finding the doctor, and realizes the answer was right under his nose. Fifty miles below the border is the town of Doctor Velasquez! Sgt. Ortez tells Johnny that it will take a long time to get the proper authorization, but Johnny tells him he will go on his own. Johnny wants to beat Hernandez to the city and tells Sgt. Ortez that what he is going to do is none of his business. Johnny wonders where he could get a light plane, and Sgt. Ortez suggests they take a ride. Johnny rents a plane and flies to the town of Doctor Velasquez, Mexico using a highway map for navigation. The town is a group of ram shackle buildings in the desert. Johnny manages to land the plane and taxis onto the road into town to block any cars coming in. Johnny hides as a car comes and Johnny recognizes Hernandez as the driver. Johnny calls him down and Hernandez tells him he will kill him. Johnny takes his gun for a souvenir and tells him to put his hands behind his back. Hernandez pulls a gun from his sleeve and Johnny shoots him. "Why don't I ever learn to frisk the punks before I tell them to lower their hands? Next time I might not be so lucky."

"It was well after dark when I finally got us back to Corpus Christi, and I had quite a time landing in the small private field from which I had borrowed the plane. Sgt. Ortez, of course, denied any knowledge of the whole thing, but I noticed the landing lights were on and waiting for me. And also by pure coincidence a young fellow from the narcotics squad just happened to be there to meet me. Nor did he suggest that I might have picked up my prisoner anywhere but this side of the border. Just the same Jackson, maybe it would not hurt to keep this report under wraps for a while."

NOTES:
- THE FIRST COMMERCIAL IS THE KINGSTON TRIO FOR SEVEN-UP.
- THE FINAL COMMERCIAL IS FOR MENTHOLATUM DEEP HEAT RUB.
- RALPH CAMAGO IS DIEGO, BOB DRYDEN IS THE SERGEANT, NELLIE SONNENBERG IS CONSUELO, LAWSON ZERBE IS THE VOICE, MAURICE

- TARPLIN IS PRICE, HILDA HAINES IS THE MAID.
- THE ANNOUNCER IS STUART METZ
- MUSICAL SUPERVISION IS BY ETHEL HUBER

Producer:	Bruno Zirato, Jr.	**Writers:**	Jack Johnstone
Cast:	Ralph Camago, Bob Dryden, Nellie Sonnenberg, Lawson Zerbe, Maurice Tarplin, Hilda Haines		

◆   ❖   ◆

SHOW:	TOO MANY CROOKS MATTER
SHOW DATE:	8/20/1961
COMPANY:	MONO GUARANTEE INSURANCE COMPANY
AGENT:	FREDDIE FREIDKIN
EXP. ACCT:	$0.00

SYNOPSIS: Freddie Friedkin calls and wants Johnny to do him a favor. Ever hear of Mrs. Ambrose Winifred Van Turkle? She is an old fuss-budget and lives over at 1227 South Terone. They have just under a million dollars on her jewelry. "You're kidding. My regular commission on a million dollars! I'll take the case."

Johnny muses, "Too many cooks spoil the broth, but too many crooks can mess up an insurance investigation." Johnny drives to see Freddie Friedkin who meets him on the street. Freddie tells Johnny that Mrs. Van Turkle is an important client, and keeps her jewelry in her home in Hartford, Connecticut. Nothing has happened to her, but it has to Freddie. Today is the servant's day off, so Freddie had promised to drive Mrs. Van Turkle into the office to look at her policies. But the Vice President has called a meeting and Freddie dare not leave. So Freddie told Mrs. Van Turkle that Johnny would drive her into the office. Mrs. Van Turkle knows all about Johnny and listens to his program every week. She will be waiting for Johnny to pick her up. Johnny agrees to do the task, not as a favor to Freddie, but to see the female that has put a scare into "Fearless Freddie Friedkin." Johnny drives to the Van Turkle house, a huge brownstone with a large yard. Johnny drives into the portcullis, and toots the horn and waits. Johnny gets out of his car to get Mrs. Van Turkle and is slugged. Johnny recognizes Willie McPeak, a second story man with a record as long as your arm as the man who slugged him. Johnny staggers into the house and finds Mrs. Van Turkle unconscious in the drawing room. Johnny phones Dr. Blakey and tells him what has happened. Mrs. Van Turkle is a patient of his, and he agrees to come right away. Johnny calls Sgt. Harry Simmons, who promises to send someone over right away. Johnny decides to look around the house and finds the safe in the library broken open and emptied. On the floor is a diamond that had been dislodged from its setting. Johnny pockets the stone and calls Freddie to ask how much her jewelry is insured for. Johnny tells him to send her a check, if she stays alive.

Johnny goes to visit Sgt. Simmons who tells Johnny that an old friend just left town an hour ago, a strong-arm man named Willie McPeak. The police just put him on a train to New York. Johnny tells Sgt. Simmons that Willie is also a burglar, and is the man he saw in Van Turkle's house and who hit him. Sgt. Simmons agrees to call the New York police and have them grab McPeak. Johnny thinks that he can find Willie faster than the police. Johnny flies to New York and cabs to 18th precinct to see Randy Singer. First, Johnny makes five calls to old friends who are willing to give him information, for money that is, and then talks to Randy. Johnny tells Randy what has happened and Randy tells him that a lot of fake diamonds are floating around the city. The police have tried to catch who is fencing the goods, but have been unsuccessful so far. Randy thinks that an intermediary is involved. Everyone is complaining to Randy, and now Johnny wants something. While Johnny talks to Randy, he is rubbing the diamond he found on the glass top of Randy's desk. Johnny tells Randy about McPeak and Randy tells Johnny that McPeak has tried a number of rackets, but is only successful at burglary. Johnny tells Randy that McPeak has stolen almost a million dollars in jewels. Johnny gets a phone call from "Spotty," who tells Johnny that McPeak was just seen going into apartment 2-A at 718 East 49th with a briefcase. Johnny takes a cab to the building and pushes all the buttons but 2-A to get into the building. Johnny finally slips the lock on the front door and goes to apartment 2-A where he hears voices arguing. A voice is about to tell Willie something about the stones, but Willie pulls a gun and shoots the other person in the room. Johnny breaks in and gets the drop on Willie. Johnny checks the other man who is dead. Johnny opens Willie's brief case and discovers [?].

Johnny calls Randy and tells him what has happened. Randy tells Johnny that there is a guy living there named Horace Petersley who deals in hot jewelry, and Johnny tells Randy that he lived there. Willie just shot him. Johnny tells Randy to send another man over, as he is coming to the office with Willie McPeak and the Van Turkle jewels. Johnny asks Randy to call the gemologist Fritz Melchior and have him come to Randy's office. Johnny cabs to Randy's office and Melchior is there and waiting. Johnny gives him the Van Turkle jewels and tells him to get to work. Randy wants to book Willie as Conroy is tired of holding his gun on him. Johnny believes that if he is right, Willie might want to use the gun on himself. Johnny reminds Randy that he had been rubbing the jewels on the glass, but not scratching it. When Petersley told Willie the deal was off and gave the paste back to Willie, Johnny suddenly remembered that the diamond had not scratched the glass. Johnny realizes that there are too many crooks involved in this case, including a little old lady who figured on collecting a million dollars on her fake jewels. Mr. Melchior confirms that the jewels are fakes. Melchior uses several tests to prove his point that the jewels are just glass. Willie gets really upset and tells them that he stole the jewels and killed a man to make a deal with him. "I've been robbed!" Willie yells as he is taken down to be booked. Randy hates to admit that Johnny has done a good day's work.

"As for the phony jewels, well (old Mrs. Van Turkle has completely recovered from the beating by the way) they are fakes. The real jewels she always keeps in the vault in the bank. The paste she had there in the wall safe was for casual wear."

NOTES:
- THE FIRST COMMERCIAL IS FOR NO-DOZ.
- THE SECOND COMMERCIAL IS FOR NEWPORT MENTHOL CIGARETTES.
- THE THIRD COMMERCIAL IS FOR SINCLAIR DINO GASOLINE.
- WALTER OTTO IS CREDITED FOR THE SOUND PATTERNS
- THIS PROGRAM IS EXTREMELY NOISY AND SOME OF THE DETAILS MIGHT NOT BE CORRECT, ESPECIALLY THE NAMES.
- THE ANNOUNCER IS ART HANNES
- MUSICAL SUPERVISION IS BY ETHEL HUBER

Producer: **Fred Hendrickson**   **Writers:** **Jack Johnstone**
Cast: **Court Benson, Sam Gray, Jackson Beck, Bill Smith, James Stevens, Tom Gorman, Maurice Tarplin**

SHOW:	**THE SHIFTY LOOKER MATTER**
SHOW DATE:	**8/27/1961**
COMPANY:	**FLOYDS OF ENGLAND**
AGENT:	**GEOFFREY REED**
EXP. ACCT:	**$4.40**

SYNOPSIS: Geoffrey Reed calls Johnny from Floyds. He is George's younger brother and has taken over here because George has been transferred to the head office. Johnny recounts the cases that George had Johnny working on. Geoffrey tells Johnny that George had told him that if Geoff had any problems of an unusual nature, he could call on Johnny for assistance. (uh, oh) This policy was written by George himself (I shudder) and is for $100,000 on the return of a child. The term of the policy forbids bringing in the police. Johnny wants to call in the FBI, but Geoff tells him he cannot. Geoffrey wants Johnny to come over and read the policy and meet the father; that will change his mind.

Johnny buys gas and drives to Geoffrey's office. Geoffrey looks like his brother, but is decidedly British and always makes his point by the longest possible route. Geoffrey starts by telling Johnny that he will be keeping an eye on Johnny's expense accounts, as they get out of hand on occasion. Geoffrey also tells Johnny that he understands the nature of George's policies. Johnny is told to read the policy on Steven Looker and his seven-year-old daughter Cynthia. Johnny thinks he knows the name, but cannot remember from where. Mr. Looker is retired and lives in the Wakefield Towers in Hartford, Connecticut. Mr. Looker had been out late the previous evening and Cynthia was alone. When he returned this morning, she was gone. A tape-recorded ransom message was left on his telephone demanding $100,000, the exact amount of the policy. Johnny reads the policy, which is written to insure her specifically against kidnapping. The terms are for payment in unmarked bills up to $100,000, and no law enforcement or the press are to be brought into the case until Mr. Looker has attempted payment or gets the child back. Johnny tells Geoff that the policy is illegal. Geoff tells Johnny that he is being brought in because he is not one of the groups excluded in the policy. The policy was issued just after Cynthia was born which was just shortly after the Bealer kidnapping and the abduction and murder of the Hammerwait child. The ransom is supposed to be paid tonight and Mr. Looker is coming to pick up the money. The secretary Sarah announces Mr. Looker and Johnny stays, acting as the employee who picked up the money.

Johnny seems to recognize Looker, who complains that Johnny being there was a breech of policy. Looker knows all about kidnappings, and what happens if you do not do what they say. Cynthia is all he has, and no one will take her away. Johnny asks for proof that Cynthia was kidnapped. Looker gives the tape to Geoff to play for this "doubting Thompson." Johnny asks why he records his phone conversations and Looker tells Johnny that he used to work in electronics and tape recordings. After his wife died, he hooked up a tape recorder to record messages. It will also record calls when Looker answers if he chooses to. Johnny tells Looker that the only reason an individual would need a recorder is if he expects to be threatened and wants a record of it for the police. Suppose he had contacts with people of questionable reputations? Geoff plays the tape, which tells Looker that they have Cynthia and to leave them 100G's in unmarked bills. They will let Looker see her before he gives them the money. Looker stops the tape when the caller tells him to "put the money in a paper bag at 11:00 and bring it to . . ." Johnny tells Looker that the tape must be left as evidence, but he takes it with him. Looker tells Geoff that he will call from his apartment when he gets Cynthia back. Johnny knows that the apartment has a switchboard, so there will be a record of the call as evidence. Johnny tries to follow Looker and loses him after five minutes. Johnny remembers where he knows the name and goes to the library to look up Steve "Shifty" Looker in the newspaper files. Johnny finds a story from September of 1954, about the breakup of the Maroni mob in Chicago. Everyone got off without a prison term. Shifty had used a clever elaborate radio hookup to jam the police radios whenever the gang was pulling a job. Shifty got off by turning state's evidence, but Maroni got a seven-year stretch and swore he would get even. Maroni was also involved in kidnapping. Johnny calls the police and asks about "Stinky" Maroni. The police agree to check on it for Johnny.

Johnny goes to see the police but there is no word yet. The police Lieutenant accuses Johnny of knowing that one of Maroni's henchmen, Steven Looker, is living in Hartford now. He has been here for seven years and has been behaving. The worst thing Maroni could do would be to harm the girl, as Looker has no money. The police are about to put a watch on Looker when the Conroy brings the teletype message in. The message tells Johnny that Maroni does not get out of the pen for another two weeks. Johnny realizes he has been blind and runs out. Was it was Maroni's upcoming release, or something Looker had planned all along? How would a kidnapper expect Looker to come up with the money unless he knew about the insurance policy? But the policy was a secret and the demands were for the exact amount of the policy. Looker must have known who Johnny was? Johnny decides to go to Looker's apartment. Johnny knocks at the door, tells Looker it is special delivery, and when the door is opened he sees Looker's bags packed. Johnny opens the bags and asks why the money is packed in the bag. Shifty pulls a gun and tells Johnny he was waiting for him. Looker starts to shoot Johnny when the police arrive. The Lieutenant tells Johnny that he had put a tail on Johnny when he left headquarters, and Johnny did not even notice. "You must be slipping."

"Well, lets see now. Expense account total is exactly $4.40? Ok, Geoffrey, it's perfectly all right, as long as you don't forget my commission on just exactly 100,000 clams. Not bad for a single days work. I'll take it anytime."

NOTES:
- COMMERCIAL BREAK #1 IS FOR MENTHOLATUM DEEP HEAT RUB.
- COURT BENSON IS REED, ROGER DEKOVEN IS LOOKER, CARL FRANK IS THE LT., ALLAN MANSON IS THE VOICE ON THE TAPE, GUY REPP IS CONROY, BARBARA CASSAR IS SARAH.
- THE ANNOUNCER IS ART HANNES
- MUSICAL SUPERVISION IS BY ETHEL HUBER

Producer:	Bruno Zirato, Jr.	**Writers:**	Jack Johnstone
Cast:	Court Benson, Roger De Koven, Carl Frank, Allan Manson, Guy Repp, Barbara Cassar		

◆ ❖ ◆

SHOW:	THE ALL WET MATTER
SHOW DATE:	9/3/1961
COMPANY:	STATE UNITY LIFE INSURANCE COMPANY
AGENT:	LAWRENCE PENWORTHY THURSTON
EXP. ACCT:	$300.00

SYNOPSIS: Lawrence Penworthy Thurston calls. He is the local representative of State Unity Life Insurance Company in Cayce, South Carolina. He wants Johnny to make sure he visits all the sights in South Carolina while he is there in Columbia. You can come right away? One of their most important clients is sure that someone wants to kill her.

Johnny flies to Columbia and cabs to the DeSoto Hotel. The next morning Johnny visits the State Unity office on State Street, which is close to station WCAY that carries Johnny's cases. Thurston is a nice old southern gentleman who offers Johnny a cigar. The client is Mrs. Melanie Ramsey Pembrooke who comes from one of the oldest families in the area. The Ramsey side of the family has the money in the family, and Mrs. Pembrooke lives in Ramseyville, South Carolina. Thurston is sure that someone is trying to kill her because of the package she received yesterday. Thurston called Johnny because Ramseyville does not have a police department. Mrs. Pembrooke told Thurston that the package had an "infernal machine" in it. Johnny clarifies that to mean a bomb. Johnny rents a car and drives to Ramseyville, which is not very big. Mrs. Pembrooke, who is in her late forties, meets Johnny at the door of her home. She tells Johnny that her husband Peter is away, he is a salesman who sells machine tools, but is not very good at it. Her husband is eleven years younger than she is, and is no way near as wealthy as she is. He had gone to Minneapolis, Milwaukee and Duluth on his last trip and should be home any time. She received the badly wrapped package yesterday. She shook the package and noticed a ticking sound inside it. She threw the package out the window and into a fishpond. When she went out to look at it later, it had fallen apart. Mrs. Pembrooke shows Johnny the contents and Johnny describes it as a crude time bomb and tells her that throwing it into the fishpond broke the wiring and ruined the detonating device. She tells Johnny that the package was meant for her. Mrs. Pembrooke tells Johnny the package was mailed from Chicago. When Johnny notes that Chicago could have been a stopover on her husband's trip she is sure that her husband is not involved.

Johnny notes that any fingerprints were long gone. Johnny checks the hotel in Duluth, and Peter had left to come home. Johnny wonders if someone mailed the package from Chicago for him. Mrs. Pembrooke is positive that her husband would not do such a thing as he is too good hearted and not to suspect him. Johnny tells her that she is not to tell her husband about the bomb until Johnny has had a chance to talk to him. Johnny visits station WCAY and speaks with Bill Barrett of the news bureau. Johnny asks Bill about any fine plantation homes in the area, and Bill tells Johnny about the Ramsey place. Mrs. Pembrooke, the last of the Ramsey line, owns it. Bill tells Johnny that Pete Pembrooke was smart and married into money; that is if she does not catch him. Bill calls Pete a Romeo who married for the money. Bill tells Johnny that Melanie is a really shrewd person, manners not withstanding. Bill tells Johnny that she seems to be the only person in the area who is not wise to Pete's a playing around. Bill tells Johnny that she would throw Pete out if she ever caught him. Johnny receives a call from Mrs. Pembrooke, who tells Johnny that her husband just came home. Johnny goes to the Pembrooke home, where Pete has and has been in the bath for an hour. Mrs. Pembrooke and Johnny go up to the bathroom and find the door locked. Johnny breaks down the door and they fund Pete dead in the bathtub.

Dr. Eustus Culpepper is called and declares the cause of death a heart attack. He asks Johnny if the radio above the tub was on when Johnny got there, and Johnny tells him no. Too bad, as Pete had a history of heart problems. Dr. Culpepper tells Johnny he can make preparations for the body, but Johnny has a better idea. Johnny calls the police and thinks about the package mailed from Chicago. Johnny ponders about Pete mailing the package or having it mailed. "Have it mailed?" Johnny has an idea and finds a pile of pulp magazines in the living room and finds what he is looking for. "Surprise your friends with mail from all over the world, signed and sent by you. For only fifty cents plus regular postage we'll mail your letter, your package from anywhere in the United States." And the address of the re-mailing outfit, Chicago, Illinois of course. Johnny could call the company to find out who paid to have the package sent, but goes back upstairs to poke around. The police arrive and join Johnny after talking with the doctor. Johnny wonders about what the autopsy will reveal, if anything. Johnny shows the officer that the door was locked from the outside and uses the hem of his handkerchief to show how it could be done. Johnny is sure that someone came in, killed Peter and then locked the door. Johnny shows the officer the radio on the shelf above the tub and tells him that a radio should never be anywhere near water. Johnny shows how the cord is unplugged, like someone pulled it from the wall to keep from shocking themselves after using it as a murder weapon. Johnny shows him how the radio is wet inside and the switch is still on. Bad heart or good, he didn't have a chance. Johnny tells the officer that the only other person in the house murdered him after she found out he was playing around, and only married her for her money. And that was too much for the fine old family pride. The phony "infernal machine" was a cover to keep her from being suspected. Mrs. Pembrooke comes in with a gun to shoot Johnny and the police officer, but the officer hits her and gets the gun away from her. "And to think that I, a gentleman sir, would ever strike a woman that way!" Johnny tells him not to worry about it; he will get over it.

"So from here on in it's up to the courts. It is not to be broadcast, but a tidy hunk of this expense account went to that officer who so fortunately for a moment forgot to be a gentleman. You'll notice I haven't given his name."

NOTES:
- THE FIRST COMMERCIAL IS ABOUT THE NEW NET ALERT NEWS SYSTEM IN USE FOR IMPORTANT NEWS BULLETINS.
- THE SECOND COMMERCIAL IS FOR THE UNITED CAMPAIGN.
- TONI DARNEY AS MELANIE, LAWSON ZERBE IS THURSTON, DAN OCKO IS DR. CULPEPPER, CLIFF CARPENTER IS THE POLICEMAN.
- THE ANNOUNCER IS ART HANNES
- MUSICAL SUPERVISION IS BY ETHEL HUBER

Producer: Bruno Zirato, Jr.   Writers: Jack Johnstone
Cast: Toni Darney, Lawson Zerbe, Dan Ocko, Cliff Carpenter

SHOW:	THE BUYER AND THE CELLAR MATTER
SHOW DATE:	9/10/1961
COMPANY:	WORLDWIDE MUTUAL INSURANCE COMPANY
AGENT:	DON REAGLE
EXP. ACCT:	$477.30

SYNOPSIS: Don Reagle calls and tells Johnny that he has been moved from Chicago to San Francisco. Johnny has some fine memories of San Francisco; fine memories of fat fees. "Is this going to be another one?" Johnny wonders. Don tells Johnny that Harvey Layman is missing and inured for $250,000. Johnny is on his way.

Johnny flies to San Francisco, California and cabs to the Huntington Hotel on Nob Hill. The next morning Johnny visits Don in his office near station KCBS, which carries his reports for CBS and helped him solve an arson case once. Don tells Johnny not to unpack his bags. Harvey Layman has disappeared, and his wife is the beneficiary. They have not really been getting along lately, but he has a good business, and would be worth more money later on. His wife is not domineering, she is overpowering! While Layman is working, she is spending on herself. Layman is stubborn and will not give up hope for her changing her ways. Layman is a commission buyer of antiques and left her a week ago for Beverly Hills to see a man, but he never came back. Layman is extremely punctual, and would not just up and change his schedule. Don has checked the hotels, and there is no sign of him. Layman went to see John Arthur Whitington Maynard, who has told Don that Layman never showed up. Maynard was a big movie producer thirty years ago, and made a number of big-money horror films. Layman was a buyer of unusual things, and Johnny remembers that Maynard had an old movie castle set moved to his property to use as a home. Johnny gets the description of Layman and is told that the wife has promised to send a picture. Johnny drives to the Layman house in Marin County. Johnny notes that the house was definitely decorated by a woman for a woman. Johnny is convinced after talking to Doris Layman, that he either left to get away from her or she did him in.

Mrs. Layman tells Johnny that she would not dirty her hands by murdering Harvey; he is worth more alive than dead. She refuses to believe that he would run off. The police, those "big talking, do nothing men," have accomplished nothing, and the movie-struck police in Beverly Hills are just as bad. Mrs. Laymen tells Johnny that Harvey had called her from Maynard's home. He always calls, she insists on it, and Harvey always obeys. She had forgotten to tell that to the police, but they should have known. Harvey had gone there to collect $10,000. Doris tells Johnny that Maynard had told Harvey he should feel honored to have helped decorate the place, and threatened Harvey. Doris told Harvey to go down there and collect the money or else. Doris tells Johnny to leave and forget about the case. From his hotel Johnny calls an old friend, "Sgt. Brady" at the Beverly Hills Police Department. Sgt. Brady tells Johnny that there was a phone call made to Marin County number from Maynard's house. Sgt. Brady thinks Maynard might have called Layman, but Johnny tells him that Maynard did not know Layman was coming. The police know Maynard, and he is a nut. The police have searched the place and found nothing. Brady tells Johnny that if Maynard ever did kill anyone, he would invite the police over to show the body to them. Johnny flies to Los Angeles, rents a car and drives to Beverly Hills and to police headquarters. Sgt. Brady is out so Johnny drives up to the Maynard house up in the mountains. Johnny gets that wee small voice in his brain that says, "Watch it Dollar, you may be getting into more than you bargained for. So, watch it Dollar. Watch it."

Johnny describes the house, once a movie set, as a medieval castle. The drawbridge is lowered as Johnny approaches and Johnny sees Maynard standing there, a short, fat unkempt man resembling Quasimodo. Maynard invites Johnny into the castle. When Johnny tells Maynard he is an investigator he starts to throw Johnny out mistaking him for a salesman. Johnny tells him he is there about Harvey Layman. Maynard takes Johnny in to show him all the things his dear friend Layman had bought for him. Johnny is sure that most of the things in the house deserved to be in a museum, and especially the things in the basement torture chamber. Maynard tells Johnny that he was the master of murder, mayhem and torture. Johnny is taken to the wine cellar, which is full of dusty wine bottles that have been there for twenty-nine years, according to Maynard. Maynard tells Johnny that he has not seen Layman for over a year. Maynard also tells Johnny that he never drinks the wine in the cellar. Maynard holds a bottle up to the light for Johnny, and Johnny sees what Maynard really means. Johnny tells Maynard that everything just looks real, that most of the house is just imitation. Johnny tells Maynard that the dust and cobwebs even fooled the police. Johnny tells him that the dust is just Fuller's Earth. Johnny would have been fooled if Maynard had not picked up the wine and held it up to the light. Maynard protests when Johnny starts to investigate a pile of bottles and pulls a gun. Johnny remembers a movie where Maynard had a man buried under bottles of wine, and Maynard tells Johnny that Harvey Layman is buried there, and Johnny will join him. Maynard is about to shoot when Sgt. Brady comes in. Maynard fires and Sgt. Brady shoots him. Johnny is glad he left word at headquarters for Sgt. Brady to join him. Johnny tells him that the bottle of sherry, which was supposed to have been there for twenty-nine years, did not have any sediment in it. The age dust and cobwebs were all fake. Johnny tells Sgt. Brady that he just took a wild guess.

"Needless to say, wild as the whole thing may seem, they found Layman's body buried there in the cellar."

NOTES:
- THE FIRST COMMERCIAL IS FOR DUPONT ZEREX ANTIFREEZE.
- THE SECOND COMMERCIAL IS FOR THE UNITED FUND DRIVE.
- FULLER'S EARTH WAS ALSO MENTIONED IN THE MEI-LING BUDDHA MATTER
- LEON JANNEY IS MAYNARD, GERTRUDE WARNER IS DORIS, WILLIAM REDFIELD IS BRADY, CARL FRANK IS DON.
- THE ANNOUNCER IS ART HANNES
- MUSICAL SUPERVISION IS BY ETHEL HUBER

Producer: Bruno Zirato, Jr.   Writers: Jack Johnstone
Cast: Leon Janney, Gertrude Warner, William Redfield, Carl Frank

◆ ❖ ◆

SHOW: THE DOUBLE-BARRELED MATTER
SHOW DATE: 9/24/1961
COMPANY: MONO GUARANTEE INSURANCE COMPANY
AGENT: PHIL EASTERDAY
EXP. ACCT: $760.00

SYNOPSIS: Phil Easterday calls Johnny from San Diego, and Johnny tells him it has been a long time. Phil wants Johnny to come out to sunny California. The problem is a series of burglaries against the same couple. But exactly nothing has been taken in any of them. Phil will meet Johnny at the airport. Goodbye.

Johnny flies to Los Angeles and then on to San Diego, California, landing around noon. Johnny notes that San Diego is the oldest settlement in California, and has the perfect climate that Los Angeles brags about. Johnny likes it there. Phil meets Johnny and tells him that whether anything is taken or not, burglary is breaking and entering with the intent to commit a felony. Mr. Charles Hastings Warner and Mrs. Trudy Warner's apartment has been broken into seven times in the past two months. Phil does not know what Hastings does for a living, but he has several policies worth over a million. The burglaries were never reported to the police. Phil's wife plays bridge with Mrs. Warner who told her, and she told Phil. Phil called Mrs. Warner who did not want to report them because nothing was stolen, but she is worried. Johnny thinks the whole thing is suspicious. Johnny gets the address and decides not to tell the Warners he is coming. Johnny rents a car and drives to the apartment, which is a cottage behind a local hotel, and very well furnished. Mrs. Warner is in her mid twenties and very dignified and well-appointed with diamond earrings. Johnny senses a blue blood, but the nasal twang and poor grammar in her voice says otherwise. Johnny uses the old foot in the door trick to get in the door to talk to her about the burglaries. She tells Johnny that she should not have talked to that insurance man's wife. Trudy wonders what would happen if she came home and found somebody in the apartment with a gun. All of the burglaries have taken place after Charlie has come home and they have gone out at night, as they do a lot of night clubbing. Who ever did it was very thorough, and Charlie told her not to worry about it, as it was probably some psychopath. Charlie is so cool and casual about everything. Over a drink, Trudy tells Johnny that Charlie is not employed, at least since she married him, and does not know what he did before that. Trudy tells Johnny that Charlie tells her his money comes from the stock market. Charlie is out hunting near El Centro, and he goes almost every week. Charlie is hunting for doves, or pigeons or what ever. Charlie stays at the Blue Bird Motor court and he left this morning. After a second short drink (just to keep her company, believe me) Johnny leaves and starts making calls to stock brokerages, and no one has ever heard of Warner. Johnny calls an old friend, Pete Fuller on the Chicago Sun Times, and Pete tells Johnny all about "Chicky" Warner. Johnny gets the rundown, and realizes he is involved in one of the most important and dangerous cases in his career.

Johnny decides to act fast and follow a hunch, based on Warner's character. Johnny buys a collection of sporting clothes and a 12-gauge double-barreled shotgun and three boxes of shells with #9 birdshot, and a hunting license. Johnny ages his new clothes by driving over his car over them and drives to El Centro and gets a room at the Blue Bird Motor court. In the bar Johnny meets Warner, a man of 50. Johnny strikes up a conversation and hopes Warner can tell Johnny where to go to find doves. Warner tells Johnny that he can tell him where to find so many doves he will call them pigeons. Johnny asks if he can tag along, and Warner agrees. There will be two of you, as he is going with some other guy named Al Milford. It is good to have some witnesses along to make sure Warner does not go over his limit. Warner tells Johnny that he can watch Milford to make sure he does not blow Warner's head off by mistake. "When a man has a gun on him, you never know. Remember that." Very early the next morning, the three men take off to Colexico and onto a dirt road that winds very close to Mexico. Johnny does not like Milford, who is very shifty. Warner places Johnny and Milford together, and when the sun comes up Johnny has more action than he can handle. Johnny notices that Warner was only shooting one shot at a time, and Milford was not shooting at all after the first big flurry. Johnny edges towards Warner and finds Milford lying in the brush aiming at Warner with his shotgun, and a .38 by his side. Milford aims the .38 at Johnny and shows his credentials. He knows who Johnny is, and Al tells Johnny that he is with the narcotics squad. They know how Warner gets the pure uncut heroin across the border. He picks it up from a contact on these hunting trips and always has a witness with him. Johnny surmises that the Feds had searched Warner's apartment, but Al cannot confirm that. No one has ever found the dope on him and Al has to find out how he brings it in. Warner walks up and tells Al he will never find out and shoots him in the arm with a shotgun slug. Warner tells Johnny to toss him the .38 or he will get the other barrel, but Johnny takes his time. Johnny tells Warner that he does want the other barrel and walks towards him, complementing him on the hiding place for the dope. "Only one shot at a time is what gave you away," Johnny tells him. Johnny tells Warner that if he shoots, the hammer will fall on the white stuff it is loaded with. Warner tries to bribe Johnny, but he only deal he will make is to slug Warner. Johnny tells Al that, as a reward for his cleverness, Warner can carry him back to the car.

"That one shotgun barrel loaded with heroin, sure it was only a guess, but thank heavens it was the right one. You know, for a second there I was afraid he might have a shell in it."

NOTES:
- THE COMMERCIAL BREAK IS FOR MENTHOLATUM DEEP HEATING RUB.
- SANTOS ORTEGA IS WARNER, ELIZABETH LAWRENCE IS TRUDY, COURT BENSON IS EASTERDAY, CARL FRANK IS AL, ROBERT DRYDEN IS PETE.
- THE ANNOUNCER IS ART HANNES
- MUSICAL SUPERVISION IS BY ETHEL HUBER

Producer: Bruno Zirato, Jr.   Writers: Jack Johnstone
Cast: Santos Ortega, Elizabeth Lawrence, Court Benson, Carl
            Frank, Robert Dryden

SHOW: THE MEDIUM RARE MATTER
SHOW DATE: 10/8/1961
COMPANY: TRI-WESTERN LIFE INSURANCE COMPANY
AGENT: JACK PRICE
EXP. ACCT: $465.30

SYNOPSIS: "I am thy father's spirit, Doom'd for a certain term to walk the night."
(Well good for you replies Johnny.) "And for the day confined to fast in fires till
the foul crimes done in my days of nature are burnt and purged away." (Bravo,
Mr. Shakespeare!) Johnny asks Jack Price why the long quote from act one of
Hamlet. Jack asks Johnny if he believes in ghosts. A lot of innocent people in
Corpus are beginning to, because of a psychic medium that has moved in on
them. He has been holding séances and doing the clairvoyance thing. Johnny
asks if the medium is rare, medium or, maybe well done? Jack asks Johnny to
come down and help him save the company's money.

Johnny flies to Corpus Christi, Texas and gets a room at the Robert Driscol
Hotel. Later, Johnny asks Jack if the police have looked into this phony. They
have, but there is no proof. The man operates outside the city limits, and uses
the name Udi Vishnu, but Jack thinks that the Hindu accent is tinted with
Brooklynese. Udi does not charge for his act, but relies on contributions. He is
operating out beyond the Ranch 66 roadhouse, in an old abandoned theater
called the Temple of the Living Truth. Every night the place is packed with the
people who think he is a new prophet, and the floor is covered with their
contributions that include insurance policies that have been cashed in. People are
coming from all over the area, and are staying at a hotel that Vishnu owns
nearby. Jack thinks he is committing murder; in the past two weeks two clients
have been murdered. Johnny suggests that he go out and to see the show, and
Jack gives him a reserved seat ticket for the show. Johnny rents a car and drives
to the temple, where only those with reserved seat are admitted. Inside Johnny
sees a bare stage with a reading platform. Most of the audience looks like poor
folks, the most likely to be taken in. At 8:27 the organ music starts and then Udi
Vishnu glides onto the stage at 8:30. Johnny notes an almost hypnotic stare in
his eyes. Udi starts with a statement about his powers and urges to audience to
join him in gaining the super natural powers within them. Udi calls on number
H-41, and a woman tells Johnny that the number is her seat number. Vishnu sees
a vision of a farm on Oklahoma near El Reno, and a small girl named Martha
Winters and a dog she was not supposed to have named Skipper. Vishnu sees her
school and the teacher, Miss Albright, who helped Martha decide not to run
away. Martha believes in Vishnu, as does the crowd for two more hours. Johnny
talks with the people after the program, but none had told anyone anything that

Vishnu knew about them. Later, Jack tells Johnny that he has to find out how Vishnu gets all of the information about the people. Even Houdini or Thurston or Blackstone would have to take a backseat to this punk. Suddenly, Johnny has an idea about the reserved seats. Johnny remembers that a magician had set out to expose the phony mediums in all the big cities, but Vishnu only plays to the small towns that would never have heard of the other magician. Johnny tells Jack to get two tickets for tonight's show and get the county authorities and the newspapers there as well. Johnny is going to prove that the mystic is a mistake. Johnny spends several hours to get the answer to a key question, the amount of the phone bill of the mystic's hotel. Johnny visits the hotel and looks at the register, which shows two critical things—the home address and the ticket number of each person. Johnny goes back to town and runs up $120 in very necessary phone calls. Jack has the tickets and they go to the show with a number of county authorities and members of the national press. The program begins as usual and within an hour he has the audience in his grasp. Finally Vishnu calls on one of the numbers Johnny had compiled. Vishnu calls the number L-13. Vishnu starts to tell a man what he knows, but Johnny jumps up and takes over. Johnny tells the man that he was there last night and has the same powers as Vishnu. Johnny tells seat L-13 that he knows all about him by using the same sort of trickery Vishnu uses. His name is Martin Mefford, and he lives in Cotton Valley, Louisiana, and his car license number is CFU160, and he is a plumber's helper. The man agrees and Vishnu tells the crowd not to believe Johnny. Johnny continues and tells Mefford that he walks with a limp because he broke his leg when he was six and Tommy Parkins shoved him from a tree. Miss Bruster in the first grade promised him a book if he stopped chewing his nails and Mefford agrees. Johnny calls out seat number C-41 and repeats the same sort of thing as Vishnu protests.

"By the time I got through telling those people things even Vishnu had not found out about them, and some of it was pretty personal, they fairly tore the place apart. Then when Udi dragged a gun from under his robes to protect himself and pulled off a couple of shots, well then the police moved in. As for the radio and newspaper story that followed, well believe me that Udi Vishnu, whose real name turned out to be Bernie Bildrick, will not try that trick again, even if he does get out of the pen." Jack asks Johnny how he got all the information, and Johnny tells him he used the same trick that the magician in New York had used. He would call the ticket agent at the hotel and get the names and addresses of a guest who had bought a ticket to the show. All Johnny had to do was look at the register. Johnny got on the phone and called the police chief and the mayor of the town and then called a few other people to get the information. So, that's that.

"Whether they can pin the two murders on him that Jack told me about remains to be seen, that's up to the authorities and is out of my hands now."

NOTES:
- THERE ARE SEVERAL PLAYS ON THE TITLE OF A PREVIOUS STORY,

"THE MEDIUM WELL DONE MATTER" IN THIS STORY.
- MAURICE TARPLIN IS JACK, DAN OCKO IS UDI, EVELYN JUSTER IS THE FIRST WOMAN, BILL LIPTON IS MEFFORD, TONI DARNEY IS THE SECOND WOMAN. ALSO GUY REPP AND SAM RASKYN
- THE QUOTE FROM HAMLET ACT I IS SPOKEN BY THE GHOST CHARACTER.
- THE ANNOUNCER IS ART HANNES
- MUSICAL SUPERVISION IS BY ETHEL HUBER

Producer: Bruno Zirato, Jr.   Writers: Jack Johnstone
Cast: Maurice Tarplin, Dan Ocko, Evelyn Juster, Bill Lipton, Toni Darney, Guy Repp, Sam Raskyn

◆   ❖   ◆

SHOW: THE THREE FOR ONE MATTER
SHOW DATE: 10/22/1961
COMPANY: INTERNATIONAL LIFE & CASUALTY INSURANCE COMPANY
AGENT: CHRISTIAN ALBECK
EXP. ACCT: $81.50

SYNOPSIS: Christian Albeck calls Johnny from Boston and he has bit of a problem. He wants Johnny to come up and Johnny agrees if he will pay his expenses, commission and maybe a little fee. Christian tells Johnny that there is a $250,000 policy involved, and Johnny is on his way.

Johnny flies to Boston, Massachusetts and cabs to Christian's office, not too far from station WEEI which broadcasts Johnny's reports. Christian is a sharp individual, who Johnny feels is often one step ahead of him. Johnny suggests that Christian spring for lunch at the Union Oyster House, and he agrees. He also tells Johnny that he will need a rental car to drive up to Center Harbor, New Hampshire near Lake Winnipesaukee where Johnny handled another case. Over lunch Johnny is told that he is to find out what happened to John Stuart Kirkman, who lives on Red Hill Road. Kirkman is retired and is worth a lot of money. Kirkman left the house after dinner last night and has not come back. Johnny tells Chris that if he had told Johnny of his suspicions on the last case, it would have saved the company a lot of money. Chris tells Johnny that the beneficiary of the policy is the wife Mona, and she will get half a million if it was an accident. Chris tells Johnny that there are three people were might be worth looking into. The first is Charles D. Hockaway, a junior partner in Kirkman's firm. Hockaway had borrowed a lot of money from Kirkman and has not paid it back. It was almost $100,000, and Kirkman was going to take legal action, and Hockaway is worried and resentful because Kirkman did not really need the money. Hockaway has recently rented a cabin in Center Harbor. The second person is Mildred Armstrong, Kirkman's first wife. The divorce was generous, but he did not add to the settlement when Kirkman started making money and she swore she would get him. She too has moved to Center Harbor. Third is Tony Benson who lives across the lake. He is an irresponsible bum and is just no good.

Tony is a dental assistant with the local dentist. He was in love with Mona, or rather her fortune, but Kirkman married her and used her fortune to enlarge his. Tony will stop at nothing to get even with Kirkman. Johnny rents a car and drives to Center Harbor. Johnny checks in at the Garnet Inn and gets a visit from Police Chief Mike Sharp. The Chief tells Johnny that he has just found Kirkman, or rather his body.

Johnny and Chief Sharp drive to the spot where Kirkman slid off the road. Johnny spots the tire tracks and Chief Sharp tells Johnny that Kirkman lost control and went over the edge of the cliff. Doc Higby, the coroner, is inspecting the body and Johnny notes that there were no skid marks on the road. Johnny wonders if Kirkman was dead before he went over. Doc Higby tells Johnny that the only mark on Kirkman is the one on his head that killed him when the car rolled over. Doc is irritated that Johnny would question him, until he finds out just who Johnny is. Doc listens to Johnny's cases on WGAN in Portland and WEEI in Boston. Doc Higby decides to do an autopsy and Chief Sharp tells Johnny that here are three people he wants to keep in the area. They are the same three Johnny is interested in. Johnny requests that a mechanic look at the car while the Chief Sharp rounds up the suspects. Johnny goes to clean up for dinner and finds Tony Benson in his room. He saw the note Johnny had left for Chief Sharp and decided to wait for Johnny in his room. Better breaking and entering than murder. Tony tells Johnny that he did not have a grudge against Kirkman, but did against Mona. Tony knows he will get a fair deal from Johnny. Johnny asks him why he thinks it was murder rather than an accident and Tony tries to back pedal and saying that the police will try to pin anything on him. Johnny gets a call from Mildred Armstrong who must see Johnny right away. She is not the one who murdered or, um, had Kirkman murdered. Johnny asks her why she thinks it is murder. She is glad when Johnny tells her it looks like an accident. Johnny tells her to come to the hotel. There is a knock at the door, and it is Charles Hockaway. Johnny surmises that Charles came to tell Johnny that he did not murder Kirkman. Johnny again asks why Charles thinks it was murder? Charlie tells Johnny that Kirkman and he were not on good terms, but he did not do it. Chief Sharp shows up with Mildred, and all three suspects are in the room with Johnny. Johnny goes into the hallway and the Chief tells Johnny that Kirkman did die in an accident. Also, Frank Marshall the mechanic can find nothing wrong with the car. There was no fluid in the brake line, but that was caused by a tiny hole in the break line, maybe it was a defective piece of tubing. Johnny tells Sharp to keep an eye on the suspects while he goes to look at the car. At the garage Frank tells Johnny that if the brake lines were tampered with he would have seen it because of the mud in the undercarriage. Frank tells Johnny that the hole in the brake line is smaller than his smallest drill bit, which is 1/128th of an inch, and the hole is smaller than that. Johnny inspects the brake line and under a magnifying glass Johnny sees that it was drilled, but not by a drill bit, which leaves a burr. There is no burr on the hole. Back at the hotel Johnny asks Tony if he is a dental assistant. Johnny tells Tony he should be more careful with the drills he borrows from the office and uses to drill holes in brake lines. Johnny tells him he forgot to clean off the bits of copper off the drill after he used it. Tony tells Johnny he is pretty smart. "No, just smart enough" Johnny replies.

"So once again its up to the courts. And how about the switch on this one? I mean the logical suspect being the logical suspect for once?"

NOTES:

- THE ONLY COMMERCIAL BREAK IS FOR DUPONT ZEREX ANTIFREEZE.
- LEORA THATCHER IS MILDRED, WILLIAM MASON IS TONY, ROBERT DONLEY IS CHRIS, ROBERT DRYDEN IS THE CHIEF, REYNOLD OSBORNE IS CHARLES, ARTHUR KOHL IS THE DOCTOR, BILL LIPTON IS FRANK.
- JOHNNY REFERENCES ANOTHER CASE IN COLD HARBOR, PROBABLY "THE WINNIPESAUKEE WONDER MATTER."
- THE ANNOUNCER IS ART HANNES
- MUSICAL SUPERVISION IS BY ETHEL HUBER

Producer: Bruno Zirato, Jr.   **Writers:** Jack Johnstone
Cast: Leora Thatcher, William Mason, Robert Donley, Robert Dryden, Reynold Osborne, Arthur Kohl, Bill Lipton

◆ ❖ ◆

SHOW: THE BEE OR NOT TO BEE MATTER
SHOW DATE: 10/29/1961
COMPANY: UNIVERSAL ADJUSTMENT BUREAU
AGENT: PAT FULLER
EXP. ACCT: $471.00

SYNOPSIS: Pat Fuller calls Johnny from the Universal Adjustment Bureau. Pat Fuller tells Johnny that Pat McCracken has retired. Pat tells Johnny he may have to cover the whole country on this thing. It is one of the simplest and oldest rackets and the hardest to catch up on. Come on over and lets talk.

Johnny cabs to Pat's office and finds Pat to be a sharp operator, just like his predecessor. Pat tells Johnny that the Universal Adjustment Bureau only handles the larger claims for the companies that they cover. Pat has uncovered thirteen claims ranging from $250 to $4,000. The racket is false injury. Johnny recalls handling a similar case on the West Coast some time ago. The reported injuries Pat has were falls in a hotel. A couple registers and makes the hotel aware that they have important business out of town the next day. The wife manages to fall in the lobby and the man yells for the manager. When he gets there the manager is threatened for a suit of $100,000, but the managers usually settle for cash. This couple is smart as the woman usually slips on a spot of oil or grease. Also, a doctor is called in for a quick examination and agrees it was an accident. Thirteen cases in less than four months. Pat is sure that the same couple is pulling the stunts but they do not use the same names or appearances. Pat has a picture taken of a model in the lobby of a hotel, and they happen to be in the background. The home address is always the same—21st Street and Fairmont Avenue in Philadelphia. Johnny recognizes the address as the Eastern Penitentiary.

Johnny tells Pat that sending the pictures to all the hotels would accomplish nothing. Johnny thinks that they have to be caught in the act. Pat shows Johnny a list of where they have hit, and Pat cannot see a pattern. Johnny has a hunch and borrows the photo and the list of cases. Johnny flies to Philadelphia, Pennsylvania and goes to the penitentiary. One of the assistant wardens recognizes the man as Harry Bain, who got out last year after serving a term for burglary, and has a record a mile long. He pulled jobs all over the country, and would always hire a lawyer before each job to have an alibi. He was only convicted after he was caught with the goods in his possession. The warden cannot figure out how a woman could recover from the injuries in so short a time. Johnny gets a list of the places where Harry pulled jobs before he was caught, and the list matches Johnny's list of hotel jobs. All of the cities are places where Harry had contacts with a lawyer. But there are three new names: Little Rock, Duluth and New Orleans. Johnny bets that Bain will hit one of these cities. Johnny receives a call from Pat Fuller. They have hit again in Little Rock. So, where does Johnny go?

Johnny goes to the Belleview Stratford Hotel, and rings up $181.40 calling the managers of all of the larger hotels in both New Orleans and Duluth. Johnny buys an armload of reading materials and after three days he finally gets a call. Mr. Devereau in New Orleans calls and tells him that here is a couple named Chatsworth from Philadelphia, and they gave 21st and Fairmont as their address. Johnny tells him to hang on to them and he will get there as soon as he can. Johnny flies to New Orleans, Louisiana and arrives early in the morning. Johnny cabs to the Hotel de Phillipe and meets with the manager, who cannot believe that the Chatsworths are those nasty people, and refuses to let Johnny into their rooms. The Chatsworths come through the lobby and Johnny hopes Devereau will not tip them off. They start toward the café and Johnny bribes a bellboy for the room number of the Chatsworth suite. Johnny and the Bellboy dicker over the use of his uniform, and Johnny must to resort to "other" tactics. Johnny ties him up in the linen closet and goes up to the Chatsworth suite where he searches the bags. In one bag Johnny finds something you will never believe. Johnny hears the lock and hides under the bed. Chatsworth comes in and tells a bellboy to call the manager and the doctor. He opens the bag and takes a bottle out and puts it on her leg. Already the ankle is swelling. Later the doctor demands a hospital visit. Chatsworth tells the manager he will sue for $50,000. Chatsworth relents and will settle for $10,000 and tells the manager that their lawyer Franky Tobello will see to it. Devereau wants to pay the doctor's bill and will give Chatsworth $1,000 to avoid any publicity. Chatsworth wants a decent offer and Devereau settles on $2,000 cash.

"The price they settled on? Two thousand bucks cash. Immediately. But as Devereau, the poor excited sucker was about to go down stairs and get it, I crawled out from my uncomfortable spot under the bed. And you know something? Surprised, Henry Bain and the woman gave up with out a struggle when they found out who I was and what I was doing there. And the manager, when I pulled the little glass jar out of their suit case and showed him how they made their phony accidents look so real, real enough to fool a doctor, well believe it or not the shock was too much for him and he almost fainted. So, that was that. And the expense account total comes to $471. Wait a minute. I forgot to tell you about the trick. Their little trick for making the ankles swell up and look like the worst sprain on record? Well you see that jar, the one that Bain had opened and then clapped against her ankle, contained exactly three nasty little yellow jackets. Bees. Yes, clever."

NOTES:
* THE FIRST COMMERCIAL BREAK IS FOR DUPONT ZEREX ANTIFREEZE.
* THE FIRST COMMERCIAL BREAK IS FOR THE EFFORTS OF THE RELIGIOUS CHARITIES ABROAD.
* JOHN THOMAS IS PAT, IVOR FRANCIS IS THE MANAGER, ROBERT DRYDEN IS BAIN, GERTRUDE WARNER IS MRS. CHATSWORTH, BOB DONNELLY IS THE WARDEN.
* I THINK THAT THERE IS A LITTLE CONFUSION AT THE END OVER THE NAMES. HARRY BAIN USED THE NAME HENRY CHATSWORTH, BUT AT THE END JOHNNY CALLS HIM HENRY BAIN.
* THE ANNOUNCER IS ART HANNES
* MUSICAL SUPERVISION IS BY ETHEL HUBER

Producer: Bruno Zirato, Jr. **Writers:** Jack Johnstone
Cast: John Thomas, Ivor Francis, Robert Dryden, Gertrude Warner, Bob Donnelly

◆ ❖ ◆

SHOW: THE MONTICELLO MYSTERY MATTER
SHOW DATE: 11/5/1961
COMPANY: INTER-ALLIED INSURANCE COMPANY
AGENT: HENRY FOREMAN
EXP. ACCT: $71.70
SYNOPSIS: Henry Foreman calls Johnny from Port Jarvis, New York. Johnny tells Henry that he is really fortunate to have the Delaware River and the Neversink so close by. Johnny tells Henry that the Neversink is his favorite trout stream. Henry wants Johnny to do work on a case for the wife of an important client, Mr. Rudolph Teckler who lives near Monticello, when they are not in the city. Henry has no idea what the problem is and Teckler had asked that Johnny come up if the has the free time, which could be a couple days or weeks. Teckler told Henry that the case is very important to Johnny, and Teckler would pay the expenses. Johnny is on his way.

Johnny flies to New York and rents a car for the drive to Port Jarvis. Johnny meets with Foreman who still does not know what Teckler's problem is. Mrs.

Teckler has a sizeable policy and is the widow of Horace Rathbone Mellinger, of the steel and oil fortune. Johnny drives to Monticello, New York and on to Bethel and to a spot near Swan Lake and Canoza Lake. A steel fence surrounds the estate but the gate is unlocked. Johnny goes in to find a delightful two-story log cabin surrounded by huge trees and a 20-acre lake that is full of lunker bass. Johnny meets Rudy Teckler who is also a fisherman. Johnny suggests that they go fishing but remembers that he is there on business and it is out of season. Rudy tells Johnny that his is a private lake and he can tell the game warden to go away if he shows up. He and his wife have invited Johnny to come to there, but not on business. Johnny realizes that his is too good to be true. When Johnny meets Mrs. Teckler that little bell in his head rings out loud and clear.

Mrs. Teckler was a short sweet pert and pretty woman with a lovely complexion who is almost sixty. Nancy tells Johnny that they love the place, which belonged to her late husband who used it for a hunting lodge. Rudy tells Nancy that she works too hard when they come up there, and next year they will bring the servants. "Next year?" she asks. Rudy does not like hunting so he put in the lake and stocked it with fish. She remembered that Johnny likes fishing, and decided to invite him, as she is an old fan of his radio program. Bringing Johnny there was much better than inviting him to a party in New York. Nancy tells Johnny to go fishing, and he better bring back some fish. Johnny recalls that Nancy is short, sweet, pert and pretty—and adds smart. Johnny wonders what her real reason for him being there is. Johnny and Rudy go fishing but before they can start to fish a storm blows in. Rudy tells Johnny that the rain will ruin the fishing and they head to the dock during a downpour. After cocktails and dinner, Johnny starts to worry as he has sensed a tension between Rudy and Nancy. Rudy gets a little too liberal with the highballs and Johnny tries to talk to him after Nancy retires. Rudy tells Johnny that he does not have a thing to worry about as long as he can drown his sorrows. Johnny helps Rudy to his room and puts him to bed. Johnny sleeps soundly and just after sunup Rudy pounds on Johnny's door. Something has happened to Nancy!

Rudy tells Johnny that Nancy has disappeared. Her bed has been slept in, but she is not there. The only thing missing are her nightgown, robe and slippers. There is no sign of her anywhere. Johnny dresses and Rudy hopes she is all right. Rudy tells Johnny that last night he had gotten the feeling that she was worried about something, but he does not know what. Johnny searches the estate and does not find Nancy. Johnny asks Rudy about problems because the difference in their ages or over money, but Rudy insists that there are none. Johnny goes to mix a couple drinks and notices the lack of a hangover in Rudy. Johnny and Nancy had been drinking Scotch so Johnny checks the bourbon Rudy had been drinking from and discovers that it held only weak tea. Johnny wonders if Nancy was the sorrow he had to drown because she was wise that he married her for her money. And was Nancy the one who was afraid? But where is the body? Johnny decides to check the obvious place. Johnny tells Rudy his is going to play a hunch and goes to the dam at the foot of the lake and removes the top layers. Rudy comes out and Johnny tells him he is going to lower the lake to find where Rudy put the body after he killed Nancy last night. Rudy tells Johnny he will show him the place, but now all the insurance and the whole estate will be his, without her there to dole it out to him. There is plenty for both of them; they will be rich! Johnny suggests that Rudy tell that to a judge.

"Any comments? Why bother, I hate this kind of case, but it does happen."

NOTES:

- THE FIRST COMMERCIAL IS FOR THE EXPANDED CBS NEWS COVERAGE.
- THE SECOND COMMERCIAL IS FOR ENTERTAINMENT LIKE BUSTER DAVENPORT AND HIS TALKING MYNA BIRD, AND LUCILLE AND HER MAGIC ALKERINA AND LITTLE BILLY AND HIS FOURTEEN-PIECE JUG BAND. YOU WON'T FIND THEM ON CBS WHERE YOU WILL FIND ARTHUR GODFREY, ART LINKLETTER, GARY MOORE, BING CROSBY AND ROSEMARY CLOONEY; GUARANTEED ENTERTAINMENT AT THE STAR'S ADDRESS.
- WILLIAM REDFIELD IS RUDY, ADELE RONSON IS NANCY, REYNOLD OSBORNE IS HENRY.
- THE ANNOUNCER IS ART HANNES
- MUSICAL SUPERVISION IS BY ETHEL HUBER

Producer: Bruno Zirato, Jr. **Writers:** Jack Johnstone
Cast: William Redfield, Adele Ronson, Reynold Osborne

◆ ❖ ◆

SHOW: THE WRONG ONE MATTER
SHOW DATE: 11/12/1961
COMPANY: TRI-STATE LIFE & CASUALTY INSURANCE COMPANY
AGENT: EARLE POORMAN
EXP. ACCT: $0.00

SYNOPSIS: Earle Poorman, a welcome voice calls Johnny from warm, sunny Florida. Earle tells Johnny that the fishing is red hot, and Earle wants Johnny to come down about a broken ankle. Earle has one, and he wants Johnny to come down and handle a client for him that lives down the road. Johnny tells Earle that something is fishy about this case, but Johnny relents and agrees to come down.

Johnny flies to Sarasota, Florida and cabs to Earle's office where he finds Earle with a cast on his ankle. Johnny offers to autograph the cast, but Earle demurs. Earle wants Johnny to run the boat for him so he can get his mind off matters. Earle shows Johnny a letter mailed yesterday that is written on wrapping paper. The letter, which is written in poor grammar, tells Earle that if the company does not want to pay off the policy real quick they should come there, because his pal is away gatoring and cannot help him. The letter is from Emmett Dennery. The policy is for $2,000, and Waldo Blake is the beneficiary. Dennery is no mental giant, but he is still a client. This letter is why Johnny is here. Earle knows nothing about the client other than Dennery and Blake live in the live in the Everglades and hunt and trap for a living. Johnny is the one who will go visit

Emmett, so that he and Earle can go fishing. Earle tells Johnny that despite the tone of the letter, Dennery has nothing to fear but the game warden. Earle shows Johnny a map that was pinned on the policy that shows where Emmett lives. Earle tells Johnny that he will do all right, in spite of Johnny's concerns. Johnny recounts how in his last trip to the Everglades he had the services of a guide named Ben Osceola. Johnny takes Earle home and goes out to look for the road on the map, which is near the location of his previous case. Johnny drives up to a small shack where a man is standing with a 30/30 in his arms. Johnny reminds Ben of who he is, and Ben welcomes him. Johnny tells Ben who he is looking for, and Ben tells Johnny that Dennery is not his friend. He and the man called Lefty do not obey the law and take game they should not take from Seminole lands. The Seminole stay away from the men, as they are taboo. Ben last saw Dennery when he was a child, and tells Johnny that Dennery and Lefty look like twins. Ben will not take Johnny to the place where Dennery lives, but allows Johnny to take his airboat. Johnny gives Ben $20 for the boat, and tells Johnny that it is too bad he cannot go with him, as Johnny must be very careful. Johnny drives the airboat into the swamps and notes the large amount of animal life. Johnny reaches an island with and old shack surrounded by racks of drying hides. Johnny heads for the cabin and opens the door to find a dead body on a bed inside the dank gloomy interior of the filthy shack. Johnny can see that the man has been dead for several days. Johnny is about to cover the body with a rag when a voice tells him to stay put or he will shoot Johnny.

Johnny spots a high-powered old-fashioned rifle aimed at this head and held by an old man dressed in ragged clothes. The man's eyes remind Johnny of a maddened snake. The man takes Johnny's gun, "a real purdy one" and accuses Johnny of killing the man on the bed and sits Johnny down on the floor. The man accuses Johnny of killing Emmett Dennery, and Johnny tells him that if he is Waldo Blake, he will get the insurance Emmett had. Johnny reaches into his pocket to show Waldo the money and Waldo grabs Johnny's wallet to count the money it. Johnny grabs the rifle and throws Waldo to the floor. Johnny tells Waldo that it is good that Emmett apparently probably died of natural causes. Johnny tells the man that he could not pass up the opportunity to get back the money he had paid on premiums. Johnny knew something was wrong because the letter was only mailed yesterday, and the body had been dead for several days. Johnny tells him that he had written the letter to get the money when it really was Lefty Blake who had died. When the man tells Johnny he cannot prove that the body is Waldo, Johnny shows how the laces on the boots were tied with a left-handed bowknot, something a right-handed man would not do. Emmett admits to Johnny that after paying all those years only to have Waldo go first, it was the only thing he could have done. Johnny reminds him that he could have cashed in the policy and gotten most of his money back. Johnny tells Emmett that it is up to the company to determine what will happen to him.

"So there you are Earle. Like I said to the old rascal, it is up to the company now. As for the total on my expense account, well lets wait until I can tote up the cost of all the fishing were are going to do. Ok?"

NOTES:

- THE FIRST COMMERCIAL BREAK IS PAT SUMMERALL FOR SPORTS TIME ON CBS EVERY DAY BUT SUNDAY
- MANDEL KRAMER WELCOMES CBS RADIO STATION WNEB IN WORCHESTER, MASSACHUSETTS.
- MARTIN BLAINE IS EARLE, BILL LIPTON IS BEN, JIM BOLES IS EMMETT.
- THE PREVIOUS CASES MENTIONED ARE "THE WAYWARD MOTH MATTER" AND "THE SALKOFF SEQUEL MATTER," WHICH CONCERNED THE RESEARCH OF A ROCKET SCIENTIST, AND HOW JOHNNY ASSISTED IN THE LAUNCH OF THE EXPLORER 1 ROCKET IN 1958.
- THE ANNOUNCER IS ART HANNES
- MUSICAL SUPERVISION IS BY ETHEL HUBER

Producer: Bruno Zirato, Jr.   Writers: Jack Johnstone
Cast: Martin Blaine, Bill Lipton, Jim Boles

SHOW: THE GUIDE TO MURDER MATTER
SHOW DATE: 11/19/1961
COMPANY: TRI-STATE LIFE & CASUALTY INSURANCE COMPANY
AGENT: EARLE POORMAN
EXP. ACCT: $85.00

SYNOPSIS: Johnny answers the phone at Earle Poorman's home, and accuses Earle of running off to the office when they were supposed to go fishing. Earle reminds Johnny of the article in the Herald Tribune about him being there, and Johnny reminds him that the evening paper and WSPB mentioned it too. Earle tells Johnny that all the publicity has every fishing guide in the area bidding to take Johnny out fishing, and Earle is looking over the offers. The winner is Captain Barney Beale, who is a good captain and a client of Earle's. Earle tells Johnny to come pick him up and crosses his heart and hopes to die that there is no insurance matter for Johnny to look into. (But if he tries to get me involved in another mess . . .)

Johnny buys gas for Earle's car and drives to his office. Johnny and Earle drive to Captain Beale's boat at Lemon Bay, Florida and Johnny describes Beale as a capable captain, formerly from New England. Barney tells Johnny that he learned to fish off Cape Cod, and what he learned there serves him well there. Johnny spends the day fishing and is exhausted by mid afternoon from catching fish after fish. After picking out some fish to take home, Barney complements Earle on his new car, which is a lot fancier than the old 1922 Maxwell he drove down from New England and has in the garage. Johnny asks to see the car and Barney takes Johnny to the garage and unlocks the door. In the garage is the Maxwell with a dead man in the seat.

Johnny determines that the man had died from carbon monoxide poisoning, that the ignition switch was on and the gas tank was empty. Johnny finds no marks on the body, and Barney does not know who the man is. Barney comments on the nice clothes and the full head of hair on the man. Barney tells Johnny that he used the car a week ago last Saturday, and bought a full tank of gas for it. The garage has been locked ever since, and only Barney has the key. Barney notices a latch on a window is open, but the opening is full of spider webs. Barney leaves to call the coroner and Earle hobbles in.

The coroner, Dr. Hill, tells Johnny that the man has been dead for a day or two. The cause is carbon monoxide poisoning and he is sure that it was a suicide. Johnny tries to ask for an autopsy, but the coroner leaves to arrange for the body to be picked up. Johnny takes another look around and checks out the window. One of the panes was brand new, and glass shards are on the floor. Johnny moistens a shard and uses it to take fingerprints of the corpse. Earle and Johnny leave after Barney refuses to take any money from Earle. Earle notes that Barney was very casual about finding the body, and Johnny mentions how the suicide did not leave any note, which they typically do. After leaving Earle at home, Johnny takes the glass to the police and sees Lt. Barney Phillips, who had helped him on other cases. Johnny asks for the prints to be analyzed by the FBI and goes fishing. Two days later Lt. Phillips calls Johnny to tell him that the suicide had a record. His name was Maury Spencer, and he operated in New England selling fishing boats. He would steal a boat, fix it up and sell it to some sucker. Lt. Phillips shows Johnny a list of aliases that includes "Baldy" Spangler. In a picture the man looks a little like the corpse and has a bald spot. Johnny tells him it must have been plastic surgery, and even Barney Beale noted the full head of hair. Johnny leaves to prove that the suicide was a murder.

Johnny visits the coroner to look at the body. Johnny pulls on the hair and it comes off; it was a small toupee. Under the toupee is a hole that Johnny guesses is from a gaff like a fishing guide would have used. Dr. Hill tells Johnny that the wound would not have killed him, so he could have been put in the car to make it look like a suicide. Johnny asks the coroner to follow him to Lemon Bay to see Captain Beale. On the way Johnny tells Earle that Barney lives in a shack, has a boat held together by baling wire, and does not spend a cent he does not have to, and yet he gave away a fishing trip. And there was a repaired window in the garage to hold the fumes from the car. At the marina, Barney tells Johnny that he should not have tried to fool a smart man like Johnny, and that his conscious has been bothering him. He thought having Johnny around was a good way to keep suspicion off himself. He killed Baldy because of all the people he had hurt Down East, and got off Scot-free every time. When he came down to Florida and suggested that Barney help him, someone had to stop him to keep him from hurting all the kind people here.

"I don't know. Who am I to judge? But I hope they handle the old fellow as gently as possible in spite of what he did and must pay for."

NOTES:

- THE FIRST COMMERCIAL BREAK IS ABOUT HOW CBS IS PROUD TO BRING SUCH STARS AS BING CROSBY AND ROSEMARY CLOONEY, ART LINKLETTER, GARY MOORE AND DERWARD KIRBY AND ARTHUR GODFREY TIME.
- IVOR FRANCIS IS BARNEY, IAN MARTIN IS EARLE, LAWSON ZERBE IS DR. HILL, JIM BOLES IS LT. PHILLIPS.
- A MAXWELL, AND NOT ONE REFERENCE TO JACK BENNY!
- THIS SAME MURDER METHOD WAS USED IN "THE HAIR RAISING MATTER" OF 11/30/1958.
- THE ANNOUNCER IS ART HANNES
- MUSICAL SUPERVISION IS BY ETHEL HUBER

Producer: Bruno Zirato, Jr.   Writers: Jack Johnstone
Cast: Ivor Francis, Ian Martin, Lawson Zerbe, Jim Boles

◆ ❖ ◆

SHOW: THE MAD BOMBER MATTER
SHOW DATE: 11/26/1961
COMPANY: GREATER SOUTHWEST INSURANCE COMPANY
AGENT: HANK PARNELL
EXP. ACCT: $350.00

SYNOPSIS: Hank Parnell calls Johnny from Muddy Gap, Wyoming. Hank is the owner, editor, reporter and everything else for the local paper "The Weekly Tribune." He is also the local agent for the Great Southwest Insurance Company. Hank wants Johnny to hightail it out on expense account. There is no insurance business yet, but if Johnny cannot give him a hand, Great Southwest will not have an office, agent or a town. Hank wants Johnny to keep Muddy Gap from being blown off the map.

Johnny travels by plane, train and car to Muddy Gap. Johnny describes how Muddy Gap is in the heart of the old Indian country, and in oil country. The town's principle business is oil storage and huge storage tanks surround the town. Johnny meets with Hank, who tells Johnny that he is also the mayor and acting police chief. Hank asks Johnny what he thinks would happen if one of the oil tanks were to explode? He is sure that it will happen unless Johnny can stop Billy Benbow. Billy was born here and is a real troublemaker. During the last war Hank and his father used the paper to manage to get Billy drafted, but Billy swore he would get back at the town. While in the Army Billy worked with explosives and every blast he set off was for someone in the town, starting with the draft board. At the end of the war Billy went completely off-base and started blowing things up and ended up in a hospital. Billy has escaped from the hospital, and Hank received a phone call the other day warning him that he has not forgotten. Hank is sure that Billy is coming back to get even, and is just waiting for a chance to blow up the town. Hank has printed nothing in the paper so as to not alarm the residents. Hank tells Johnny that the state police will be glad to help, after Billy has done something. Hank tells Johnny that the phone has rung every day at noon, and the line was empty when he picked up the receiver. Johnny tells Hank that he needs more evidence. The phone rings and Johnny picks up the extension. A voice tells Hank "I better prove that I haven't forgotten." The caller confirms that he is Billy Benbow and there is an explosion in the back of the office.

Johnny crawls out from under the desk and sees that the pressroom is totally destroyed. Johnny tells Hank that he is sure that Billy only wants to put the paper out of business, but where is Billy? Johnny finds a timing device that was used to set off the blast. Pete Ranson comes in and smells dynamite, but Hanks tells him it was only a can of benzene he used to clean the type. Pete, along with Tony Backman are the whole police department. Pete gets the crowd out of the way and Johnny asks Hank about Pete's face. Hank tells Johnny that it was marred when he was drug by a horse. Johnny is not sure that the excuse about the benzene was wise, as they do not know if Billy is finished yet. Hank tells Johnny that everyone on the draft board is dead except for Grampa Wheedon. "Oh, Lord that old house of his!" Hank tells Johnny that the house is down by the terminal, and if it were blown up, it would set off the whole town. Johnny calls the operator and asks her where the call earlier came from. The operator tells Johnny that he sounds just like that Johnny Dollar on the radio, and the townspeople would really like to know that. She tells Johnny that the call came from the only phone booth in the town, outside the drug store. The phone rings again and Billy tells Johnny that the big one is coming later, maybe tonight. Hank wants to evacuate the town, but Johnny tells him that it is too late. Johnny is sure that Billy has been here for weeks, and asks Hank to let him handle things his own way. Johnny wants Hank to call the deputies and have them all follow his orders exactly. Johnny is sure that his hunch is right. When Tony arrives first, Johnny tells Hank and Tony what he wants them to do, and they cannot believe him, but agree to say nothing to anyone, even Pete. When Pete arrives, Hank and Tony leave and Johnny asks Pete for his gun and starts to go to see Grandpa Wheedon. Johnny tells Pete that he thinks that the mad bomber will hit Grandpa next. Pete asks Johnny what kind of a man he could be, and Johnny asks him how he knows it is a man? Pete does not seem to like it when Johnny mentions a madman and bets they will find nothing. Pete tells Johnny that he has not been on the force too long, and has been working on ranches lately doing odd jobs. Johnny mentions that his hands are kind of soft and he immediately knew the smell of dynamite when he came into the office earlier. Johnny tells him that the scars on his face are from an explosion, and he is sure that no one would recognize him, "would they, Billy?" Pete pulls another gun and tells Johnny to reach. Billy knew he would have trouble with Johnny, because he is not dumb like the others. He is going to kill Johnny and then go to his place and set the timer on another bomb. The bomb will be planted out by the tank farm by Grandpa Wheedon's. He will set the timer so that he will have enough time to get out of town in

Johnny's car. Hank comes in with the bomb he found in Pete's room. Pete threatens Hank and Tony warns Pete that he will get him if he shoots Hank. While Pete is distracted Johnny slugs him. "Wow, wee, that's a mighty good left you have there, Dollar!" Johnny tells Hank that Pete was right; Hank is kind of stupid for carrying the bomb so Pete could shoot at it. "Oh, my gosh!" exclaims Hank.

"Remarks, why bother on this one."

Notes:

- THE FIRST COMMERCIAL BREAK IS ABOUT THE NOISE OF OLDER CARS AND THE BETTER ENGINEERING OF TODAY'S CARS. SMOOTHER CARS INCREASE THE NEED CONTROL SPEED. TAKE CARE AND GET THERE.
- COURT BENSON IS HANK, LAWSON ZERBE IS PETE, CLIFF CARPENTER IS BILLY, BARBARA CASSAR IS THE OPERATOR.
- MUDDY GAP, WYOMING IS NORTH OF RAWLINGS.
- THE ANNOUNCER IS ART HANNES
- MUSICAL SUPERVISION IS BY ETHEL HUBER

Producer: Bruno Zirato, Jr.   **Writers:** Jack Johnstone
Cast: Court Benson, Lawson Zerbe, Cliff Carpenter, Barbara Cassar

◆ ❖ ◆

SHOW: THE CINDER ELMER MATTER
SHOW DATE: 12/3/1961
COMPANY: WORLDWIDE MUTUAL INSURANCE COMPANY
AGENT: CHARLIE WARREN
EXP. ACCT: $377.80

SYNOPSIS: Charlie Warren calls Johnny from warm, sunny California and he can just image how Johnny is doing with all the cold and snow in New England. Johnny reminds him of the beauty he is missing: the clean crisp invigorating air, the sparkle of the sun on sleet covered branches, the sound of sleigh bells, rolling fields drifted high with pure white snow. Charlie adds all the mud and slush Johnny has to plow through. Charlie asks Johnny if he can come out to California to enjoy the beauties of his area, if he can keep his expense account under control. Johnny will arrange to take a propeller driven plane so he can get some sleep, and will meet Charlie in the morning.

Johnny flies to Los Angeles and is not able to sleep on the flight. Johnny's seatmate is a cute little brunette who needs help with her vacation plans. At the airport a tall young man who plays right tackle for the Los Angeles Rams meets the girl, and Johnny's plans go out the door with them. Charlie meets Johnny and gives him the keys to the rental car, complete with snow chains. Johnny is to head out past San Bernardino for Crestline, California. Johnny can get directions for the Hillcrest Lodge in Crestline. Charlie wishes he could go with Johnny, what with all the snow and skiing, but all Johnny wants is some sleep. The case is about the disappearance of Bartley Harmon. Harmon and his wife Nora and partner Elmer Wrightson went up to the lodge for a few days. The "poor little shrimp" has disappeared. Harmon and Wrightson are both only five-feet-three and one hundred fifteen pounds and look like twins. But Nora is five-feet-eleven, blonde and built like an Olympic champion. Wow! Bartley went off for a walk and has just disappeared. The sheriff's office has been notified, and they have not been able to find anything, and they know what they are doing. The policy is $200,000 double indemnity, and Harmon has a bad heart. The business will go the partner and the insurance goes to Nora. Johnny wonders how Nora and Wrightson get along, and Charlie tells him that Nora is beautiful, rich and a lot younger than Wrightson. Johnny figures he better get up there quick.

Johnny drives through San Bernardino and the heat really gets to him because of the lack of sleep. At 4,000 feet Johnny has to stop to put on chains and is invigorated. At the lodge, Roy Turner of the sheriff's office meets Johnny and tells him that he does not like the situation. There is no love triangle as Wrightson is the same kind of "homely, pedantic, facts-and-figures little shrimp" that her husband was, and she is tired of that type. Nora is much younger and more athletic, and she makes the most of what she has. She always brings too many clothes, including a trunk full of shoes. She likes the lodge and Bartley and Wrightson come to keep an eye on each other. The hills and cabins in the area have been searched. Harmon headed over to "Old Ironsides," a mountain with a steep cliff-like face on it. Roy gets a phone call and Harmon's body has been found. Johnny and Roy go to the airport and fly to the area in a helicopter. On the snow above the tree line they spot the body. The chopper lands and Johnny and Roy get out to look at the body. Roy tells Johnny that Harmon believed in a legend about a cave full of gold, and came up to look for it every year. Johnny thinks that it was heart failure, until they spot two things: another set of smaller footprints and a cigarette butt with lipstick on it.

Roy is sure that Nora is guilty, and her alibi of being shopping at Lake Arrowhead is not so sound now. Johnny is unsure though. Wrightson was supposedly asleep in his room all afternoon. Roy tells a deputy to have the lipstick analyzed when he and Johnny take the body in. Johnny wants to go along but opts not to. In San Bernardino, Doc Hanley tells Johnny that the lipstick is quite unusual. A deputy takes Johnny back to the lodge, and Johnny bribes a bellboy to take a lipstick from Nora's room. Johnny takes it back to Doc Hanley and he confirms that it is the same type. The autopsy shows that Harmon was beaten to death, and death was so sudden that the blood stopped circulating before bruises could form. Hanley tells Johnny that Nora had the motive and the ability, but Johnny wonders why she would leave so many obvious clues. Johnny leaves to keep Roy from arresting the wrong person. In his room, Johnny meets with Roy who tells Johnny that Harmon was followed up the mountain, and every time Harmon stopped, she stopped and smoked a cigarette and left the butt in the snow. Roy tells Johnny that he found a pair of snow boots in Nora's room that matched the prints in the snow. Johnny realizes that the important clue here is the cigarette butt. Johnny asks Roy if he left any butts on the trail, and Johnny tells Roy that the position of the butts is important. On the trail Roy takes Johnny to the first location and Johnny shows him that the butt was not crushed out, and only placed on the snow. If it was lit, it would have melted some of the snow, but it didn't. The butts were put out somewhere else and left here to incriminate Nora Harmon. So it has to be Elmer Wrightson, the only other person with a motive. Roy wants to look to see if Elmer has snow boots just like Nora, but Johnny feels that, with a trunk full of shoes she probably has several pairs. So Elmer might have borrowed a pair, and Johnny suggests they try the old Cinderella trick, only they will call it the Cinder Elmer trick, and have him try on a pair of Nora's boots.

"Her snow boots fit him, all right. And little old Cinder Elmer, the dumb jerk, should have known better. He should have made us come up with some really concrete evidence. But luckily for us, Elmer just broke down and confessed to the whole bit. So, once again it is up to the courts."

NOTES:
- THE FIRST COMMERCIAL BREAK IS FOR THE HIGH VOLUME OF HOLIDAY MAIL, AND THE NEED TO MAIL EARLY AND OFTEN, AND TO USE POSTAL ZONE NUMBERS.
- CLIFF CARPENTER IS ROY, EUGENE FRANCIS IS CHARLIE, BOB DRYDEN IS HANLEY, JIM STEVENS IS THE PILOT.
- MUSICAL SUPERVISION IS BY ETHEL HUBER
- THE ANNOUNCER IS STUART METZ.

Producer: Bruno Zirato, Jr.   **Writers:** Jack Johnstone
Cast: Cliff Carpenter, Eugene Francis, Bob Dryden, Jim Stevens

◆ ❖ ◆

SHOW: THE PHONY PHONE MATTER
SHOW DATE: 12/17/1961
COMPANY: TRINITY MUTUAL INSURANCE COMPANY
                AGENT: BERT HELFER
EXP. ACCT: $0.00

SYNOPSIS: Bert Helfer calls and wishes Johnny a Merry Christmas. Johnny tells Bert he is not taking on any cases until after the holidays. Bert asks Johnny to come over to his office, but the answer is no. Bert tells Johnny that he only wants to give Johnny the money for the San Francisco job he did a few weeks ago. "Are you sure that's all?" asks Johnny.

Johnny checks out with his call service and goes to see Bert, who is alone in the office. Bert finishes up a call so that no one will bother him while he is in Florida. Bert gives Johnny his expenses in cash, as the banks are closed and he knows Johnny will need the money for shopping. Bert gives Johnny a message from his call service to call Exmont 3-5770 immediately. Johnny does not recognize the number, but Bert knows the number, and it belongs to Harvey L. Hallet, who owns Hallet Industries in Hartford, Connecticut. Bert shows Johnny the Hallet buildings from his window and relates that they have a lot of insurance on the plant. There have been a number of burglaries lately, and Bert does not trust Hallet. Bert tells Johnny that he had given Johnny's number to Hallet, and Johnny decides he will call Hallet back. Johnny relates how a phone call can be used to cover up a crime and based on Bert's mistrust, Johnny wants to call Hallet. Johnny calls Hallet's number and reaches Mary Hallet who tells Johnny that Mr. Hallet is leaving for New York. Hallet takes the phone and wants to talk to Johnny about some burglaries next week and hangs up the phone. Suddenly there is an explosion outside and a building has just blown up, the Hallet Industries building. Johnny cabs to the building to find it fully involved in flames. Johnny finds police Lt. Jimmy Harmon who tells Johnny that he is there to investigate the burglaries at Hallet's plant. Lt. Harmon tells Johnny that he has gotten nowhere and feels that Hallet did not want him to find out anything and gave him too much cooperation. Hallet was always underfoot and getting in the way. Lt. Harmon tells Johnny that he does not trust Hallet, and that he suspects arson. The arson squad is working on the building already. Mr. Hallet arrives and tells Johnny that he heard the explosion from his home, and Johnny tells Lt. Harmon that he can corroborate the fact that Hallet was on the phone with him. Johnny mentions insurance, but Hallet tells him that the money cannot make up for the business. Hallet tells Johnny that the color of the smoke and the smell are odd. There were solvents stored in the back room, but it was always locked. Hallet wonders if the night watchman was injured. Lt. Harmon comes back to confirm that arson was involved. Also, he thinks that the watchman, Ben Matthews, saw who did it and knew the person. The door had a dead-latch lock on it, and Ben's key is in the inside of the lock, so he let someone in he recognized. Lt. Harmon knew Ben, and he never would let anyone in he was not supposed to, but if his boss asked him to open it . . . But Hallet will not have to testify because there is a bullet in Ben's head. Johnny asks about the device used to start the fire, and Lt. Harmon tells him that there was no device; only a wick was used. Johnny tells Lt. Harmon that Hallet was at home, where Johnny talked to him on the phone.

Johnny calls Jonathan Buckley who verifies that Hallet's money is in his bank. After Johnny mentions the murder of the watchman, Jonathan can only tell Johnny that Hallet's financial condition is pretty bad. Lt. Harmon tells Johnny that he has checked over all of Hallet's employees, and can vouch for all of them; Hallet is the only one he does not know about. Johnny calls New York and talks to his pal Randy Singer of the New York Police. Randy asks Johnny what kind of a jam he needs to get Johnny out of in New York. Johnny asks Randy if the name Harvey Hallet means anything, and Randy tells Johnny that Hallet is really "Paraffin Peterson," who has been chased out of New York, along with his girlfriend Mary. Peterson only uses a paraffin wick to start fires. But how to prove that Hallet started the fire when he was on phone with Johnny? Johnny wonders if Hallet Electronics might have a product to help in this situation. Johnny and Lt.

Harmon go to Hallet's home where he is just returning. Johnny notices a tape device on the table that Mary had left there. Lt. Harmon runs the tape back and plays it. On the tape is the conversation that Hallet had with Johnny. So the message was prerecorded. And his wife played it when Johnny called. Then his wife called Hallet at the plant and told him to go ahead. "Any comment, Mr. Hallet?"

"Expense account total, forget it."

NOTES:

- THE FIRST COMMERCIAL BREAK IS AND **AFRS** ARTICLE ON THE BENEFITS OF DEMOCRACY.
- THE SECOND COMMERCIAL BREAK IS AN **AFRS** STORY ABOUT THE US NAVY AND THE USS PROVIDENCE THAT STOPPED IN VERA CRUZ TO HELP THE LOCAL PEOPLE WITH BLOOD DEPOSITS.
- PAT CANEL IS THE ANNOUNCER.
- MUSICAL SUPERVISION IS BY ETHEL HUBER
- CAST INFORMATION IS FROM RADIO**GOLDIN**DEX.

Producer: Bruno Zirato, Jr.   **Writers:**   Jack Johnstone
Cast: Jackson Beck, Michael Kane, William Redfield, Terri Keane,
                Eugene Francis, David Kern

◆   ❖   ◆

SHOW: THE ONE TOO MANY MATTER
SHOW DATE: 12/31/1961
COMPANY: EASTERN LIABILITY & TRUST INSURANCE COMPANY
AGENT: HAL KEMPER
EXP. ACCT: $4.80

SYNOPSIS: Hal Kemper calls Johnny and wishes him a happy New Year. Hal asks if Johnny has any plans for New Years Eve. Johnny tells Hal he will greet 1962 with other plans. Hal asks Johnny to come to his house and talk to Dr. Begley, the famous heart doctor about a patient, Mrs. Nancy Cunningham, who is an important client of Hal's. Johnny asks to wait until after New Years, but Hal tells Johnny that if he waits, Mrs. Cunningham might not live to see 1962.

Johnny drives to Hal's house in Hartford, Connecticut through an obstacle course of crazy drivers. Johnny meets Dr. Begley who tells Johnny that Mrs. Cunningham lives in a small house that she can take care of, given her heart condition. Today he learned something that will want to make Johnny go right over there. Tonight, two persons, Donald Kingman and Walter Baird, the nephews of Mrs. Cunningham, will visit. The nephews are heirs to her estate and considerable insurance. Dr. Begley has arranged for Johnny to stay there as long as the two nephews are there. Dr. Begley is sure that one of the nephews is there to murder her. Mrs. Cunningham had called Hal and wants to change the beneficiary of the estate to a charity. The nephews will be there before they are cut out of the will. The only time they have been there before was for money, but now they are "good-hearted Joes." Johnny learns that on Donald's last visit, gunshots broke a window narrowly missing Mrs. Cunningham, but Donald reported it and made the police investigate. The police said the bullets were strays fired in the woods, but Dr. Begley remembered that Donald was a good rifle shot. That evening the heat was on low, but went off. And Dr. Begely found a cotter pin in the mechanism that jammed the thermostat, and she could have frozen to death. Dr. Begley is sure that the boys were there to get to her before the will is changed. Johnny agrees to go see Mrs. Cunningham.

Johnny drives to Mrs. Cunningham's house, where Don Kingman opens the door and invites Johnny in and introduces him to Walt. Johnny talks to the nephews, who have fixed up a nice party with, catered food and a portable bar. Walt fixes drinks (scotch and soda for Johnny) and Don is surprised that Aunt Nancy knows Johnny. The boys admit that it is time they paid more attention to their aunt; after all she has done for them. The clock chimes nine, and Walt leaves to drive to a liquor store to buy some champagne. Don asks Johnny how long he has known Nancy when there is the sound of an automobile accident outside. Don tells Johnny that they knew Nancy was going to cut them off, and that is one reason they decided to be nice. She told them that she was leaving them in the will after all. Don starts acting woozy, drops his glass and collapses on the floor. Johnny starts to feel the same way, and he falls to the floor. When Johnny wakes up a policeman is slapping him awake. Sgt. Rogan gives Johnny a drink of brandy and asks what he knows about what has happened. Sgt. Rogan tells Johnny that Mrs. Cunningham is dead in the bedroom with a bullet in her.

Sgt. Rogan tells Johnny that a .22 bullet is in Mrs. Cunningham's head. An officer was investigating a crash, heard the shot and radioed for Sgt. Rogan to investigate. Sgt. Rogan broke in and found them. Johnny tells Sgt. Rogan about the drinks, and Sgt. Rogan tells Johnny that there is sediment in his and Don's glass. Also, an envelope of penorphene was found under the bar. Walter's glass had some in it also but Walter had left before drinking any. Johnny tells Sgt. Rogan about Walter pouring the drinks and leaving on an errand to the liquor store. The time is now ten forty, so Sgt. Rogan needs to find Walter. The phone rings and Sgt. Rogan takes the call. Sgt. Rogan asks Johnny what time Walter left, and Johnny tells him it was at nine. Sgt. Rogan tells Johnny that the accident down the street involved Walter Baird, who is in the hospital. Sgt. Rogan tells Johnny that the door was locked when he got there, so who killed Mrs. Cunningham? Johnny wonders if Dr. Begley was the killer who found out that she was not leaving the money to a hospital or a charity. Sgt. Rogan wonders if Johnny had anything to do with the killing, but Johnny tells him not to kid about that. Sgt. Rogan wonders if the doctor would know about the penorphene, but Johnny tells him that anyone could get the drug, and the only ones who would benefit were Walter and Don. Johnny has an idea and notes Don's glass on the table. Johnny is sure that Donald killed Mrs. Cunningham and then drank from his drink. All of the glasses had the drug, but it was Walter who suggested going out before Don would have had to tell him before he touched his drink. By leaving, Walter was the obvious suspect, except for the accident, which Don could not for see. Don had gotten up to stiffen his drink, but it was really to pour a new one without the drug. When Johnny started to go out, Don faked his collapse, got up and killed Mrs. Cunningham, came back and put the drugs in his drink and went out with an alibi that Johnny would have to corroborate. Johnny tells Sgt. Rogan that the glass is on the table now, but earlier when he faked the collapse, Donald dropped his glass and it rolled on the floor. Only Don could have put the glass on the table. "Satisfied?"

"When he came to, and we told him how he had worked it, how he had made the mistake of setting the glass back on the table, told him that we made a paraffin test of his hand to prove our point, well Don not only confessed, he showed us where he had hidden the gun."

Notes:

- The first commercial break is about the Cotton Bowl between the Mississippi Rebels and the Texas Longhorns, a CBS special. The man to stop is Jimmy Saxton
- Mandel Kramer wishes everyone the very best of New Years.
- Lawson Zerbe is Begley, Allan Manson is Don, Nat Polen is Hal, Robert Dryden is Rogan, Doug Parkhurst is Walter, Ethel Everett is Nancy.
- Art Hannes is the announcer.
- Musical supervision is by Ethel Huber

Producer: Bruno Zirato, Jr.   **Writers:** Jack Johnstone
Cast: Lawson Zerbe, Allan Manson, Nat Polen, Robert Dryden, Doug Parkhurst, Ethel Everett

◆ ❖ ◆

Show: The Hot Chocolate Matter
Show Date: 1/7/1962
Company: Tri-Eastern Indemnity Associates
Agent: Harvey Weller
Exp. Acct: $49.35

Synopsis: Harvey Weller calls, and Johnny knows why he is calling. Johnny has heard on the radio that $100,000 in diamonds was stolen from MacDilby's jewelry store. Harvey wants Johnny to work on the case, but Johnny asks if he has thought about how much Johnny's commission will be. As Harvey starts to calculate it, Johnny tells him he is on his way.

Johnny flies to New York City and cabs to MacDilby's House of Jewels on Madison near 57th Street. In the store Johnny meets Randy Singer who wants to know how Johnny found out so quickly. "Never underestimate the power of radio," Johnny tells him. Mr. MacDilby is introduced to Johnny, and he knows all about Johnny and his fine work. So far the loss is $104,218.51, approximately. There was one witness, but Mr. MacDuggan the night watchman is in the hospital. There was no sign of forced entry, so MacDuggan must have let the thief in. Miss Tavish, who always opens the store in the morning, discovered the robbery. So far the only missing employee is Daniel Fairling, the cleaning boy. Mr. MacDilby tells Johnny that the safe was not opened and the jewels were in the display cases because the store was open late last evening. Johnny decides to visit MacDuggan in Belleview Hospital. Johnny cabs to the hospital and sees Officer Rogan trying to get the attention of the nurse. Rogan had been trying to get her attention because MacDuggan was conscious again. Johnny arranges to watch MacDuggan while Rogan goes to call Randy. MacDuggan tells Johnny to "Ask Fairling. Ask Danny Fairling," and goes out again.

Johnny runs to the phone, and runs into Rogan who tells him Randy is on the way. Johnny looks up Danny Fairling in the phone book and cabs to his apartment. Johnny finds the apartment house door open and goes up to apartment 3-B. A neighbor tells Johnny that Danny and his wife have split up. She thinks that they are going to make up because a delivery boy just delivered a box of chocolates to her. The neighbor tells Johnny to knock again and then there is an explosion. Johnny breaks down the door to find that the box of chocolate had contained a bomb. Mrs. Fairling is dead, and Johnny asks the neighbor to stay until the police arrive. Johnny calls Randy's office and learns that MacDuggan has died. Johnny tells Randy what MacDuggan had said about Danny Fairling, and Randy tells Johnny to get over to his office. Johnny cabs to the 18th precinct and in Randy's office he is told that they have discovered that Danny has a record, and that Danny was picked up earlier that morning. Danny's wife had told the police where to find him. Johnny tells Randy about the bomb and asks to talk to Danny. Randy asks Danny about the jewelry and Danny tells Johnny that he cannot prove that he took the jewels. Danny tells Johnny that he was late this morning and left when he saw the crowd. Johnny asks if he knows anything about the robbery, and offers Danny legal assistance if he can help them. After briefing Randy, Johnny asks Randy not to tell Danny about his wife or to tell the other precinct that they have Danny in custody until he can check on some things. Johnny is sure not convinced that they are holding the right man. He has a better idea, but he does not like it

Johnny goes to talk to MacDilby and the loss is just as he had estimated. Randy tells MacDilby that they suspect Danny because of his record. Johnny asks to look around the store and Miss Tavish gladly offers to show him around. Johnny wants to follow up on his idea and finds what he is looking for in a cleaning closet, a box of chocolates. Miss Tavish tells Johnny that Danny loves chocolate, especially the French ones he cannot afford. Johnny goes to the candy shop and learns that a box of chocolates was delivered to the Fairling apartment that morning. A man bought them last evening, and came back an hour later to ask that the box be delivered today. The customer was a well-dressed Scottish gentleman. Johnny talks to Danny and tells him that he suspects MacDilby because the store was not broken into. MacDuggan knew who was at the door and let him in. Johnny tells Danny that he got to work early and saw what MacDilby had done and threatened to blackmail him, because MacDilby had told Danny to stay home that morning. Johnny tells Danny that MacDilby had promised to give him a share of the money and offered him legal help, but MacDilby had other plans for Danny. When Johnny asks Danny about his wife, Danny tells Johnny that he had walked out on her for a couple days, but was going back to her, because he loves her. Johnny asks if Danny likes French chocolates, and tells Danny that MacDilby did not know that he had moved out. MacDilby thought that Danny would be there in the apartment, so he sent a box of chocolates with a bomb in it. Danny is upset when he learns that his wife is dead and tells Johnny that if the law does not kill MacDilby, he will.

"Don't worry, the law will take care of MacDilby. And Danny, his term will be a short one because of his testimony, and my testimony. Expense account total, including the ride back to Hartford, $49.35, and uh, don't forget the commission."

NOTES:
- THE FIRST COMMERCIAL BREAK IS FOR NO-DOZ.
- THE SECOND COMMERCIAL BREAK IS FOR KENT CIGARETTES.
- THE THIRD COMMERCIAL BREAK IS FOR REGULAR PRICED SINCLAIR DINO GASOLINE THAT PERFORMS LIKE PREMIUM.
- EUGENE SIMES DOES THE MUSIC SUPERVISION, AND THE MUSIC IS HEAVY WITH BONGO DRUMS AND JAZZY SOUNDS.
- WALTER OTTO IS MENTIONED FOR THE SOUND PATTERNS, AND MIKE SHOSKUS FOR TECHNICAL SUPERVISON.
- ART HANNES IS THE ANNOUNCER.

Producer: Fred Hendrickson   **Writers:** Jack Johnstone
Cast: Jackson Beck, Sam Gray, Gilbert Mack, Bill Lipton, Guy Repp, Betty Garde, Ivor Francis, Vicki Vola

◆ ❖ ◆

SHOW: THE TERRIBLE TORCH MATTER
SHOW DATE: 1/21/1962
COMPANY: NEW JERSEY FIRE & CASUALTY INSURANCE COMPANY
AGENT: FRED LARKIN
EXP. ACCT: $1,500.00

SYNOPSIS: Fred Larkin calls from Trenton and gets Johnny out of bed. There is trouble in the town of Woodbine where Johnny handled a case several years ago. Johnny remembers something about a mattress factory that charged its clients less than they invoiced for mattresses. Fred remembers that he covered the business for more insurance than necessary and really lost on that one. The trouble this time is a couple of fires. Fred asks Johnny to come on down so he can tell Johnny all about it. Fred tells Johnny that if he can help end what he thinks is going on, Johnny can count on his expenses and a nice big fat commission. "Freddy, you speak the language I love to hear. I'm on my way."

Johnny flies to Philadelphia, rents a car and drives to Trenton, New Jersey using the same route George Washington did. Fred takes Johnny to Hildebrechts Restaurant for lunch and tells Johnny that he thinks that the fires were arson, and there will be more of them. The area around Woodbine is mainly farmland, but there are a number of factories in the town. The two fires occurred just outside of town. A promoter has opened up an industrial area. Fred agrees with Johnny that it is a bad area for the development as there is no high rent area for the factories in town to get out of. The development is slowly going broke, and there have been two fires so far. When someone gets away with it, fire can be a catchy idea. The first fire was a week ago and the last was yesterday. There are eleven factories in the development. However, the other eight are owned by people who are related to each other. Johnny tells Fred he is going to call in some help, Smokey Sullivan. Fred is surprised when Johnny tells him that Smokey was one of the best arsonists in the business and got away with a lot of fires, but has gone legitimate now. Smokey knows all about firebugs, and has been a real help to Johnny. Right now he is a consultant for the arson squad in Boston. Johnny asks about a bank, and Fred tells him that there is a loan office there that cashes checks. Johnny tells Fred he will use it for getting information. Johnny arranges with Smokey to come to Trenton. Over dinner Johnny convinces Smokey that the area would be a great place for a firebug, especially if the owners got the arsonist from where they came from. Johnny wants Smokey to find out if the fires were arson. The next morning Smokey and Johnny leave for Woodbine, New Jersey where Smokey goes to investigate the fires and Johnny talks to the one-man loan office. Johnny tells the owner, Mr. Hanley M. Becker that he wants to know the financial condition on all eleven of the factories in the development. Becker tells Johnny that the financial information is confidential and there are only nine companies out there now. Becker starts to stutter when he tells Johnny that the insurance company had better pay of the claims, so that he can collect the loans he has made out there. Johnny tells Becker that he thinks that arson is involved, and if so, there will be no pay off, which really flusters Becker. Becker tells Johnny that the loans were to pay off the properties and build housing for the workers that no longer work there. Only the warehouses are of any value now. Johnny tells Becker that if the remaining plants burn and arson is involved he will get nothing. Suddenly Becker is more than willing to tell Johnny anything.

Johnny goes to wait for Smokey and by 2 PM Smokey is not back. At five o'clock Smokey is still not back, so Johnny goes back to the loan office to see Becker. Johnny asks Becker where the newcomers came from, and the answer is Patterson. Johnny remembers some arson jobs there and thinks that Smokey has found something. Johnny mentions that Smokey has his car and Becker loans Johnny his. Johnny wonders about Becker and drives to the factory area. The area is empty and overgrown with weeds. Johnny spots his car by a windowless warehouse and stops there. Johnny goes in and finds Smokey unconscious on the floor.

Smokey is still alive and Johnny drives him to the motel where Dr. Rosenberg brings Smokey around. Smokey tells Johnny that it was Pete Larrison from Patterson. He must have thought that Smokey was trying to muscle into his territory. Smokey tells Johnny that Pete is going to fire the warehouse tonight. Smokey tries to tell Johnny about the others as he runs out the door to go to the warehouse. Johnny goes to the warehouse and smells the strong odor of gasoline. Johnny turns on the lights to find Pete Larrison there with a gun. Walter is there behind Johnny and takes his gun. Pete shows Johnny the arrangements for the fire, which will look like spontaneous combustion. Johnny sees strips of heavy felt soaked in gasoline leading to stacks of upholstered material and cardboard cartons. Pete sets the fuse by the door and tells Johnny that the police will suspect him. Johnny tells Pete that Smokey is still alive, but Pete tells Johnny that no one would believe Smokey because Pete has a perfect alibi. He and Walter will be playing Pinochle with Hanley Becker when the fire starts. Becker does not know about the fires, only the owners who have hired Pete know what is going to happen. Walter starts to take the gas cans out and Johnny swings around, grabs a can and throws it at Pete as he rolls out the door. Pete shoots several times and the factory goes up like a bomb.

"Me? I guess I was OK. The blast rolled me a hundred yards or so across that sandy ground, and I came to only a couple of minutes later. Walter, who was blown up against the side of my car, ended up with a concussion. As for Pete, well I don't think I need to tell you. And that's it Freddy. The company can prosecute the factory owners any way it sees fit."

Expenses include a hunk for Smokey, and damage to the rental car.

NOTES:
- THE FIRST COMMERCIAL BREAK IS FOR **YMCA** WEEK.
- LEON JANNEY IS HANLEY, SAM GRAY IS FRED, MASON ADAMS IS PETE, LARRY HAINES IS SMOKEY, JAMES DEMETRIE IS WALTER
- ART HANNES IS THE ANNOUNCER.
- MUSICAL SUPERVISION IS BY ETHEL HUBER

Producer: Bruno Zirato, Jr.   **Writers:** Jack Johnstone
Cast: Leon Janney, Sam Gray, Mason Adams, Larry Haines, James Demetrie

SHOW: THE CAN'T BE SO MATTER
SHOW DATE: 1/28/1962
COMPANY: WORLDWIDE MUTUAL INSURANCE COMPANY
AGENT: LES WALTERS
EXP. ACCT: $0.00
SYNOPSIS: Mary, the operator at the Worldwide Mutual office calls Johnny. She has a call that Johnny thinks from Les Walters. After Johnny address Les as "a big

bum," the voice on the phone turns out to be Jonathan Harmon. Johnny was expecting Les to call about going to a hockey game to celebrate a recent birthday, if Les can get away from his wife that is. Jonathan tells Johnny it is too bad about Les' wife and tells Johnny that William Willoby was found dead this morning from "lead poisoning." Jonathan tells Johnny to go on out there and find out what happened. "I wonder what he meant about Les and his wife?"

Johnny cabs to the Hartford, Connecticut address of Willoby and in Apartment 5-B Johnny meets Sgt. Bravo. Sgt. Bravo had called the insurance company and had been watching Willoby since he moved there. They thought he might be involved in narcotics, but had left here to get away from some debts. He came back with a lot of money recently and the police were suspicious. Sgt. Bravo tells Johnny that someone Willoby knew must have killed him. One of the glasses on a table had smudged prints, and Willoby was shot by a .45. When Johnny mentions Les Walters, Sgt. Bravo tells Johnny that he had seen Les' wife Connie having lunch with Willoby in a cozy bar on Route 44. Johnny remembers that Willoby had made a play for Connie before she married Les. Johnny wonders if Les found out about it and killed Willoby. Johnny cabs to the Worldwide Mutual office where Jonathan tells Johnny that Walters had not come in that day and had not called in. Jonathan tells Johnny that he was concerned that there was some worry between Les and his wife. Johnny leaves to check with the switchboard operator and she tells Johnny that Les had not called in today. Johnny tells her to call him if Les were to call, and not to tell him know Johnny was looking for him. Johnny goes to see Connie Walters, and she wishes him a happy birthday. Johnny asks Connie if Les owns a gun, and she mentions that Johnny is the big gun collector. Connie tells Johnny that Les has been trying to find something to give Johnny to thank him for solving an embezzlement case that got him promoted. Johnny asks where Les is, and she does not know where he is. Johnny asks Connie about Willoby and she tells Johnny that he had a crush on her once. She went to lunch with him once last week after seeing Willoby at a gas station; but that was all. Connie tells Johnny that Les did not know about the date. The phone rings and the operator at Worldwide is calling. Les had called earlier and said he would not be in today or tomorrow. He called collect from EQuity 3-0114, which is over in Waterbury. Johnny calls the Equity number, hoping he is wrong. The number is for Berghoff's Gun Shop. Johnny asks Berghoff if Les Walters had bought a gun lately, and he tells Johnny that Les had bought a gun this morning—a .45.

Johnny still cannot believe the circumstantial evidence that points to Les Walters; his failure to check in, the slip-up on the date for the hockey game, Connie seeing Willoby, and her being so evasive about where Les was. But did Connie know about Willoby? But what is Johnny to do? Johnny calls Sgt. Bravo and he tells Johnny that progress has been made, and he will call Johnny when they make an arrest. Back at Connie's place she asks Johnny why he is asking so strangely. The doorbell rings, and Les is there. In the foyer he tells Connie he got it at the gun shop while she is trying to keep him quiet. Les tells her he finally got it—a genuine single-action Army Colt .45. Connie tells Les that Johnny is there and the phone rings. Les goes in to tell Johnny he spoiled the big surprise and tosses the gun at a not too happy Johnny. Les tells Johnny that he bought the gun as a surprise for Johnny's birthday. Connie tells Johnny that Sgt. Bravo is on the line. Bravo tells Johnny that the prints led the police straight to Shorty Scarpone, who confessed to the whole thing. A relieved Johnny hangs up and joins Les and Connie. He can finally tell them that not a thing is wrong with him now.

"I can only tell you this, I was never so glad to be wrong in my life. And I mean all wrong about a case."

NOTES:
- THE FIRST COMMERCIAL BREAK IS FOR JUNIOR ACHIEVEMENT.
- MASON ADAMS IS BRAVO, MARGARET DRAPER IS CONNIE, ARTHUR KOHL IS HARMON, PAT HOSLEY IS THE OPERATOR, CASEY ALLEN IS LES, SAM GRAY IS BERGHOFF.
- ART HANNES IS THE ANNOUNCER.
- MUSICAL SUPERVISION IS BY ETHEL HUBER

Producer: Bruno Zirato, Jr.   Writers: Jack Johnstone
Cast: Arthur Kohl, Casey Allen, Margaret Draper, Mason Adams,
             Pat Hosley, Sam Gray

◆   ❖   ◆

SHOW: THE NUGGET OF TRUTH MATTER
SHOW DATE: 2/4/1962
COMPANY: UNION STATES CASUALTY INSURANCE COMPANY
AGENT: TED NEWBERRY
EXP. ACCT: $20.00

SYNOPSIS: Ted Newberry calls, and Johnny congratulates him on getting engaged. Ted tells Johnny that the announcement in the papers was just a bit of skullduggery by Maryanne's mother, and now she will not talk to her mother or Ted. Johnny reminds Ted that when he does fall, the world will hear it. Ted tells Johnny that the only woman for him is Pandora Peters, the most beautiful girl he has ever met. When she did come to visit Ted, all she wanted was to find out how to talk to Johnny! Ted has set up a date for Johnny at 2:30, in his office.

Johnny shaves and showers, puts on a new tie, and cabs to Ted's Hartford, Connecticut office, arriving at 2:18. Ted tells Johnny that he forgot to tell Johnny that Pandora is married. She is married to Phillip Truesdale Peers, a nice family, but with not too much money. Phil has invented some electronic gadget, and is using his wife's money to get started. Both have $100,000 policies with each other as the beneficiaries. Johnny is curious, but Ted tells him that Phillip does not need Pandora dead to get her money. Pandora arrives and she is as lovely as Ted described her. Johnny can only stare at her, and she is worth staring at; but there was something there, a coldness that did not belong.

Pandora has a serious problem and tells Johnny that someone is threatening to kill her. Pandora drops her car keys, and Johnny notices that the key chain has a golden skull on it. Pandora tells him that it was carved from a single nugget found by her grandfather in Alaska. It is her good luck talisman. Pandora started getting notes in the mailbox about two months ago, just after Phil got the final patent on his invention, a little battery kind of thing. Pandora was not too enthusiastic at first, but she told Phil to go ahead when the notes started. The first one started with a quotation, "What profiteth a man if he gain the whole world but suffer the loss of his own soul" and it added that it was sinful for one man to profit from the device, and it should be given to the world. Phil laughed at it, and the police thought it came from a religious fanatic. More notes came with increasing levels of threats they thought were for Phil. Yesterday another note came addressed to Pandora and she shows a copy of it to Johnny. The note says, "Blind foolish woman, it is you who are guilty because of your money and that device of the devil. It is you who must die. And very soon." The police have the originals of the notes, and now Pandora is frightened. Pandora wants Johnny to find out who is behind the notes. Pandora has some errands to run and will then go home to fix dinner. Johnny tells her to continue her plans while he talks to the police. Johnny thinks that there is something very fishy about this deal. Johnny cabs to his apartment to get his car, which promptly breaks down on him. Johnny drives to police headquarters after the carburetor is fixed and talks to Sgt. Bill Budd who has been on the case from the beginning. Sgt. Budd tells Johnny that they had put a tail on Phil and looked at all the kooks, but found nothing. Sgt. Budd tells Johnny that the Peters have some problems and she has some money and he thinks that Pandora was writing the notes to scare Phil out of spending her money. That would explain how the noted got past the police. Johnny suggests that maybe Phil was writing the notes to scare her, so that he could kill her and get all her money. Phil Peters comes in all hysterical and tells Sgt. Budd and Johnny that it has finally happened and it is terrible. Officer Conroy tells Sgt. Budd and Johnny that he was the one who found the body. Pandora has been murdered.

Phil tells them that Pandora has been murdered, and they should have taken the letters seriously. Sgt. Budd gives Phil a slug of brandy to calm him down. Officer Conroy tells them that he was on patrol and investigated a call about a car blocking the road. When he got there he found no one in the car, and the motor running. Conroy looked around and found the body by a nearby pond. Conroy turned off the engine and called homicide. Lt. Briggs and Doc Campbell got there and Conroy left. Conroy is sure that the weapon is in the pond. Conroy then drove to the Peters home to tell Mr. Peters what had happened, and he insisted in being brought to headquarters. The phone rings and the call is for Conroy who tells the Lt. he will be right back because he has the Peter's car keys. Johnny looks at them and discovers the answer to the whole thing. Johnny asks for Phil's keys and he gives them to Johnny. The key chain has a golden skull on it, for good luck. Johnny tells Phil that it is not good luck for him, as his keys are the ones Pandora had when Johnny talked to her earlier. That means that Phil had to be with her, and that he killed her. Phil tells them he had to kill her to get the money for his invention, and Sgt. Budd calls for someone to record the confession.

"So with that full confession, complete with signature, there will be no problem. He did it, he'll pay for it."

NOTES:

- THE FIRST COMMERCIAL BREAK IS ABOUT THE EFFORTS OF CBS NEWS TO BREAK IN TO SPACE AND EXPAND THEIR COVERAGE.
- RITA LLOYD IS PANDORA, JIM STEVENS IS TED, DON MACLAUGHLIN IS BUDD, COURT BENSON IS PHIL, BILL LIPTON IS CONROY.
- ART HANNES IS THE ANNOUNCER.
- MUSICAL SUPERVISION IS BY ETHEL HUBER

Producer: Bruno Zirato, Jr.   **Writers:** Jack Johnstone
Cast: Rita Lloyd, Jim Stevens, Don MacLaughlin, Court Benson, Bill Lipton

◆ ❖ ◆

SHOW: THE DO IT YOURSELF MATTER
SHOW DATE: 2/11/1962
COMPANY: GREATER SOUTHWEST INSURANCE COMPANY
AGENT: ROY HARKINS
EXP. ACCT: $833.70

SYNOPSIS: Royal B. Harkin calls Johnny from Los Angeles, and tells Johnny that one of their offices in the Simi Valley is having a problem with fires. Roy is sure that a firebug is at work, and they are willing to pay Johnny's expenses. When Johnny mentions his usual fee, Roy starts to get upset, and when Johnny mentions a commission if money is saved, Roy is ready to call off the case, but relents.

Johnny flies to Los Angeles, California and arrives just after noon. Johnny cabs to Royal Harkin's office, where Roy is hesitant about Johnny's unknown fees. Johnny reminds Roy that he has saved them a lot on money on his other assignments. Roy reminds Johnny of the Bel Aire and Topanga Canyon fires the previous year, where 450 homes were destroyed and Greater Southwest insured many of them. Roy had decided to make up for the losses by selling more and more insurance. There is a great deal of development in the Simi Valley and Roy has established an autonomous office in Moorpark, California, just north of Thousand Oaks. The office has full authority to settle all claims, as that is the best way to compete with the bigger companies. A young man, Harry Walterson, took their course and passed, and has sold more insurance in three months than Roy has sold in three years. The premiums have been rolling in, but there have been nine fires in less than six weeks. The losses were high, but Walterson has been able to sell even more insurance. The premiums are not covering the losses though. The Police and Fire Departments are good, but they cannot keep up with the development of homes, and have not found anything to prove arson. With all the brush-covered hills, the new homes are at risk. Johnny wonders if the new homeowners are setting the fires, and Roy tells Johnny he has to find out. Johnny rents a car and drives to Moorpark and the office of Harry Walterson. Johnny asks Harry about the homeowners setting the fires and Harry tells Johnny, in between numerous phone calls, that the homes are new and the homeowners want to stay. The policies do not cover everything, and homeowners would not want to risk losing everything in a fire. Harry tells Johnny that the first fire was probably caused by sunlight refracted through some glass bottles, even though the owner, Mr. Orloff, did not like all of the development in the area. And the other fires started at night. Harry tells Johnny that the fires always start on windy nights, which occur often here. Harry offers to take Johnny to dinner and buzzes the receptionist who tells Harry that he has a number of calls, so Johnny prepares to drive back to Los Angeles. Johnny buys some dinner and finds a county fire chief at home, but he cannot help Johnny. The chief tells Johnny that it only takes one cigarette to start these fires, and with more people coming in the new people do not know how to handle the brushy country. The chief gets a call, and another fire is burning.

Johnny and the chief drive to the fire to find a new house burnt to the ground. The owner had no idea how the fire started, and Johnny is sure that he did not set it. Johnny inspects the ruins for hours and finds nothing. The chief tells Johnny that a cigarette probably started the fire. Harry arrives and tells Johnny that he heard about the fire from a neighbor. Harry tells Johnny that he had gone to Hollywood to see a movie, and found out about the fire when he came back. Harry tells the chief that old Timothy Handler was the one who told him about the fire and the chief remembers that Timothy was there before the fire department got there. Johnny gets a motel room and goes to Harry's office the next morning where Harry pays off the previous night's fire and collects more and more insurance applications. Harry tells Johnny that the people are scared, but he checks to make sure that the owners do not over insure. Johnny tells Harry he has to fly back to Hartford, but Johnny gets a motel room for the week and calls Pat Fuller at the Universal Adjustment Bureau for information on fire claims. Pat calls back and tells Johnny that Greater Southwest is the only company in the Simi Valley that is paying off on house fires, nine or ten in a row. Johnny tells Pat that he does not like what he thinks. Johnny gets two more rental cars and an old truck, some old clothes and several fire extinguishers. Johnny starts a tailing job because of the Latin phrase he remembers from school, "cui bono," who benefits? And how benefits? The one big beneficiary was not the homeowners, but the man who collected the commissions on all the policies. After a week of trailing Harry 24 hours a day, Johnny finally gets a windy moonlit night and follows Harry to a new home where Harry lights the brush to start another fire. Johnny uses a fire extinguisher to put out the fire, and gives one to Harry to use. Harry asks Johnny how he knew, and Johnny tells Harry it was by remembering his Latin.

"He didn't have a leg to stand on; he knew it. And he confessed to the whole dirty rotten business. For my money, they can lock him up for life, because if there is one thing I can't take, it's a crooked insurance man. I'm glad they are few and far between."

NOTES:

- THE FIRST COMMERCIAL BREAK IS ABOUT MENTAL ILLNESS—AMERICA'S NUMBER ONE ILLNESS.
- HERB DUNCAN IS HARRY, RAYMOND EDWARD JOHNSON IS ROYAL, JOSEPH JULIAN IS THE CHIEF, JOHN THOMAS IS PAT,
- BILL GILLIAN IS THE ANNOUNCER.
- MUSICAL SUPERVISION IS BY ETHEL HUBER

Producer: Bruno Zirato, Jr.   **Writers:** Jack Johnstone
Cast: Herb Duncan, Raymond Edward Johnson, Joseph Julian, John Thomas

◆ ❖ ◆

SHOW: THE TAKES A CROOK MATTER
SHOW DATE: 2/18/1962
COMPANY: WORLDWIDE MUTUAL INSURANCE COMPANY
AGENT: LES WALTERS
EXP. ACCT: $0.00

SYNOPSIS: A man calls Johnny to ask if he remembers a case Johnny was accidentally involved in four weeks, three days, thirteen hours ago, in the course if which he saved a man's life. Johnny recognizes the caller as Hal Leonard of the Federal Bureau, who is ok now. Hal thanks Johnny for walking in and saving his life. Johnny asks how Hal has recovered from his amnesia. Johnny tells him he was in the print shop because he thought Becker was fencing loot from a burglary, but Hal reminds Johnny that he found out what Hal had been tracking Becker for. Hal tells Johnny that now he is eligible for a nice long prison term. The crime is possession of evidence. Hal reminds Johnny that he was packing up the burglary evidence into his car, evidence that was really evidence in Hal's case. Hal tells Johnny he will fly up and relieve Johnny of the evidence.

Johnny recalls how he had forgotten all about the evidence in his car, which he had not used in four weeks. Les Walters calls, and he wants to see Johnny about the Morre Madonna, a picture painted by Marcel Morre that is worth a couple hundred thousand. It was in an exhibition at the Manhart Gallery in Hartford, Connecticut. Johnny tells Les that he cannot imagine why anyone would pay $200,000 for that impressionistic atrocity. Les tells Johnny that Worldwide insured it, and it has disappeared. Johnny tells Les that he must wait for a Federal man to come up, and Les is happy that Johnny has finally been caught! Johnny will be able to start on the case later that night, but Johnny will come over for an update. Johnny decides to drive his car to verify that the evidence is still there, or better yet to remove it from the car. Johnny outlines the layout of the garage as he opens the quick-lift door. Johnny opens the trunk, the garage door closes, and Johnny is slugged.

Johnny wakes up in the garage and opens the door to find the car trunk empty. Johnny passes out and then tries to get up to his apartment, holding something in his hand. Johnny bumps into Hal Leonard in the hallway. Hal takes Johnny up to his apartment where Johnny tells him what happened. Johnny gives Hal the keys to the garage and his car, and Hal leaves. The phone interrupts Johnny and Les Walters is wondering what happened to Johnny. Les tells Johnny to go see Thaddeus Brittingham, who lives in the Selfridge, a swanky apartment house in Hartford. Johnny cabs to a rooming house to see Little Willie, a stool pigeon that has an uncanny knowledge of art and art thieves. Willie tells Johnny that, for $100, he has been waiting for Johnny to visit him so that he can tell Johnny all about the Madonna. Willie tells Johnny that "he" had been watching the Madonna, and finally took the painting home to copy it. Johnny had better act fast because he probably has a buyer for it. For $150, Willie tells Johnny that the man is Charlie Starkey, who is out of the pen again. He is living at 324 South Crocus. Johnny arranges to mail $150 in cash to Willie and cabs to the address on Crocus, but Charlie has left in a big hurry, leaving all his clothes and paints. Mrs. Botz the landlady shows Johnny the money that Charlie paid her with and Johnny grabs it only to discover that it is counterfeit. Johnny searches the room and finds the Madonna. Johnny stashes the painting in his apartment and remembers that he had grabbed a part of the attacker and has a receipt with the name of Harvey Twiller on it. It was a receipt for an apartment at the Selfridge. Johnny cabs to the Selfridge and the doorman knows that Mr. Brittingham is expecting Johnny, but Mr. Twiller is not. Johnny convinces the doorman to let him in and Johnny goes to apartment 5-A to find Scotty Bagney, not Mr. Twiller. Scotty is out of the pen now, and is holding a gun on Johnny. Scotty invites Johnny in, and asks him to drop his gun, and Johnny obliges. Scotty tells Johnny that he had been trailing Johnny after hearing about the job in Becker's print shop. Scotty is about to shoot Johnny when Hal Leonard walks in and tells Johnny that he had found Scotty's prints on Johnny's garage door. Scotty tells Johnny and Hal that he does not have the stuff, as he used it to make a purchase. Johnny tells Scotty and Hal that the purchase was a copy of the Morre Madonna. Johnny tells Scotty that Starkey was a master copyist and a good fence that could sell to the rich who would buy such things. Scotty did not know that Starkey would steal the paintings and copy them, give the sucker the copy and skip town, while letting the original be discovered or even returned. Johnny tells Scotty that he original is in his apartment. Hal wants the counterfeit money he was looking for, and Johnny starts to search Scotty when there is a knock at the door. Charlie Bagney comes in ranting that Scotty gave him counterfeit money and Hal arrests Charlie. Johnny describes the whole affair as a quadruple play: Dollar to Scotty to Charlie to Hal.

"It's kind of a complicated mess, I know, but the painting is back to its owner, the counterfeit money is recovered, I'm in the clear with Uncle Sam, and all is well. Expense Account total, well why not just pay me the commission on that lovely Madonna."

NOTES:
- HERE IS NO "IT" IN THE TITLE OF THIS PROGRAM WHEN MANDEL KRAMER INTRODUCES IT.
- THE MUSIC ON THIS PROGRAM IS DECIDEDLY JAZZIER.
- THE FIRST COMMERCIAL BREAK IS FOR ADVENTURE IN THE FORM OF JOINING THE PEACE CORPS.
- MARTIN BLAINE IS HAL, RALPH BELL IS SCOTTY, JACK GRIMES IS LES, LEORA THATCHER IS THE LANDLADY, BILL KRAMER IS WILLIE, GUY REPP IS THE DOORMAN, LUIS VAN ROOTEN IS CHARLIE.
- ART HANNES IS THE ANNOUNCER
- MUSICAL SUPERVISION IS BY ETHEL HUBER

Producer: Bruno Zirato, Jr.   **Writers:** Jack Johnstone
Cast: Martin Blaine, Ralph Bell, Jack Grimes, Leora Thatcher, Bill Kramer, Guy Repp, Luis Van Rooten

◆ ❖ ◆

SHOW: THE MIXED BLESSING MATTER
SHOW DATE: 2/25/1962
COMPANY: WORLDWIDE MUTUAL INSURANCE COMPANY
AGENT: CHARLIE WARREN
EXP. ACCT: $0.00
SYNOPSIS: Charlie Warren calls from Los Angeles and Johnny calls him a bum and yells at him for assigning him to a case high in the mountains. Charlie tells Johnny that he has an assignment for Johnny in the Mojave Desert, out near Lake Mojave. Johnny tells Charlie he will grab all of his fishing tackle and head right out, but Charlie tells Johnny to bring a .38 also. Charlie will meet Johnny at the airport and give him the whole story.

Johnny flies to Los Angeles and Charlie meets him there. Over cocktails Charlie tells Johnny that he was only kidding about bringing a gun along. Charlie has called Ham Pratt and arranged for Johnny to have a boat and all the necessities for the next day. When Charlie mentions that the fishing is better in the afternoon, Johnny gets suspicious. Charlie tells Johnny that he has to pick up some money from Jake Kessler over in Kingman. The money is $40,000 to payoff a retirement policy. After making the delivery, Charlie tells Johnny that he can spend the rest of the week fishing, on expense account. Johnny knows that there is only one problem with this assignment; it sounds too easy.

Johnny describes Jake Kessler as he goes to meet him. Jake had made a fool of himself, took a dare and tried to ride a horse and ended up breaking an ankle and dislocating a knee. The injuries are why Jake needed to call someone to pay Barney Blessing. The policy was originally set up to pay Barney a monthly income, but now Barney wants the money all at once. Jake wonders if the company is suspicious just like he is. Jake tells Johnny that Barney Blessing was a gunman for the mobs, and moved here only last year with his dog Ricky and a man named Harry Higby. Harry was called "The Twin" and was the reason why Barney never got caught. Whenever Barney went out to do a job, Harry was planted somewhere as an alibi. Harry came west with Barney to blackmail him. Barney must have read the fine print and has demanded to be paid "in hand." Jake has never met Barney or Harry, and no one has seen either of them for a year. Johnny asks Jake why he sent for Johnny, and Jake tells him that he has a nose for trouble, and Barney told Jake that if he showed up without the money, well um . . . Johnny gets the money gets and directions to Barney's ranch, along with the necessary paperwork. Johnny wants to borrow the policy to copy it, but Jake has already done that for Johnny.

Johnny drives to Hackberry, Arizona and then on to the Cottonwood Mountains. The ranch is a tidy little farm with a lot of greenery and beef cattle. An old man meets Johnny with a high-powered rifle and tells Johnny to leave. When Johnny mentions the insurance money, the attitude changes. Barney recognizes who Johnny is, and Johnny tells Barney that Jake is laid up so he brought the money. Johnny asks Barney to sign the papers and compares it to the signature on the policy. Johnny asks about Higby "The Twin" and Barney tells Johnny that he paid Harry off and threw him out. Johnny asks about the dog, Ricky, and Barney tells Johnny that he died, and is buried outside. Johnny tells Barney he saw the mound of earth and wants to see what is under it. Barney gets anxious and waves the rifle at Johnny. Johnny pulls his gun and shoots the rifle out of Barney's hands. Johnny tells Barney to dig up the mound of earth. Barney digs up the grave and finds the remains of Ricky, but Johnny wants him to dig some more, but Barney hesitates. Johnny tells Barney that he is really Harry Higby, and had killed Barney when Harry found out that Barney was taking the money in cash so he could get out of the country, and away from Harry. Johnny tells Harry he decided to claim the money, and that Barney's fingerprints are on file, and they will match the body. Harry admits that Barney is under the dog.

Jake admits that it was just a hunch and did not know how to prove it. Johnny tells him to hang on to that nose of his.

"Dog gone it, because of a call from Hartford I again had to miss out on the fishing. But I am going to keep on trying, you can depend on that."

NOTES:

- THE FIRST COMMERCIAL BREAK IS FOR SAVING FOR COLLEGE EDUCATION AND THE NEED TO SUPPORT YOUR COLLEGE.
- LUIS VAN ROOTEN IS HARRY, CLIFF CARPENTER IS JAKE, MAURICE TARPLIN IS CHARLIE.
- ART HANNES IS THE ANNOUNCER
- MUSICAL SUPERVISION IS BY ETHEL HUBER

Producer: Bruno Zirato, Jr.   **Writers:** Jack Johnstone
Cast: Luis Van Rooten, Cliff Carpenter, Maurice Tarplin

SHOW:	THE TOP SECRET MATTER
SHOW DATE:	3/4/1962
COMPANY:	SURETY MUTUAL INSURANCE COMPANY
AGENT:	LEN WALKER
EXP. ACCT:	$993.70

SYNOPSIS: Len Walker calls Johnny from San Francisco. Len tells Johnny that three little explosions have cost him over a million dollars apiece. The explosions were caused by rocket fuel at the Bascom Development Company. Len tells Johnny to come on out, maybe Johnny can be sent aloft on their next blowup. Len tells Johnny that if he can get to the bottom of this, they will pay Johnny enough to fly high and wide and handsome for a long time. Johnny will catch the first plane.

Johnny flies to San Francisco, California via New York City. In New York Johnny meets his old friend George Langley, who is only going as far as Chicago. He is a vice President of a big chemical company, so Johnny wants to pick his brain. George tells Johnny that he is trying to turn down a rocket fuel contract. George asks Johnny if he still has a top security clearance, and Johnny shows him his credentials from the OSI, CIA, and the CIC. George tells Johnny that a new solid rocket fuel is about to hit the market. It was developed by sheer luck by an East German scientist at their plant. The scientist came for a nondescript job, developed the formula, and turned it over lock, stock and barrel. The fuel puts them light years ahead of the competition. Johnny asks George about Bascom, and he tells Johnny that he has never heard of them. Johnny is left to talk to George about fishing for the rest of the flight. Johnny lands in San Francisco and cabs to Len's office near station KCBS. Len tells Johnny to get dinner and prepare to drive to Bascom tomorrow. Bascom is located south of San Francisco, near Big Sur on a hidden dirt road. The three explosions resulted in three deaths, which is the major cause of the losses. Bascom was the beneficiary, along with the families. Len tells Johnny to ask Bascom about the particulars. The next day, Johnny drives down beautiful Highway 1 along the coast. At Point Sur Johnny finds the road and arrives at what looks like summer cottages with an armed guard. Johnny passes a building and is immediately caught in an explosion.

Johnny almost gets past the explosion but the rental car is turned over. Johnny is taken out of the car and to Horace Bascom's office, where Johnny is held at gunpoint until he tells Bascom who he is. Bascom tells Johnny that he is very fortunate, and could have ended up on the rocks below the plant. Bascom is not upset about the explosion, as others more knowledgeable will look into it. Bascom tells Johnny that they are working on a revolutionary semi-liquid rocket fuel, a powerful gelatinous propellant. Bascom is sure that they will succeed, and he will be on top of the industry with sole ownership of the secret. Johnny goes out to look at the ruined building with Bascom and Dr. Welcome, but nothing is found. Johnny speaks with Dr. Welcome later, and he tells Johnny that the chemicals are unstable, but they take all the necessary precautions. And each of the men who died was alone in the labs when the explosions occurred. Welcome tells Johnny that they are very close to finding the formula, even in light of the salary cuts, and that an East German named Hans Kellerhaus gave the idea of the fuels to Bascom. Bascom comes in, and reports finding nothing. Johnny tells Bascom that he has to go back to San Francisco for the evening, so Bascom loans Johnny his car. Johnny drives south, finds a phone and makes a series of calls that blow the case wide open. First, Johnny calls George Langley in Chicago; and then he calls Hans Kellerhaus, who left Bascom to work at a larger, more established company. Johnny is talking to the gas station owner when one of the tires explodes and the car goes over the side of the road onto the rocks. Johnny gives the station owner $100 to borrow his car and then drives back to Bascom's plant. Johnny slips the lock in Bascom's office and searches it until he finds a hidden switch with wires running to Building 1. Bascom comes into his office and Johnny asks him "why," the reason for the explosions. Johnny tells Bascom about the explosion that happened because he knew Johnny was coming, the switch in his office, and Bascom's help in combing the ruins that only misdirected Johnny away from the detonator. Also, the salary cutbacks for needed money, and the statement that he alone would have the secret of the fuel. Bascom tells Johnny that he had gone to Europe "on vacation," but was really there to contact Kellerhaus. Bascom got Kellerhaus into the country and he agreed that Bascom was to have complete control of his discoveries. Kellerhaus found out what Bascom was doing and decided to leave after signing over everything to Bascom. But Kellerhaus had not finished the fuel. The only way he could continue was to cash in on the insurance. Johnny asks Bascom to leave with him, but Bascom tells Johnny he will not leave, as he has a loaded .38. Johnny convinces him that it would not make any difference, and they leave.

"It's almost unbelievable, I mean the length to which some people will go to promote their own selfish interests at the sacrifice of others. Don't they know that somehow, sometime there has to be a showdown?"

NOTES:
- MELVILLE RUICK IS BASCOM, COURT BENSON IS DR. WELCOME, FRANK CAMPANELLA IS GEORGE, WILLIAM MASON IS THE GAS STATION ATTENDANT.
- ART HANNES IS THE ANNOUNCER
- MUSICAL SUPERVISION IS BY ETHEL HUBER

Producer: Bruno Zirato, Jr.   **Writers:** Jack Johnstone
Cast: Melville Ruick, Court Benson, Frank Campanella, William Mason

◆ ❖ ◆

SHOW:	THE GOLDEN DREAM MATTER
SHOW DATE:	3/11/1962
COMPANY:	GREATER SOUTHWEST INSURANCE COMPANY
AGENT:	JAKE KESSLER
EXP. ACCT:	$451.80

SYNOPSIS: Jake Kessler of Worldwide Mutual in Kingman, Arizona calls Johnny. Jake has a problem with a Greater Southwest client. Jake has retired and the two companies want him to keep an eye on their offices for them. The problem is a client who was insured by the San Francisco office. The client is a mining engineer, and he has disappeared. Johnny tells Jake he will grab his fishing rod and come out for some great bass fishing while he tries to help Jake.

Johnny flies to Los Vegas and rents a car the next day, and drives across the desert and the Hoover Dam to Kingman, Arizona. Jake tells Johnny he might have a chance to get some fishing done, as the one person who can help Johnny find Myron Kingsley is Ham Pratt. The old mine, the Golden Dream is very close to the Lake Mojave Resort. It seems that a man named Marty Spiller has been selling stock in the mine, mostly to people in the East who could not afford to check on the mine. One stockholder got suspicious and hired Kingsley to look around. It has been several days since Ham has seen Kingsley in his room. The phone rings and Ham is calling for Johnny. Ham tells Johnny that he came for nothing, as they just found Kingsley's body at the bottom of a mineshaft.

Johnny drives to Lake Mojave Resort and goes out with Ham to the mine. Ham has been carrying a gun since he thinks that Kingsley might not have fallen into the mineshaft, being an experienced engineer and all. Ham tells Johnny that the people in the area do not like Marty Spiller. After a very rough jeep ride across the desert Johnny and Ham arrive at the mine at sunset. Ham tells Johnny that they stopped working the mine back in the late thirties. Spiller came along four years ago and has done just enough to keep his rights by re-washing the tailings, which is mostly worthless rock. Spiller has not taken any gold from the mine, but he is selling stock in it though. At the mine Ham tells Johnny that when Kingsley arrived, Spiller supposedly left for California. In the mineshaft Johnny spots Kingsley's body about a hundred feet below in the water. Johnny convinces Ham to lower him down on a rope to retrieve the body. On the way down, Johnny notes small tunnels leading off the shaft. Near the bottom Johnny tells Ham that there is a big shaft at the bottom. Johnny yells and there is no response from Ham, except for some falling rocks. Then there are gunshots aimed at Johnny as the rope slips and Johnny falls into the water.

Johnny notes that he cheated when the ropes slacked and threw a rock into the water from the tunnel entrance. After the gunshots, huge boulders were rolled into the water. A voice yells at Johnny, who remains quiet as several more boulders crash into the water. Johnny struggles up the tunnel to get to the main shaft of the mine and the surface. Johnny reaches the surface and edges towards the jeep where he spots a man tying another one to a 10 by 10 timber. Johnny crawls across the desert as he stalks Spiller. Johnny rushes across an open spot only to have Ham tell Johnny he is ok. Spiller had hit Ham with a gun, and when Ham came to, he tied up Spiller and decided to go down after Johnny. When Johnny asks how Ham was certain that he was alive, Ham tells Johnny "If a lousy punk like Spiller could kill off a man like you, well this I gotta see." "I hope you never do," replies Johnny.

"We brought up Kingsley's body the next morning. The bullet that had killed Kingsley before he had been dropped into the mineshaft had come from Spiller's gun. A simple ballistics test proved that conclusively. So again, it is up to the courts."

NOTES:
- THE FIRST COMMERCIAL BREAK IS FOR THE PAYROLL SAVINGS PLAN TO BUY US SAVINGS BONDS.
- THIS PROGRAM DOES NOT LIST THE ROLES PLAYED BY THE ACTORS.
- WARREN SWEENEY IS THE ANNOUNCER.
- MUSICAL SUPERVISION IS BY ETHEL HUBER

Producer: Bruno Zirato, Jr.   Writers: Jack Johnstone
Cast: Cliff Carpenter, Bob Dryden, Sam Raskyn

SHOW: THE IKE AND MIKE MATTER
SHOW DATE: 3/18/1962
COMPANY: TRI-WESTERN LIFE INSURANCE COMPANY
AGENT: JACK PRICE
EXP. ACCT: $0.00

SYNOPSIS: A voice asks Johnny if he wants to hop aboard the next plane for the mighty sovereign state of Texas. Jack Price tells Johnny that there is no way Johnny can save Jack any money on this case. Johnny can come down, but only on a bare minimum expense account with no service fees or commission. Johnny asks Jack if he thinks Johnny would accept such and assignment from Jack of all people, and Jack tells him yes, he would. Johnny tells Jack that he is right!

Johnny flies to Corpus Christi, Texas and takes the airport limousine to the Robert Driscol hotel where he gets a room, not a suite mind you, just a room. Jack meets Johnny in his room and Johnny wants to order drinks, but Jack tells him not to, as it is too late for Johnny to do what Jack wanted him to do. Also it is too late to cancel the policy because of what happened after Jack called Johnny. Jack tells Johnny that the policy was for $25,000 straight life, with double indemnity. Jack asks Johnny if he remembers a character named Lou Livercum. Johnny remembers that Little Louie Livercum was a slippery stock promoter Johnny had chased all over the country a couple years ago, only to have a slick lawyer get him off. Jack tells Johnny that a new man in the office sold a policy to Isaac Prelinger, who was known as "Smarty Ike" in the local pool halls. He had no visible means of support, and was just a smart fast-talking bum from San Antonio. Jack was checking the policy and discovered that Livercum was the beneficiary. Jack realized that something was wrong and Johnny suggests that Livercum fronted the money for the policy, and planned to have Ike killed to get the money. Jack tells Johnny that Livercum's last address was in Oregon. So that is why Jack called Johnny so he could look into the policy to see if Jack could cancel it. Jack tells Johnny that the shack Ike lived in burnt to the ground just a few hours ago. Jack identified the body based on the policy medical information, and is sure that it was Ike Prelinger that died. Jack tells Johnny that the arson squad called the death accidental and typical: Ike got drunk and fell on the bed with a lighted cigarette and the shack went up. Johnny rents a car and drives to Jack's office to read the policy and the physical details about Ike. Johnny calls Pete Frawley of the Arson Squad at home, and arranges to meet Pete at the morgue to look at Ike's body. Pete tells Johnny that there were no prints, and the ID was made from general physical characteristics. The autopsy proved that the body was Ike's. Pete tells Johnny that there were a flock of empty liquor bottles around, and Pete had been able to isolate the ashes from the cigarette in Ike's hand. Johnny tells Pete he suspects someone wanted to kill Ike, and used the fire as a cover up. Pete tells Johnny he had thought the same thing, but the autopsy proved that Ike was not injured or poisoned before the fire, and that there was smoke in Ike's lungs. Johnny suggests that maybe someone smothered him enough to knock him unconscious, but Pete tells him he needs evidence to prove that. Johnny tells Pete about the beneficiary angle, and Johnny thinks he better fly out to Oregon. On a hunch, Johnny drives to Jerry Deek's poolroom and Jerry convinces Johnny that his hunch is right. Deeks tells Johnny that Ike made his money playing pool, and was a very consistent player. Deeks tells Johnny that Ike never used liquor. Deeks had given Ike some once, and Ike told him that liquor was nothing but poison.

Johnny calls Jack and tells him what he has learned, and that he is sure that murder was involved and is flying out to Oregon. Johnny reminds Jack of the old saying, "Ike and Mike, they look alike," and tells Jack to meet him in his office. In Jack's office Johnny reviews the application and calls Pete Frawley to tell him that he is sure that murder was involved because Ike did not drink. Johnny wants a further autopsy to look for a fracture on the first metatarsal on the right foot. Johnny tells him that if they do not find the fracture to call missing persons in San Antonio with a complete description of Ike. They might be looking for somebody who looks like Ike. If they are not, call every other town in Texas until he gets a match. Johnny flies to Eugene, Oregon via Houston, Los Angeles, and Portland and arrives the next morning. Johnny cabs to Lou's house and asks the cab to wait. Livercum was the same suave, slippery character Johnny remembers. Lou has heard about Ike's death, and has filed a claim. Lou tells Johnny that they worked together once, but Johnny asks if they are still working together. Lou tells Johnny that his neighbors can prove he has been home all week, and that Johnny cannot prove that Lou was involved in Ike getting killed. Johnny makes a call to Pete and learns that the body did not have a broken bone. It was a dead ringer for Prelinger. Pete had called San Antonio, and they have a missing man named Mike Ringler. Johnny tells Pete that when Ike learned he had a double, he moved to Corpus, called Lou Livercum and set up the scheme to split the $50,000. Johnny tells Pete he will stay there until Ike shows up. A man enters with a gun and tells Johnny to hang up. Lou tells Ike who Johnny is and Ike prepares to shoot Johnny. The cabby comes in asking for Johnny, and in the confusion Johnny slugs Ike. Johnny has the cabby help him take Lou and Ike to police headquarters.

"Yup, it was good hunting. Not only because Ike will have to pay for the murder of Mike Ringler. But more important to me, because Lou Livercum is finally ending up where he belongs, behind bars. Expense account total? Oh, you figure it up Jackson. And don't forget my commission on the insurance that won't have to be paid out."

NOTES:
- THE FIRST COMMERCIAL BREAK IS ABOUT THE FOLKS WHO DROP IN TO VISIT EVERY DAY; ARTHUR GODFREY, GARY MOORE, BING CROSBY AND ROSE MARY CLOONEY, CBS RADIO'S STARS.
- WILLIAM REDFIELD IS PETE, MAURICE TARPLIN IS JACK, REYNOLD OSBORNE IS LOUIE, LAWSON ZERBE IS DEEKS, RALPH BELL IS IKE, BILL LIPTON IS THE CABBY.
- THE ANNOUNCER IS BILL GILLIAN
- MUSICAL SUPERVISION IS BY ETHEL HUBER

Producer: Bruno Zirato, Jr.   Writers: Jack Johnstone
Cast: William Redfield, Maurice Tarplin, Reynold Osborne,
             Lawson Zerbe, Ralph Bell, Bill Lipton

◆ ❖ ◆

SHOW: THE SHADOW OF A DOUBT MATTER
SHOW DATE: 3/25/1962
COMPANY: WESTERN INDEMNITY COMPANY
AGENT: TED ORLOFF
EXP. ACCT: $450.00

SYNOPSIS: Ted Orloff calls Johnny from Los Angeles. Ted wants Johnny to come out to see Barney Garrison, who owns a small bottling plant. Barney told Ted that someone has embezzled $170,000 from the till. Johnny will be right out.

Johnny flies to Los Angeles and Ted meets Johnny at the airport. While Ted complains about the California drivers, he tells Johnny that Barney owns a bottling plant that handles all types of drinks. Barney Garrison got the money to set up the plant somehow and Ralph Betterly is the Vice President and handles the bookkeeping. It is a partnership, but they are really opposites. Betterly is a quiet neat little man and has a nice home on Pandora Avenue in Westwood. Barney is a big well-fed backslapping salesman type. He is a bachelor and thinks he is a lady's man and has a new home in Palm Springs. Barney called yesterday to say he had been going over the books, and discovered the missing money. Barney is waiting for Johnny in Palm Springs, California. Barney has arranged for Johnny and Ted to take his private plane to Palm Springs. Johnny and Ted fly on Barney's private twin engine Beech and Johnny in Palm Springs notices some long thin clouds that turn out to be skywriting for "Poppola," Barney's new product. Ted tells Johnny that today is the announcement of the product. Barney arrives and tells Ted that he has discovered that Betterly has taken the money.

Barney takes Johnny and Ted to his new home and shows them around. Johnny describes a big neon sign with a clock in it advertising "Now is the time to drink Poppola." The sign is for a photo shoot planned for the next day. Barney shows Johnny some instant photos of himself in front of the sign at 10:05AM, and one of the skywriting. Johnny forces Barney to talk about the theft, and Barney tells Johnny that Ralph is not a full partner and only gets a quarter of the profits, which have been pretty low because of the startup costs of Poppola. Also, Ralph has a lot of hospital bills and his wife died just a few days earlier. Barney is sure that Ralph is the only one who could have stolen the money, as Ralph is the only other man with the combination to the safe, and who knew that the money was in the safe. Barney tells Johnny he needs a lot of cash to pay off the Mexican boys who, uh . . . Barney tells Johnny that a secret ingredient does not cross the border legally, and that is why he needs the cash. Johnny gets angry and asks Ted if he knew about the smuggling, which he did not. Also, Barney tells Johnny that he had not told the police, and Johnny tells him that if the police found out, they would put him out of business. Barney tells Johnny that he is too smart to get caught. Johnny wants to leave and Ted wants to cancel the policies, but Barney tells Ted that he still owes Barney the money. Johnny rents a car for the drive back to Los Angles so Johnny can follow a hunch. When Johnny gets to 1308 Pandora Ave., the police are there and they tell Johnny that Garrison had called them. They broke in the door and found Betterly dead of suicide. Lt. Harvey May tells Johnny that if Betterly had shot himself, there should be powder burns. The doctor thinks Betterly was shot from a distance and died between 9:30 and 11:30, but no one in the area heard anything. Lt. May tells Johnny that Garrison had proof he had been in Palm Springs since yesterday, but Johnny is almost sure he can prove otherwise. Johnny asks Lt. May to call the Palm Springs police, but to give Johnny time to get there first.

Johnny drives to Palm Springs alone, not quite as sure as the thought he was, but the facts added up. Garrison needed money to support his life style. Also the call to the police to insure the body would be found and establish a time of death set to remove suspicion from Barney. Johnny knew he would be called on to support Barney's alibi. At Barney's house there is a party in progress and Barney invites Johnny in. Barney tells Johnny that he had called Ralph to see how he was. Johnny tells Barney that he had tried to plant the idea of suicide with Johnny earlier. In Barney's office Johnny tells Barney that he tried hard to plant an alibi with Johnny. Johnny asks Barney if he is pretending that he does not know that Ralph is dead, and Barney acts shocked and tells Johnny "suicide, too bad." Johnny tells Barney that Ralph was murdered, and that Barney did it and knows when it happened. Barney asks when Ralph died but Johnny does not answer. Barney shows Johnny the photo of the clock taken at 10:05 with the sky writing in the background. Johnny looks at the picture and Barney tells Johnny that the picture had to be taken today, because of the skywriting. Johnny tells Barney that the pool in the picture runs north to south, and Barney faced south in the picture. But the shadows in the picture indicate that the picture was taken in the afternoon, shortly before Johnny arrived. Barney pulls his gun, complete with silencer, but a police sergeant walks in and Johnny tells him to give the gun to him.

"Once again it is up to the courts, but when the West Los Angles police run down the $170,000, where ever Garrison put it, and I am sure they will, he won't have a leg to stand on."

NOTES:
- THE FIRST COMMERCIAL BREAK IS ABOUT THE PROGRAM "DIMENSION OF A WOMAN'S WORLD" WITH BETTY FURNESS HEARD THREE TIMES A DAY ON CBS.
- BOB DRYDEN IS BARNEY, BERNARD GRANT IS LT. MAY, JAMES STEVENS IS TED, EUGENE FRANCIS IS THE SGT., JOCELYN SUMMERS IS THE GIRL.
- PAT CANEL IS THE ANNOUNCER.
- MUSICAL SUPERVISION IS BY ETHEL HUBER

Producer: Bruno Zirato, Jr.   **Writers:** Jack Johnstone
Cast: Bob Dryden, Bernard Grant, James Stevens, Eugene Francis, Jocelyn Summers

◆ ❖ ◆

SHOW: THE BLUE ROCK MATTER
SHOW DATE: 4/1/1962
COMPANY: STATE UNITY LIFE INSURANCE COMPANY
AGENT: PHIL?
EXP. ACCT: $200.00

SYNOPSIS: Phil calls Johnny from New York and tells Johnny he is slowly going mad. Johnny tells him that he is ready to open the trout season by dropping flies in front of ravenous rainbows. Johnny tells Phil he is going to a private stream not far from Hartford, but Phil tells Johnny that he is going to go fishing on the Esophus River, just out side of Mount Tremper, New York. Johnny knows the stream well, and Phil tells Johnny that they will pay his expense account. Johnny is on the way.

Johnny packs his trout fishing gear, including a pair of long johns, and flies to New York and goes to Phil's office. Phil tells Johnny that he does not have the time to go fishing, besides the man Phil wants Johnny to watch knows Phil. The man is Thomas Gerald Aspenwald, a man who would stop at nothing to get at the Emory Archibald fortune. Johnny thought that Archibald, the stockbroker was dead, but Phil tells him that he will be dead soon of an incurable disease. Tom Aspenwald was married to Nancy Archibald, and Nancy's five-year-old son Barry is the last of the family. Barry's father died about the time he was born. Originally Archibald had left half of the estate to Tom, and half to Nancy. But the new will leaves the whole estate to Nancy and the boy, unless the boy dies before the old man does in which case Tom gets the money. Phil has learned that Tom is taking the boy away for a few days. Phil has made reservations for Johnny at the home of Mr. and Mrs. Fritz Hornblock, who have a home near a big pool. Johnny tells Phil he knows all about the Blue Rock pool, which is a very dangerous place to be, and a great place to fake an accident. Tom Aspenwald and Barry are the only other guests at the Hornblock place. Johnny is ready to drive up.

Johnny spends the night and then buys a fishing license and rents a car for the drive to Mt. Tremper. Johnny arrives as the weather turns cold and windy. At the Hornblock house, Fritz insists in carrying Johnny's baggage to his room. Fritz offers Johnny a drink of schnapps, but Johnny tells him he has a bottle of scotch he carries, in case of snakebite. As Fritz finishes his drink Tom Aspenwald arrives and is introduced. Tom tells Johnny that he brought his stepson to teach him to fish. Fritz tells Johnny that Barry has gone to town with "Mama," who promised to buy him some rock candy. Barry loves the candy, even though it makes him sick, like it did last time Tom was there. Fritz promises to take care of Barry. Johnny asks Tom about his plans and Fritz tells them that the big hole below the bridge will have no one fishing there, but Fritz will not let Tom take Barry there as it is too dangerous. Maybe he can take Barry later in the day. Johnny suggests that they hit the hole first thing in the morning, but Tom tends to waffle. Johnny tells Tom that he should take Barry later in the day after he has caught his limit. Tom leaves to get some dry flies he forgot, but Fritz tells Johnny that Tom brought along every fly ever made. Johnny tells Fritz that Tom should know that dry flies are not appropriate for this time of the year. Wet flies, streamers or nymphs would be more appropriate, and Fritz tells Johnny that he has some worms ready for them. Mama returns with Barry and Johnny talks to him and learns he really is not too fond of his stepfather. Barry was clutching a bag of blue rock candy, but Johnny is vaguely reminded of something else. Johnny is told that Barry really loves the blue candies, and he would rather play with the farm animals than fish. Johnny is sure that Aspenwald will get rid of the boy in the river, but it turns out to be a fatal mistake.

Aspenwald wears a new fishing jacket at dinner with a bulging pocket, and is in a better mood. Barry asks if he bought some more "rocks" and Tom tells him that he has had too many. Fritz makes plans to go to town in the morning, and Mama must take some butter to a neighbor so Barry will be alone for a few minutes to play with the chickens. Johnny tells Tom that Fritz has given him a secret weapon to use the next morning. At dawn the temperature is in the 20's but after a hearty breakfast Johnny and Tom go fishing. Johnny notices a coating of ice on the rocks and the missing bulge in Tom's jacket pocket. Johnny manages to catch his first trout using one of Fritz's secret weapons, a fat worm. Tom tells Johnny that he knows who he is, and pushes Johnny off a slippery rock into the water. Johnny manages to hold on to Tom's leg and pulls him in. After they both get out Tom admits he brought the boy up here to kill him. Tom tells Johnny that he goofed by telling Tom how old Barry was before he met him, so he made other arrangements. Johnny notices a blue-green stain on the jacket and recognizes that is it blue vitriol, or copper sulfate that Tom had bought in Kingston. The copper sulfate looks just like the candy Barry loves and Tom had left it for Barry to eat. Johnny slugs Tom and runs to the farmhouse to find Barry.

"The big dramatic ending, I'm sorry. Not this time. Thanks to the fact that Mrs. Hornblock had changed her mind and taken Barry along on her morning errand. By the time they got back, I'd cleaned up every chunk of the Blue Vitriol that Aspenwald had planted, mostly around the chicken coop. So the only casualty was Aspenwald, who had nearly frozen to death in his wet clothes on the frozen ground where I had knocked him out. And he was a very docile prisoner when I handed him in at the Kingston hoosegow."

NOTES:
- THE FIRST COMMERCIAL BREAK IS FOR NEWPORT FILTER CIGARETTES.
- CAST INFORMATION FROM RADIOGOLDINDEX.
- BLUE VITRIOL IS A BLUE, CRYSTALLINE HYDROUS SOLUTION OF COPPER SULFATE USED IN INSECTICIDES, GERMICIDES, AND HAIR DYES AND IN THE PROCESSING OF LEATHER AND TEXTILES.
- THE ESOPHUS IS A FAMOUS TROUT STREAM IN EASTERN NEW YORK STATE.
- ART HANNES IS THE ANNOUNCER

Producer: Bruno Zirato, Jr.   Writers: Jack Johnstone
Cast: Bryna Raeburn, Karl Weber, Luis Van Rooten, Sarah Fussell, William Mason

◆ ❖ ◆

SHOW: THE IVY EMERALD MATTER
SHOW DATE: 4/8/1962
COMPANY: SURETY MUTUAL INSURANCE, LTD.
AGENT: BOB BAKER
EXP. ACCT: $0.00

SYNOPSIS: Bob Baker calls Johnny from Boston. Johnny hopes there is a big fat commission on this call. Bob asks Johnny if he has ever heard of the Ivy Emerald, the biggest green emerald in the world, but Johnny is only interested in the folding green stuff. Bill tells Johnny that the emerald has been stolen, and Johnny must find it before it is cut up. The emerald is insured for $600,000, so Johnny is on his way.

Johnny flies to Boston, Massachusetts and meets with Bob Baker in his office. Bob tells Johnny the client is Mrs. Oscar B. Sterlingwaite, Emily Sterlingwaite, a rich old widow. The emerald is called the Ivy Emerald because of the mounting, which looks like an ivy plant. The emerald was placed in the safe last night, but this morning it was missing. Also, the safe was opened the old-fashioned way, with the dial. Normally the jewelry is in a vault, but it was in the safe with the paste copies of her real diamond because she had just worn it. The fact the paste diamonds were not taken means that the thief was an expert. No one else knows the combination to the safe that has an oil-dampened movement made by the Darlington Safe Company in Boston. Bill knows Mr. Darlington, and tries to convince Johnny that he is honest. Johnny rents a car and drives to the Sterlingwaite home on Beacon Hill. The uniformed butler shows Johnny in to Mrs. Sterlingwaite, who shows Johnny the safe, which is hidden behind a panel. Mr. Darlington had installed it just for her when he was dating her many years earlier. The dial is oversized because of her eyes, as she does not see very well. No one knows about the safe except Hendricks, the butler, but he has been with her for forty years. But only she knows the combination. Johnny learns that Arnold Bixby, the former chauffeur left about a month ago and Emily gives Johnny a picture of him. Johnny wonders at the picture, and is sure that he has seen the man before. Johnny tells Emily that he can open the safe for her. Johnny tells her to open the safe while he goes out and closes the big double doors.

Johnny waits outside and goes in when Emily has opened and then closed the safe. Johnny then opens the safe with the combination. Johnny tells Emily that there is a crack in the doors that allowed him to watch her turn the large combination dial at arms-length to open the safe. Johnny is sure that others could have watched also. Johnny is sure that Arnold is still in the area and has an idea. Johnny thinks there are three possibilities: Mrs. Sterlingwaite, but she is not the type. Then there is the ex-chauffeur who was familiar to Johnny, but only vaguely. Third was Darlington. After Johnny meets with Darlington, there is no doubt that he is innocent. Darling is truly upset at the loss of Mrs. Sterlingwaite's jewels, as he has let her down. Johnny tells him that Emily would love to have him there to comfort her, and suggests he call her. Johnny shows Darlington the picture of Arnold, and he tells Johnny that the man was employed there under the name of Roger Gove. Roger was a truck driver and loader, but Darlington fired him when he found Roger in his office one night. Darlington confirms that his safe has a record of combinations for all safes he sold, and Johnny is convinced that is how Roger got the combination, but Darlington tells Johnny that the safe was locked. Johnny next takes the case in the right direction by contacting an old friend, an ex-con who knows the underworld, Smokey Sullivan. Smokey is still working with the Fire Department and he tells Johnny that he does not know where the emerald it is or who took it, but he does have a lead.

Smokey tells Johnny that five blocks away is a man who is a fence and gem cutter from Chicago, Fritz Bildow. Smokey tells Johnny that Fritz has a shop where he makes cheap jewels for the kids. Johnny shows Smokey the picture of the chauffeur, and he tells Johnny that the man is Manny Breed, a jewel thief. Johnny figures out the plot and Smokey tells Johnny that he had spotted a pile of trash outside the shop and had started watching Bildow thinking he was going to burn the place. Smokey had called Lt. Tommy Winkler to check up on Bildow, and at three this morning Smokey had seen Bildow working on a big gold setting, like an ivy leaf. Johnny and Smokey rush to the shop in an alley. Manny gets the drop on Johnny and Smokey, and tells them that Bildow had recognized Smokey, and that is why he is ready for anything. Manny knocks on the door and takes Johnny and Smokey inside, where Johnny spots the stone. Manny gets Johnny's gun and is about to close the door and shoot Johnny when Lt. Winkler rushes in and shoots Manny. Tommy had come to follow up on the arson angle from Smokey, and Johnny tells him he has helped recover the Ivy Emerald.

"So, the emerald's back, and all's right with the world. Just one thing though, my commission on this one is to be split three ways; a third to Smokey, and a third to Tommy Winkler. As for the expense account, well if you pay the commission promptly, you can forget about it."

NOTES:
- THE FIRST COMMERCIAL BREAK IS FOR NEWPORT MENTHOL CIGARETTES.
- ABBY LEWIS IS EMILY, LAWSON ZERBE IS DARLINGTON, JOSEPH JULIAN IS SMOKEY, WILLIAM GRIFFIS IS BOB, JACK GRIMES IS BREED, SAM GRAY IS FRITZ, WILLIAM MASON IS WINKLER.
- WARREN SWEENEY IS THE ANNOUNCER
- MUSICAL SUPERVISION IS BY ETHEL HUBER

Producer: Bruno Zirato, Jr.   Writers: Jack Johnstone
Cast: Abby Lewis, Lawson Zerbe, Joseph Julian, William Griffis,
             Jack Grimes, Sam Gray, William Mason

◆   ❖   ◆

SHOW: THE WRONG IDEA MATTER
SHOW DATE: 4/15/1962
COMPANY: ETERNITY MUTUAL INSURANCE COMPANY
AGENT: TIM HARRINGTON
EXP. ACCT: $229.57

SYNOPSIS: A voice tells Johnny that he is not going to like this. Tim Harrington from Knoxville, Tennessee tells Johnny that Alphius Brannigan, the kid who Johnny got sent up for embezzlement based on a tip from his pretty wife, had sworn he would get even with Johnny and his wife. Alfie got out of prison a couple weeks ago on good behavior. Tim thinks they were suckers, and his wife is a client. Tim has tried to find her but she has disappeared, so Johnny is on his way.

Johnny flies to Knoxville, Tennessee and takes a limousine to Tim's office. Tim tells Johnny that the policy on Marylyn Brannigan is only $7,500 and her brother Charlie is the beneficiary. Johnny tells Tim he should not worry about the courtroom threats to get even, as Johnny has seen too many of them. Tim is sure that Tim was not kidding. Marylyn has not seen Alfie, because he would not let her see him, and would not answer her letters. She called Tim and asked for advice and Tim told her to call the police. Sgt. Piper of the police called the other day and told Tim that Marylyn has disappeared. Tim tells Johnny that he better watch out for himself, too.

Johnny goes to see Sgt. Piper, who is a big florid man who chews a cigar. Sgt. Piper tells Johnny that he has found no signs of Marylyn or Alfie. Marylyn had her own car, and is an accountant. The license on the car was ULL166, and an APB has not been put out, because she is not guilty of any crime. Johnny yells at Sgt. Piper that Alfie did nothing until the police dropped their guard, and then he acted. Johnny is sure that Alfie has gotten to Marylyn and taken her away. Johnny grabs the phone to call the state police and the FBI but Sgt. Piper relents and issues an ABP and apologizes to Johnny for not acting sooner. Johnny tells Sgt. Piper to call him at the Andrew Johnson Hotel. After dinner at the Rathskeller, Johnny gets a room at the hotel, and is called by Sgt. Piper. He has located Marylyn at 21270 South Peachtree Street in Jefferson City. Sgt. Piper has not told the police to keep an eye on her, so Johnny rents a car and drives to the address in Jefferson City where Johnny finds Marylyn's car is out side. Johnny gets in to find a scared Marylyn Brannigan. She had not heard from Alfie for three years, wondering what he meant in the courtroom. She tells Johnny that Alfie never changed his mind about what he says. She tells Johnny that she had to tell Johnny about where Alfie was, and that the money he embezzled was for a holiday present for her. They had only been married a few weeks but she really loves him. Because Alfie would not see her or answer her letters, she is not sure of what to do. Johnny tells her that the police should be there. She has no phone so Johnny goes out to call the police and tells her to keep the door locked. Marylyn kisses Johnny on the cheek as he leaves. Outside Alfie stops Johnny in the dark and slugs him.

Johnny wakes up in his car to the slaps of a police officer and a whiff of smelling salts. The police tell Johnny that Sgt. Piper had called them about Marylyn, and they went out to check the address. There is there is no one in the house when they got there, and they had seen a car drive away when they got there. The police give Johnny his wallet and he tells them to go back to headquarters and spread the word. Johnny makes a difficult drive back to Knoxville and visits Sgt. Piper and then goes back to his room to get some sleep. Alfie and Marylyn meet Johnny in his room. She tells Johnny that Alfie came back to her. Alfie had seen Johnny at the cottage and assumed that he was there to take her away. Marylyn is so happy about all the things he had done for her. Alfie tells Johnny that it was the least he could do for her. He had to prove that he was worthy of her. He was serious about what he said in court, about how he would show everyone and make up for the crazy thing he did. He has worked hard and studied to improve himself. When he got out he went to see her brother Charlie, who had liked him. Now he has a steady job and a place to live far away from all the bad memories. Now they can start again, the right way. Johnny tells Alfie that if he wants to keep things right, to hold his temper, even when he sees his wife kissing another man. Johnny is glad to have a case end on a happy note for once as they help him to his bed.

"Well, you know something? Sure, those two are even younger than they realized, but I think that those kids will do all right. I hope so."

NOTES:

- THE FIRST COMMERCIAL BREAK IS FOR WINSTON BURDETTE, ARTHUR GODFREY AND MANY MORE OF THE EXCLUSIVE STARS OF CBS RADIO.
- THE SECOND COMMERCIAL BREAK IS FOR NEWPORT MENTHOL CIGARETTES.
- JIMSEY SOMMERS IS MARYLYN, LAWSON ZERBE IS PIPER, RICHARD HOLLAND IS ALFIE, HERB DUNCAN IS TIM, BILL LIPTON IS THE POLICEMAN.
- ART HANNES IS THE ANNOUNCER.
- MUSICAL SUPERVISION IS BY ETHEL HUBER

Producer: Bruno Zirato, Jr.   Writers: Jack Johnstone
Cast: Jimsey Sommers, Lawson Zerbe, Richard Holland, Herb
            Duncan, Bill Lipton

◆   ❖   ◆

SHOW: THE SKIDMORE MATTER
SHOW DATE: 4/22/1962
COMPANY: TRI-WESTERN LIFE INSURANCE COMPANY
AGENT: JACK PRICE
EXP. ACCT: $276.28

SYNOPSIS: Jack Price calls and Johnny tells Jack that he is one of the few people in the country who tack on an extra fee to his expense reports. Jack tells Johnny that this time he does not need any extra fees. Doug Johnstone has a problem and has suffered a considerable loss already. So if Johnny will not come down without the lure of an extra fee to help an old friend, Jack will find someone else. Johnny is on the way and Jack will meet Johnny at the airport.

Johnny flies to Corpus Christi and Jack meets Johnny with a rental car. Jack tells Johnny that he is going to Skidmore, and that Doug is running a retirement home. Doug has done well in the stock market and other investments related to the oil business, but he has been losing heavy equipment from a warehouse in Skidmore, and Jack has to pay for all the stolen equipment. There is a guard now, but no police department in Skidmore. The watchman is Joe Hernandez. Johnny drives to Skidmore, Texas and at the warehouse Johnny is met by a small man about 4 feet 10, and 100 pounds. As Johnny approaches, the man pulls a huge old revolver and waves it in Johnny's face. Johnny tells him who he is, and Joe knows who "Juanito Dollar" is, the famous, how you say, investigate. Joe is expecting Johnny and introduces him self as Jose Algere di Santiago McPherson Julio al Hernandez. The McPherson is a most honorable ancestor. Joe tells Johnny that Mr. Price will not lose any more equipment, so Johnny can go home now.

Nothing has disappeared since Joe started working, except for a skip loader. Joe tells Johnny that no one will bother him now because of his .45 caliber pistola, and proves it by shooting out a window in Johnny's rental car. Johnny is not so sure.

Joe introduces Johnny to his wife Carmilla and then shows Johnny the warehouse with the equipment waiting to be sold. Johnny sees tractors, bulldozers, graders, power shovels, skip loaders and spare parts. The last robbery was just after the wedding of Joe's 32nd cousin Fernando. Joe had thrown a party there, and Johnny tells Joe he must have been boiled to the ears to sleep while all the equipment was stolen. Joe's cousin, Fernando Ortiz, had recommended him to Doug Johnstone. Ortiz operates heavy equipment and repairs it in his shop in Tres Rios, Three Rivers. Johnny tells Joe he is going to see Doug Johnstone and tells Joe to pack his bags. Johnny meets with Doug, but Doug did not even know that Joe and Ortiz were related. Doug has just found out that Ortiz owns a piece of an equipment repair shop. Ortiz had done some jobs for Doug doing earth moving. Johnny tells Doug to replace Joe with someone smarter. Doug tells Johnny that Ortiz is coming that evening asking for more work, even though Doug has told him there is none. Johnny arranges to be there later. Johnny drives to Skidmore to check up on Joe. Johnny gets a room at the Robert Driscol hotel and has dinner. Johnny goes to meet with Doug and Ortiz, who really is a sharp character. Doug tells Ortiz that there is no more work at the rest home and Ortiz is insistent that he be called if there is any more work. Johnny is concerned that Ortiz was not surprised to see Johnny at the meeting, and that he was stalling for time during the meeting, which lasted from 8:30 to 9:00. Doug gets a call from Jack Price who tells Johnny that Joe has been murdered, and Jack will meet Johnny to go to Skidmore. Joe was murdered at 8:25 according to Joe's wife, and Johnny is sure that Ortiz did it.

Johnny finds the warehouse crawling with State Police, and meets and old friend, Sgt. Billy Roscoe who is in charge. Sgt. Roscoe tells Johnny that someone used Joe's clothes to muffle the shot from Joe's 45, and that any prints on the gun had been wiped off. Carmilla had not seen anyone, but Johnny and Fernandez there all day. Carmilla had told an officer that Ortiz had been there just before dinner to give Joe some wine, but he did not want it and chased Ortiz away. Joe went to the warehouse, and Carmilla got a call from Ortiz at exactly 8:25. The time is right because Ortiz asked Carmilla what time it was. He told her to get Joe to the phone, so she went to the shed and was opening the sliding doors when she heard a loud noise. Doug notes that Ortiz had been at his office at 8:30. Carmilla found the body and called the police. The police do not know if Ortiz was on the phone when she got back. Johnny thinks that Ortiz had talked to Joe about Johnny and knew Joe was supposed to be in the warehouse. Johnny is sure that he made the call so Carmilla would find the body when he was in Doug's office in Corpus. When Sgt. Roscoe mentions that Carmilla heard a loud bang when she opened the door, Johnny has an idea. Johnny realizes that she should have heard a muffled thump, not a loud bang. Jack notices a burn mark on the door and the smell of iodine. Johnny tells them that Ortiz killed Joe earlier in the evening, came to Corpus and called Carmilla who set off the noise when she opened the door. Johnny tells them that the answer is like the old schoolboy chemistry trick to make stink bombs with carbon di-sulfide. This one was nitrogen iodide. It was made into a paste and spread on the door, and when it was disturbed it exploded to make Ortiz's alibi. Johnny asks Sgt. Roscoe to take a sample for analysis.

"That's really all there is to the case. It was nitrogen iodide all right. And the run down on Fernando Ortiz brought out the fact that he had been quite a prankster in his high school days. But you know what gave me a big surprise? The way he made a full confession after I told him exactly how he had set up his alibi."

NOTES:
- THE FIRST COMMERCIAL BREAK IS FOR THE PEACE CORP.
- THE SECOND COMMERCIAL BREAK IS FOR NEWPORT MENTHOL CIGARETTES.
- JOSEPH CABIBBO IS NOTED FOR THE SOUND PATTERNS.
- SANTOS ORTEGA IS JOSE, MAURICE TARPLIN IS JACK, RICHARD KEITH IS DOUG, RALPH CAMAGO IS ORTIZ, ALSO HEARD WERE BILL LIPTON AND SAM RASKYN.
- GAYLORD AVERY IS THE ANNOUNCER.
- MUSICAL SUPERVISION IS BY ETHEL HUBER

Producer: Bruno Zirato, Jr.   **Writers:** Jack Johnstone
Cast: Santos Ortega, Maurice Tarplin, Richard Keith, Ralph Camago, Bill Lipton, Sam Raskyn

◆ ❖ ◆

SHOW: THE GRAND CANYON MATTER
SHOW DATE: 4/29/1962
COMPANY: NORTHEAST INDEMNITY ASSOCIATES
AGENT: BILL WALKER
EXP. ACCT: $550.00

SYNOPSIS: Bill Walker calls from New York, and asks Johnny if he has ever seen the Grand Canyon. Johnny replies that he has always wanted to, but not at this time of the year. Bill tells him the canyon is always beautiful, especially when someone is paying him to look at it. Bill asks if the name Orloff means anything, and Johnny mentions Ted Orloff in Los Angeles. Bill means Kristie Orloff, well, come on down and I'll give you the whole story.

Johnny flies to New York City and cabs to Bill's office at 5th Avenue and 42nd Street. Bill has made reservations for Johnny at the Waldorf, and Johnny has tickets to Phoenix in the morning. Bill tells Johnny that tonight cocktails, dinner and a show are on him. Bill tells Johnny that most people have never heard of Kristie Orloff and reminds Johnny of a summit meeting in 1957 that took place in Apalacan, New York between all the crime bosses. Kristie was there as one of the small fish. Bill is sure that Kristie has the Oterez necklace that belonged to a countess. It was sold to Winkler and Winkler and has been quietly stolen. Bill has the insurance on the necklace for just under a million. Johnny remembers that the necklace could have been broken up and sold very easily. Bill is working with Randy Singer at the 18th precinct, and Randy is sure that Kristie has the necklace. Randy suggested that Bill call for Johnny. Johnny asks why he is going to the Grand Canyon, and Bill tells him to get the details from Randy. And remember Kristie's background if you meet him.

Johnny goes to Randy's office and talks with him after some good-natured jesting. Randy tells Johnny that they have nabbed the men who actually took the necklace: Izzy Frambless and Opie Norton. Both Izzy and Opie told the police that the rocks had been given to Kristie Orloff, but the police could not find any trace of the jewels when they searched Orloff's apartment. Kristie is a great passer of hot goods, and has contacts on the West Coast. The Los Angeles police are watching the contacts, and Johnny is on his way to the Grand Canyon because that is where Orloff is. Randy has an officer watching Orloff on the train as far as Chicago, but after that Orloff is alone until he gets to the Grand Canyon. Johnny questions the information from the stoolies but Randy is sure that Orloff is going to the canyon. Johnny gets a description of Orloff, who looks like a sweet old man.

Johnny spends a pleasant evening with Billy Walker and buys a camera for the trip. Johnny flies to Phoenix and rents a car for the drive to the Grand Canyon, Arizona. Johnny is hard pressed to describe the vast beauty of the canyon and the Colorado River. Johnny gets a room at the El Tovar hotel and gets a phone call from Randy. Randy tells Johnny that Orloff will arrive the next day by train, and that the Los Angeles police have advised Randy that Ricky Fortino, a big-time criminal who is into all sorts of rackets, is going to the canyon also. Randy wonders why the criminals always travel by train when they could fly. Randy tells Johnny to be careful. Johnny wanders outside after dinner to view the canyon by moonlight. Johnny puts his camera on a post to get a picture and climbs over the railing to set the camera. Johnny is hit by a boot and feels himself falling, falling into the darkness. When Johnny wakes up he is tangled in a bush over a trail 20 feet below the handrail. Johnny realizes that Ricky Fortino is there and has recognized him and might suspect why Johnny is there. Johnny does not know what Fortino looks like, so Johnny figures Fortino will stay away from Johnny, thinking that Johnny knows him. At breakfast Johnny looks over the guests and does not find any one suspicious. When Orloff arrives, Johnny follows him and watches his room. Johnny goes on a bus trip with Orloff, and they turn out to be active shutterbugs. Kristie notes that Johnny likes to take pictures and Johnny, using the name Jerry Glenn, notes he has used two rolls of film just on the bus trip. Kristie asks about the mule trip the next morning and Johnny agrees to accompany him the next day, and to join him for dinner that night. Johnny realizes that the hiding place for the necklace is in the one thing Orloff kept with him at all times except meals. Johnny notes that Orloff had taken over 60 pictures without changing the film. Johnny calls Randy and arranges for him to call Orloff later. Johnny watches the room until dinner when they go to dinner during which Orloff gets a phone call from New York. Johnny goes to Orloff's room and searches for the camera and finds the necklace inside. Johnny takes the necklace and pockets it. When Johnny hears footsteps he exits out an open window. Johnny watches Orloff give a small wiry man the camera, but the necklace is gone! Ricky pulls a gun and accuses Orloff of pulling a dodge on "Big Hugo" and gets ready to shoot Orloff.

"With one quick movement from somewhere under his coat Orloff pulled a gun and got off a shot. So did Fortino. And then, by the time it is over, the two of them lay on the floor, both very dead. Come to think of it, there is an extra dividend on this case, Fortino's mention of Big Hugo, who ever he is. So now the police know of another big shot to gun for."

NOTES:
- THE FIRST COMMERCIAL BREAK IS FOR A REXALL 1 CENT SALE.
- SOUND PATTERNS BY JOSEPH CABIBBO.
- EUGENE FRANCIS IS RANDY, CASEY ALLEN IS BILL, ARTHUR KOHL IS KRISTIE, RALPH BELL IS RICKY, GUY REPP IS THE GUIDE, SAM RASKYN IS THE HOTEL CLERK.
- ART HANNES IS THE ANNOUNCER
- MUSICAL SUPERVISION IS BY ETHEL HUBER

Producer: Bruno Zirato, Jr.   Writers: Jack Johnstone
Cast: Eugene Francis, Casey Allen, Arthur Kohl, Ralph Bell, Guy Repp, Sam Raskyn

◆ ❖ ◆

SHOW: THE BURMA RED MATTER
SHOW DATE: 5/6/1962
COMPANY: MONO GUARANTEE INSURANCE COMPANY
AGENT: JIMMY BARTELL
EXP. ACCT: $0.00

SYNOPSIS: Jimmy Bartell from Mono Guarantee calls, and tells Johnny that it is high time he answered the phone. Jimmy has been trying to reach Johnny for four weeks. When Johnny asks if he tried his call service, Jimmy had forgotten about that. Johnny recounts to Jimmy that he has been in Grand Canyon, then Corpus Christi, then Knoxville and then Boston over the past four weeks. Jimmy tells Johnny that he has been up to his neck in trouble and beating his brain out while Johnny has been out gallivanting. Jimmy tells Johnny that the problem is the Burma Red and it is insured for half a million. Johnny has to get it back before they have to pay out. Johnny wants to know what it is before he starts gallivanting around looking for it. Jimmy tells Johnny to come on over and get the details.

Johnny cabs to the office of Jimmy's Bartell, who specializes in property insurance and fine art works. Jimmy tells Johnny that the Burma Red may not even be in the country now. It was brought into the country by a countess a couple years ago as part of a collection and written up in all the picture magazines. It was part of the Buckingham collection in England and bought by Winkler and Winkler. Johnny thinks that this case is just like the case of the Ivy Emerald he just finished. The stone is a single un-mounted Ruby that was sold to Mrs. Harvey Laraman Brittingham who lives in Hartford. It was stolen from the safe a few weeks ago, and Jimmy needs Johnny to get the stone back. The prime suspect in the case is Oscar Mayfield, but the police have not been able to pin anything on him and he is back in New York. Jimmy is sure that Oscar got away with it, and Johnny agrees. Johnny tells Jimmy that Oscar promised him that if he ever tried to interfere with him again, he would see to it that Johnny had a very nice funeral.

Johnny cabs to the Hartford, Connecticut police headquarters and talks to Sgt. Hollie Holcum who does not provide any encouraging information. He tells Johnny that all the hallmarks on the safe were Oscars', but they could not prove anything because of his alibi and his lawyer. They have contacted Randy Singer in New York, and Sgt. Holcum suggests that Johnny go visit him. Johnny gets all of the details on the case, and the all unconfirmed evidence points to Oscar Mayfield, but Oscar had an unshakeable alibi. Johnny calls Randy who is surprised that Johnny has just found out about the robbery. Randy has kept an eye on Oscar, but they have found nothing. Johnny and Randy are both sure that Oscar has passed the stone on to someone else. Randy is sure that the stone is either on its way out of the country or being cut up into smaller stones, but they cannot find it. Randy has heard "unofficially" that an officer rolled Oscar in an alley and found nothing. Randy knows that the stone is not in Oscar's apartment, but Johnny reminds him how he found the Oterez necklace that Randy's boys overlooked in a camera. Johnny gets the address for Oscar, but Randy tells Johnny that he will not be there when Johnny gets there as Mayfield is leaving for Mexico City this afternoon. Johnny decides to play a trick to get Oscar to stick around. Johnny remembers from a previous run-in with Oscar, that he used a fence named Hugo. Johnny decides to wire Oscar "Urgent, that before you make any deal, you call me immediately at Plaza 3-9970 Signed Hugo." Johnny then flies to New York and cabs to 614 E. 49th Street. The doorman balks at telling Johnny Mr. Mayfield's apartment number until Johnny tells him that he is an investigator. Johnny shows him his credentials and gets the apartment number, 7-G. Johnny goes in and knocks and then opens the unlocked door to find and empty apartment with bags in the bedroom. Oscar comes from behind a door and puts a gun into Johnny's back and takes his gun. Oscar reminds Johnny of his promise to Johnny and tells him that the apartment is sound proof.

Oscar tells Johnny that he was expecting Johnny, but he does not have the stone, because it has been successfully dealt with. He knew the telegram was a fake and tried the phone number eight times until the phone company told him that the number always has a busy signal. Oscar waited for Johnny until the doorman called him. Randy walks in and takes the guns from Oscar. Randy tells Johnny he is off duty and just stopped by for a visit. Oscar tells Randy he will not find the Ruby, and Randy tells Oscar he will book him for the little show he just put on. There is a knock at the door and Johnny answers it. There is a delivery boy at the door and Johnny poses as Oscar. The boy is Rosy Gilliam, and he has a package from Hugo. Rosy wants a receipt and is expecting a fin or a tenner from Oscar. Johnny opens the package and learns that Hugo meets Rosy whenever he needs him to make deliveries. Inside the package is a pile of money. Johnny asks how to spell Hugo's last name and the boy tells Johnny "I should know how to spell Hemperschlag?" Randy takes Rosy into custody and promises to protect him. Johnny is sure that the money is payment for the ruby. Oscar, knowing he is beaten grudgingly gives Johnny the address for Hugo.

"Hugo Hemperschlag believe it or not, turned out to be a gem setter for the famous jewelry house of Winkler and Winkler, where he couldn't help but know about all the important stuff brought into this country, and with the know how to break it up, after he had arranged to have it stolen. Expense account total, in view of the commission I'll get on this one, forget it.

NOTES:

- THE FIRST COMMERCIAL BREAK IS FOR DUPONT DACRON CLOTHES AND SUITS FOR MEN.
- THE SECOND COMMERCIAL BREAK IS FOR KENT CIGARETTES WITH THE MICRONITE FILTER.
- SOUND PATTERNS BY JOSEPH CABIBBO.
- PAUL MCGRATH IS OSCAR, AL HODGE IS RANDY, IVOR FRANCIS IS JIMMY, JACK GRIMES IS ROSY, SANTOS ORTEGA IS HOLCUM, MERCER MCLEOD IS THE DOORMAN.
- ROGER FOSTER IS THE ANNOUNCER.
- MUSICAL SUPERVISION IS BY ETHEL HUBER
- INTERESTINGLY, IN THE "TOO MANY CROOKS MATTER," JOHNNY GOES TO ANOTHER FENCE ON E. 49TH STREET, THAT TIME AT #718.

Producer: Bruno Zirato, Jr.   Writers: Jack Johnstone
Cast: Paul McGrath, Al Hodge, Ivor Francis, Jack Grimes, Santos
             Ortega, Mercer McLeod

SHOW: THE LUST FOR GOLD MATTER
SHOW DATE: 5/13/1962
COMPANY: UNIVERSAL ADJUSTMENT BUREAU
AGENT: PAT FULLER
EXP. ACCT: $0.00

SYNOPSIS: [Introduction missing.] Johnny cabs to Pat's office and Pat confirms the invitation from Emmett Gowan to spend some time fishing off the island of Cozumel, Mexico. The trip will be on the expense account because Pat wants Johnny to fly over to Mexico City after a few days of fishing to look into a missing client, Juano Anzana. The wife wants someone to look into the matter, so Pat wants Johnny to look into it. Johnny cabs home, packs and starts the long flight to Cozumel, via New York, New Orleans and Marida, Yucatan. Once in Cozumel, Yucatan Johnny gets a room at the Cabana el Caribe, where Emmett Gowan meets Johnny. Johnny tells Emmett that he is really tired, but Emmett tells Johnny that a few days fishing will fix that. Johnny tells Emmett that he cannot understand why the Universal Adjustment Bureau is footing the bill for the trip. Emmett mentions Juano Anzana, but is evasive about giving Johnny any information except about fishing. So, Johnny goes fishing.

Johnny relates that the fishing that afternoon was almost good enough to be a lie. In a lagoon off of a mangrove island Johnny catches a large tarpon, and then a big snook, then a moon-eyed snapper, then a barrel barracuda, followed by three more tarpon. At the end of the day Johnny is bushed and has forgotten all about the insurance investigation business. The next day Johnny and Emmett go across the bay to a fishing camp Emmett runs near Matanceros, where a Spanish Galleon sank. A number of treasure hunters have worked it over, including Juano Anzana, but Anzana has found another shipwreck, the Pinafa. That is where Johnny and Emmett are heading to use their SCUBA gear to explore the ship. Emmett tells Johnny that Juano discovered the ship, when he was brought there by Emmett to do some spear fishing. Emmett tells Johnny that Juano is the most disagreeable man Emmett has ever met, and would not trust him. Juano found something but would not say anything about it, but his eyes told Emmett that he found something. Emmett tells Johnny that, in retirement, he is very content, and does not want to get involved in more money; that would ruin his paradise. He was afraid he might find something. Emmett was called by Juano's wife stating he had not come back, and then Pat Fuller's called, so that is why Johnny is here. Johnny asks if Juano would dive alone, and Emmett tells him that where treasure is involved, anything is possible, and any man can be dangerous. Johnny and Emmett arrive at the wreck and secure the boat on the beach. Johnny and Emmett don their scuba gear and see that another boat has been there. Emmett calls for Anzana, and then goes to the boat to take a look. The boat was well hidden, but Juano was not there. Johnny dives down into the clear, clean warm water to look for Anzana. Johnny notes how clean and clear the water is and how he is surrounded by all types of fish [missing dialog].

Johnny notes the body on the wreck was a Mexican, with a bullet hole in the back of his head. Johnny is able to read a name on the dog tags of a bracelet: Juano Anzana. Johnny notes that Emmett's boat has moved so Johnny surfaces and sees a very unfamiliar face. The man tells Johnny to get in his boat and helps Johnny in. The man tells Johnny that he will join the man in the water, the man who came after his treasure; the treasure that he discovered first. Johnny tries to find out what is going on, but the man starts to shoot at Johnny, so Johnny capsizes the boat and surfaces to find Emmett in the water subduing the man. After getting the man to the beach Emmett tells Johnny that the man is Anzana, who had been maddened by the treasure. Johnny is sure that Anzana killed the man, and put his bracelet on the body so that he could just disappear when he found the treasure. That way he would be free and have the treasure. Emmett tells Johnny that he knew the hidden boat was Anzana's, and there were no bubbles. So he hid his boat and dived to hide his presence. Emmett heard what was going on, so he kind of helped Johnny capsize the boat. Emmett suggests they take Anzana back to the police, and Johnny agrees.

"You know, the ironic part of it all is that there was not one single dollar's worth of treasure in the wreck of the Pinafa. So he had murdered for nothing, and now of course will have to pay for it. Expense account total, after four more days of absolutely fabulous fishing . . . aw, wait a minute. This one is on the house."

NOTES:
- THE FIRST COMMERCIAL BREAK IS FOR CLOTHES MADE FROM DACRON BY DUPONT.
- THE SECOND COMMERCIAL BREAK IS FOR KENT CIGARETTES.
- WALTER OTTO AND DON CREED PROVIDE THE SOUND PATTERNS.
- BOB DRYDEN IS EMMETT, RALPH CAMAGO IS ANZANA, LAWSON ZERBE IS PAT.
- MUSICAL SUPERVISION IS BY ETHEL HUBER

Producer: Bruno Zirato, Jr.   Writers: Jack Johnstone
Cast: Bob Dryden, Ralph Camago, Lawson Zerbe

◆ ❖ ◆

SHOW: THE TWO STEPS TO MURDER MATTER
SHOW DATE: 5/20/1962
COMPANY: WESTERN MARITIME & LIFE INSURANCE COMPANY
AGENT: PETE BRENAMAN
EXP. ACCT: $511.80

SYNOPSIS: Pete Brenaman calls Johnny from Las Vegas. Pete is checking the schedules so that Johnny can get there for breakfast. Pete has a client named Harvey Skillman with a straight life policy for $62,000 and Harvey has been poisoned. Johnny is on his way.

Johnny flies to Las Vegas, Nevada via Los Angeles and arrives for an early breakfast. Pete takes Johnny to the Silver Dollar Café for breakfast where Johnny notes a little old lady playing a slot machine at that early hour. Pete tells Johnny that the police are convinced that Johnny came out here for nothing. The police doctor told Pete that the poison was penorphene alcolaid. The doc found some in a coffee cup and the police found the sugar bowl laced with it. Johnny notes that the poison tastes terrible, and Pete tells Johnny that Harvey was almost addicted to coffee. Johnny is sure that no one would have drunken the coffee with the poison in it, so it must have been taken deliberately but Pete is sure that Harvey did not commit suicide. Pete is sure about Harvey and wants to tell Johnny why, if he will only listen.

Pete tells Johnny that Harvey was 31 when he hit it lucky at the craps table and ran a five-spot up to $44,000. He quit his job to help his sister Mary who is a nurse, and who came down with a crippling bone disease last year. Harvey used all his money and savings to take Mary to the Mayo Clinic and to a doctor back east. Now she will be cured in a year or so. However, Harvey ran low on money and came back to try and win some more to help Mary but lost everything except his insurance. Pete gave Harvey a job and all his best prospects and Harvey was able to save some money. But Lippy Lorenzo, who used to work for Al Capone and retired here, lowered the boom. Harvey told Pete that Lippy had something on Harvey and could blackmail him for everything he has, but Harvey did not tell Pete what it was. Harvey told Pete that he had paid his debts to society, but had to settle things with Lippy. Harvey decided to settle things with a deck of cards—double or nothing for the $10,000 that Harvey had. Harvey went through with it and won, and Lippy paid off. The police thought Lippy had gotten to Harvey, but the poison convinced the police doctor that it was suicide. Johnny realizes that if it were proved or declared suicide, Mary would get nothing, which is not what Harvey wanted. Pete had seen Harvey in his apartment just before he died. Pete was going to take Harvey to the airport, and the apartment door was open when he got there. They drank some coffee, and Harvey was ok until he put in the poison-laced sugar in his coffee. Johnny wants to go to Pete's office to make a phone call.

Johnny notes that a professional must know a lot about one thing, but Johnny must know a little about a lot of things, and most importantly, what pro knows the most about what things. Johnny calls Dr. Les Crutcher in Sarasota because Les had studied rare and exotic plants and herbs, the kind of drugs used by witch doctors in the jungles. Les reminds Johnny of the foul medicine he made Johnny take the last time he visited. Johnny asks about the glass of herbal tea Les gave Johnny to deaden the taste of the medicine for hours. The tea was a secret of Les' taken from a member of the milkweed plant, gymnema sylvestre. Les refers Johnny to Dr. Raymond Anthony Corberly at U.C.L.A. and tells Johnny that he came across the plant doing medical work for the Chicago police. A wayward doctor who worked for Al Capone would brew it up for a murderer who would give the tea to a victim, and then administer a rank poison. The tea disables the ability to taste sweet and bitter things. The doctor was Willie somebody. Johnny flies to Los Angeles to see Dr. Corberly who gives Johnny a sample of the plant and Johnny wonders about using the dried leaves as tea. Johnny flies back to Vegas, drives to police headquarters, and then goes to the ranch of Lippy Lorenzo. Lippy invites Johnny in and tells Johnny that he is retired. In a nearby vase is a dried up gymnema sylvestre plant. Johnny tells Lippy that he made Harvey a cup of coffee laced with the plant to dumb his mouth so that he could not taste the sugar he was going to lace with the poison. Lippy pulls a gun with a silencer on it. Johnny calls for the police, but Lippy thinks it is a gag, until the police come in and take his gun. Johnny calls the police doctor to tell him how to fill out the death certificate on Harvey.

"So, it's just the way you wanted it, Pete. The company will have to pay the insurance to Mary Skillman, $62,000."

NOTES:

- THE FIRST COMMERCIAL BREAK IS DOUGLAS EDWARDS, DIMENSION IN ENGLAND, ROSE MARY CLOONEY AND PETER KALISHER FROM MOSCOW, ART LINKLETTER AND OTHER CBS RADIO PROGRAMS.
- THE SECOND COMMERCIAL BREAK IS FOR KENT CIGARETTES.
- JOESPH CABIBBO DOES THE SOUND PATTERNS ON THIS PROGRAM.
- JIM STEVENS IS PETE, JOHN GRIGGS IS LES, BILL SMITH IS DR. CORBERLY, LAWSON ZERBE IS LIPPY, BILL LIPTON.
- MUSICAL SUPERVISION IS BY ETHEL HUBER
- THE ANNOUNCER IS ART HANNES
- GYMNEMA SYLVESTRE IS A MEMBER OF THE MILKWEED FAMILY, AND IS NATIVE TO THE TROPICAL REGIONS OF INDIA. IT IS CALLED THE "SUGAR DESTROYER" BECAUSE THE LEAVES EFFECTIVELY BLOCK SWEET TASTES IN THE MOUTH WHEN CHEWED.

Producer: Bruno Zirato, Jr.   **Writers:** Jack Johnstone
Cast: Jim Stevens, John Griggs, Bill Smith, Lawson Zerbe, Bill Lipton

◆   ❖   ◆

SHOW: THE ZIPP MATTER
SHOW DATE: 5/27/1962
COMPANY: WESTERN MARITIME & LIFE INSURANCE COMPANY
AGENT: PETE BRENAMAN
EXP. ACCT: $200.00

SYNOPSIS: Johnny gets a call from a man who knew that Johnny would still be here in Vegas. Pete Brenaman has tracked Johnny down to the Stardust because the airlines did not have a reservation for him so he started calling the big hotels. Pete has a little problem, "unless you don't care about a little extra fee on this trip, why don't you come over here to the office and let me tell you all about it?" "Ok, why not."

Johnny cabs to Pete's office, glad for the opportunity to get a better look at Las Vegas, Nevada, where everywhere there is a slot machine or a casino. Johnny notes the variety of people who come there to gamble. Pete shows Johnny a picture of Willard Rayfield Swift attached to a policy. Johnny cannot remember seeing Swift, but Pete tells Johnny that Swifty is a compulsive gambler who hangs out at the Stardust. He is only 31, and his father left him a lot of money, doled out in weekly allotments of $300. Swifty has gambled away his money and is in debt, but the lenders do not know that the money will stop coming soon. They also do not know about a policy on his uncle, Fred Payton, who died the other day leaving a policy for $120,000 to be divided up three ways. A third goes to a niece Doreen Clayford, a real good-looking girl who is married to a fellow with a feed store. A third also goes to a nephew Kenneth Kermer who is about 40 and runs a ranch north of here. The $40,000 share Swifty will get is just about what

Swifty owes. If one of the beneficiaries dies, the remainder will split the money 50-50. Johnny notes that it is worth it to them if one dies. Pete tells Johnny that Swifty and Kenneth have always had bad blood between them. Ken would not go far enough to kill anyone, but Swifty would. Pete is sure that if Johnny has not seen Swifty at the casino, he is up to something.

Pete tells Johnny that Shorty Callahan has been breathing down Swifty's neck for the $40,000 he is owed, and people who try to cheat Shorty end up dead. Pete tells Johnny to protect Ken Kermer from Swifty, as no one would complain if Swifty were killed by Shorty, or one of his boys. Pete gets a call from Doreen Clayford who tells Pete that she just met Swifty who was on his way to see Ken. Swifty had been drinking, and she is going to follow him, even though he told her not to. Doreen tells Pete to get the police and hangs up. Pete and Johnny drive to Glendale after stopping at Doreen's house. On the way Johnny and Pete spot a storm coming over the mountains and drive even faster. The storm slows Johnny and Pete when it catches them, and they must avoid mudslides and boulders on the road. Pete turns off onto the side road as Johnny wonders about whether Ken or Doreen might be planning something. Pete tells Johnny that Ken might, but not Doreen. At the ranch Johnny spots Doreen's car, with her standing at the door waving. Doreen tells them that Swifty got there ahead of her and that the door was open when she got there. She heard shouting and a shot from within a tool shop and went to investigate, but the door was locked. Johnny breaks in the door and they find one man unconscious on the floor, and the other dead.

Johnny determines that the dead man is Ken Kermer, who had been shot with a .38 that went through him and landed on the floor. Pete and Doreen work on Swifty while Johnny investigates the scene. Swifty wakes up and tells Doreen and Johnny that he came here to see if Ken would let him have some money. Ken would not let Swifty in out of the rain, but when Doreen arrived he took Swifty into the shop and locked the door. They had a big argument and Ken hit him when he turned his back on Ken. The next thing Swifty knew, Doreen was trying to wake him up. Swifty is sure that Doreen must have killed Ken. But Doreen wonders how she could have locked the door on the outside from the inside and gotten out the keyhole. Doreen accuses Swifty of killing Ken and throwing the gun out the window. Swifty is sure that Shorty must have done it after he was knocked out, but Shorty got the wrong man. Pete is sure that Swifty is right about Shorty because the glass was broken from the outside in, but Johnny tells him that a bullet would not break the glass. Johnny thinks that Swifty shot Ken for the insurance money, but Swifty asks Johnny where the gun is, after all he was outside looking for it. Johnny wonders how Swifty knew Johnny was looking for the gun, when he was supposed to be unconscious? Swifty points to he fresh mud on Johnny's feet for his reason. Johnny accuses Swifty of lying about Ken seeing Doreen's car and that he hit himself, but Swifty again asks where the gun is. Swifty tells Johnny that maybe he swallowed the gun, or maybe it was a .38 caliber zipp gun. Johnny muses about the zipp gun angle and is sure that Swifty did it, as he just told Johnny how he did it. The shop is full of enough pipe to make a zipp gun. Johnny mentions that the bullet on the floor does not have any rifling. While Pete holds Johnny's gun on Swifty, Johnny searches for a piece of pipe big enough for a .38 slug. Swifty agrees to cooperate as maybe a judge or a jury will . . . so Swifty points to a short piece of pipe on the workbench with the hammer beside it.

"So once again it's up to the courts and I'm sure Swifty will go up for life, at the least.

NOTES:
- THE FIRST COMMERCIAL BREAK IS FOR NO-DOZ.
- THE SECOND COMMERCIAL BREAK IS FOR NEWPORT MENTHOL CIGARETTES.
- JIM STEVENS IS PETE, LEON JANNEY IS SWIFTY, RITA LLOYD IS DOREEN.
- SOUND PATTERNS BY JOSEPH CABIBBO.
- MUSICAL SUPERVISION IS BY ETHEL HUBER
- THE ANNOUNCER IS ART HANNES

Producer:　Bruno Zirato, Jr.　　　**Writers:**　Jack Johnstone
Cast:　Jim Stevens, Leon Janney, Rita Lloyd

◆　❖　◆

SHOW:　THE WAYWARD GUN MATTER
SHOW DATE:　6/3/1962
COMPANY:　AMALGAMATED LIFE ASSOCIATES
AGENT:　ADOLPH DORFMAN
EXP. ACCT:　$0.00

SYNOPSIS: Adolph Dorfman calls Johnny and tells him that he has been trying to reach Johnny for days. Johnny tries to explain that he was in Los Vegas on a case. Dorfman tells Johnny to get over to his office right away because he wants to know what is happening on the Clevis Martin case. Johnny tells him that he has not solved the case yet, and tells Dorfman that he has one possible clue yet to checkout. Dorfman is also upset that Johnny has sent in an incomplete expense report, but Johnny tells him that Dorfman demanded that Johnny send in a report every Friday, whether the case was complete or not! Johnny will be glad to explain the expenses when the case is over, but Dorfman demands that Johnny come to his office and explain the report face-to-face.

Johnny explains that Dorfman has always been, and always will be a short-tempered, crotchety old maid, and nothing but trouble on a case. Johnny cabs to Dorfman's office and fights over the various items on the expense report. Johnny tells Dorfman that he is waiting for a call from New York, where their top ballistics expert will have information for Johnny that will solve the case. Dorfman has one other item to discuss but Johnny accuses him of just stalling. Dorfman stalls Johnny with inane chatter about Las Vegas. He tells Johnny that Alfred W. Berriman, the contractor and client, was shot last night. Police Sgt. Anset arrives and thanks Dorfman for catching Johnny for him. Sgt. Anset wants Johnny's great big .38, but when Johnny says that he does not have it on him, Sgt. Anset tells Johnny that they have his gun at headquarters, and they are holding Johnny on suspicion of murder.

Johnny really cannot repeat his reaction to being nailed by Dorfman and Sgt. Anset. Johnny demands his rights to a phone call and tells Dorfman he is using his phone, "and don't be surprised if you pay through the nose for the phone call." Johnny calls Randy Singer, who has no word for him yet and promises to call Johnny right back. Johnny tries to explain to Sgt. Anset who he is, but Sgt. Anset knows all about Johnny, and is just doing what Lt. Bartley told him to do. At Hartford, Connecticut police headquarters Johnny accuses Lt. Harry Bartley of pulling a boner by having him arrested. Lt. Bartley tells Johnny that he has been stalling on the Martin case, and had gone out of town, all very suspicious. Also, there was the micro-photo of the bullet that Johnny would not explain. When Berriman, who was bidding on a project in Lakewood County got shot, Lt. Bartley wondered if there was a connection. Johnny tells Lt. Bartley that he has held out certain information because of the rotten political situation in Lakewood. Lt. Bartley knows who Johnny is talking about, and Johnny tells him that the politician could make it very hot for anyone who gets in his way. Johnny tells Lt. Bartley that there was no way Berriman or Martin could have underbid the inside competition if they had kept alive. Johnny had gone to visit the politician and had noticed a collection of guns that included a gun just like the make, model and finish Johnny carries. Johnny created a diversion and switched guns so he could have the politician's gun checked by ballistics experts in New York. If it matches the gun used in the murders, Lt. Bartley will have his murderer, and Lakewood County will be clean. Lt. Bartley is suspicious despite Johnny's story and has Sgt. Anset lock Johnny up. Lt. Bartley tells Sgt. Anset that he will take care of the booking paperwork.

Johnny is visited by Lt. Bartley and he tells Johnny that the newspapers, cigarettes, coffee and reporters were brought in for Johnny. Johnny is upset about his reputation, and for Lt. Bartley letting a murder run around free. Johnny asks Lt. Bartley to let him take a special phone call when it comes in. Lt. Bartley gets an urgent phone call and leaves. Officer Handley takes Johnny to Lt. Bartley's office where he welcomes Johnny. He tells Johnny of the call from Randy Singer, who is also an old friend. Randy told Lt. Bartley that the report proves the politician's gun did kill Berriman and Martin, so Johnny is a hero again. Johnny tells him that his reputation is ruined after being booked for suspicion of murder. "Booked? You know, I must have forgotten to." Lt. Bartley tells Johnny with a grin. Lt. Bartley decided to throw the politician off course by publicizing that the police had arrested the murderer. They picked up the politician in Hartford and told him about the gun switch, and he became so confused that he broke down and made a full confession. Johnny is worried about the newspaper articles, but is told that the afternoon papers will have a story giving Johnny full credit for the whole case. The only hero is Johnny Dollar because he laid the groundwork and deserves all the credit.

"After this, I think I better keep my tricks to myself. Well now, wait a minute, how can I when every case I handle gets broadcast all over the country? Yeah, I guess I just can't win. Expense account total, well all I want now is one big fat apology from meddling old Adolph Dorfman at Amalgamated Life for having trapped me into that night in jail."

NOTES:
- THE FIRST COMMERCIAL BREAK IS FOR NEWPORT CIGARETTES.
- THE SECOND COMMERCIAL BREAK IS FOR SINCLAIR GASOLINE.
- ROBERT DRYDEN IS ADOLPH, RALPH BELL IS ANSET, MARTIN BLAINE IS BARTLEY, NAT POLEN IS HANLEY.
- SOUND PATTERNS ARE BY JOSEPH CABBIBO.
- MUSICAL SUPERVISION IS BY ETHEL HUBER
- THE ANNOUNCER IS ART HANNES

Producer: Fred Hendrickson   Writers: Jack Johnstone
Cast: Robert Dryden, Ralph Bell, Martin Blaine, Nat Polen

◆   ❖   ◆

SHOW: THE ALL TOO EASY MATTER
SHOW DATE: 6/17/1962
COMPANY: WESTERN INDEMNITY COMPANY
AGENT: TED ORLOFF
EXP. ACCT: $491.34

SYNOPSIS: Ted Orloff calls Johnny, and he has problems with fires, but someone has to prove he is right. "Can you make it?"

Johnny flies to Los Angeles, California and arrives at noon. Johnny cabs to Ted's office and runs into him at the front door. They jump in Ted's car and rush to the scene of another fire, the sixth. The building is old and uninhabited, and Ted is sure that the fire bug will set fifteen more fires before he is finished. Ted has contacted the Arson Squad and they agree the fires were arson, but they refuse to grab the guy who is doing it. Ted tells Johnny that he knows who the arsonist is just as the walls of the building collapse. Over a drink Ted tells Johnny about Altheus Brockway Broxton, a widower 82 years old who the doctor says has a heart condition, and will only live a few more years. But he does not look like he is sick. He is a playboy in spades, but has had to slow down after his last wife died. He is now living a simple live and his stepdaughter has married and is the beneficiary of his estate. Broxton is not rolling in money, but he does have a lot of property in the poorer sections of LA. The taxes are getting higher and higher each year and Broxton still has insurance on the properties. So now he is burning down the properties and collecting the insurance from Ted. Johnny wonders that the answer is too obvious, too easy.

In the office Johnny gets a list of the unburned properties and Broxton's address. Ted reminds Johnny about the phrase "cui bono," and Ted cannot think of anyone else who would benefit. The police feel that the arsonist is someone else other than poor little Mr. Broxton. Johnny wonders about Broxton's age, and Ted suggests that he might have hired a professional, so Johnny decides to assist Ted with the case. Ted gets a call from Fred Klein, the Fire Commissioner who tells Ted that there is another fire. When Ted tells him that he has hired Johnny, Fred talks to Johnny and they agree to meet. Johnny rents a car and drives to see Fred Klein. Fred tells Johnny that he is not upset at Ted's feelings about the department, because most people turn around when they get results. Fred tells Johnny that they originally thought Ted was right until they looked into the fires. Fred tells Johnny that he should talk to Broxton, and he will agree that a man with a heart condition could not set the fires. Also, a pro did not set the fires because they do not follow a pattern, and pros always follow a pattern. The department has a file on all the pros, and Fred is convinced that an amateur is setting the fires because there is a different method used on each fire. Fred tells Johnny to talk to Broxton, and then they will compare notes. Fred tells Johnny that he has only eleven men, and Johnny can spend more time on a fire than any of his men can. Johnny drives to Mr. Broxton's, and Johnny is sure he did not set the fire, and the excitement would kill him. Broxton was content with his life and not interested in making more money to give to his stepdaughter who had assured Broxton they were doing fine. As Johnny drives away convinced that Broxton is innocent, he thinks about his own phrase "cui bono" and the insurance policy. Johnny decides to follow up on the policy angle.

Johnny calls Broxton and asks for an address. Johnny buys an imitation leather portfolio with gold lettering on it that says "Federal Housing and Occupation Survey." Johnny drives to Sherman Oaks and a poorly kept house. While Johnny paces the room, the woman tells Johnny that she is Lois Claytor and her husband is Ben. Lois tells Johnny that she is a typist for Aerojet and her husband is in the import business and has an office in the back room. Also, Ben left for Mexico the previous day on business. She describes the equipment Ben imports and shows Johnny a brochure. Johnny starts to inspect the office, but it is locked. Johnny questions that the house belongs to a successful businessman, especially when he spots a repossession notice for the television. After a cursory inspection of the house Johnny leaves and makes two calls. One is to a company in East Los Angeles, one to one of the companies that Ben sells to. They tell Johnny that Ben has only been a pain to them, what with his phony deals in Mexico. A call to an air conditioner company yields the same results. Johnny visits the state employment office and learns that Claytor has had a dozen jobs in the past five years and stayed on each long enough to get fired and collect unemployment and some disability insurance. Tie that in to the fact Broxton did not have long to live and it all adds up. Johnny calls Fred Klein and updates him and goes back to the house. At the house Johnny tells Lois he did not finish the survey the last time and tells her he will have to break into the office. In the room, Johnny finds long strips of paraffin tape, candles, cans of solvent, gasoline, even a couple of crude timing devices to set off a blaze. He'd been right.

Ben Claytor was behind the fires to add every possible dollar to the old man's bank account before he died and left it to Lois. And there was all the evidence he could need. Suddenly Ben is there with a gun and tells Johnny not to move. Lois takes Johnny's gun as Ben tells Johnny he made a mistake by giving Lois his real name. Ben was going to clean out the room, but now he has no choice but to kill Johnny. Lois tells Ben she put up with the fires but she will not let him kill Johnny. Ben tries to take the gun from Lois and Johnny slugs Ben just as Fred comes in. Johnny tells him that Ben and Lois Clayton are done playing with fire.

"Not a very pretty one, I know. And I hope the shock of it all isn't too much for poor old Mr. Broxton"

NOTES:

- THE FIRST COMMERCIAL BREAK IS FOR NO-DOZ.
- THE SECOND COMMERCIAL BREAK IS FOR NEWPORT CIGARETTES.
- THE THIRD COMMERCIAL BREAK IS FOR SINCLAIR GASOLINE.
- MUSICAL SUPERVISION IS BY ETHEL HUBER
- THE ANNOUNCER IS ART HANNES
- THE CAST CREDITS HAVE BEEN EDITED FROM THIS PROGRAM.

Producer: Fred Hendrickson   Writers: Jack Johnstone
Cast: Unknown

◆   ❖   ◆

SHOW: THE HOOD OF DEATH MATTER
SHOW DATE: 6/24/1962
COMPANY: FOUR STATE INSURANCE COMPANY
AGENT: LUTHER PENNYROLL
EXP. ACCT: $200.00

SYNOPSIS: Ol' cousin Luther Pennyroll in Nashville calls Johnny, and Luther has a problem with Henry Sweetwater and his accident policy. Luther thinks that the accident he had was on purpose, and Mr. Sweetwater is trying to take them. Johnny is on his way.

Johnny flies to Nashville, Tennessee and the plane passes over the tower of station WLAC. Johnny cabs into the Andrew Jackson Hotel, and then cabs to Luther's office. Lou tells Johnny that the client is an old crook by the name of Henry Sweetwater who made a lot of money with a lot of snide property deals. Lou tells Johnny that he should not have written the policy because of the special clauses in it. Henry claims a car hit him and Doc Caroway has looked at him and does not think the claim is legitimate either. Lou and Johnny drive to the town of Laverne, where Henry lives with a pretty young wife named Billy Mae. Lou thinks Billy married Henry for his money. Lou tells Johnny that he could have married Billy Mae if she did not say she loved Henry. When Lou's car starts making noises he pulls over and Johnny pulls a bomb from the engine compartment just before it explodes.

Lou is all shook up, and tells Johnny that he is sure Henry found out Lou is investigating. Lou tells Johnny that Henry says he laid on the road until Billy Mae came back from shopping in Nashville. Henry is claiming shock and disability and everything else on top of the broken arm. Lou tells Johnny that Dr. Caroway knew Henry and used to be an osteopath. When Henry told Lou that he never heard the car coming, Lou was sure that he was faking it. Johnny and Lou look at Henry's house from the road and notice smoke coming from the chimney. Just as Lou tells Johnny that Henry always has a fire going the house explodes.

Johnny describes the explosion and sees Henry totter out of the door and collapse. Johnny rushes to him and Doc Caroway arrives and Henry is put to bed. Johnny inspects the house and finds evidence of dynamite in the fireplace. Lou is sure that Henry staged the blast. Johnny is sure that someone is out to get Henry. Doc Caroway tells Johnny that he has given Henry a mild sedative, on account of his heart condition. Johnny notes that Henry had been locked inside the house, as he had checked the locks. Doc tells Johnny that only Billy Mae and Patty have keys to the door but Henry usually kept the doors open hoping folks would come over and keep him company. When Lou suggests that Henry himself threw the dynamite in the fire, Johnny thinks maybe he did. Johnny tells Lou about an old trick used by the forty-niners, and goes to inspect the woodpile where he finds a number of logs filled with dynamite, but who did it?

Billy Mae arrives and she was the first suspect until Johnny sees the way she tends for her husband. She tells Johnny that she has called her sister because Patty has done nursing work. She tells Johnny that she is glad that Henry and Doc Caroway have let bygones be bygones, but does not explain. Billy asks Johnny if he can stay around for a while after Patty gets there. Patty arrives and is cool and calculating in the way she cares for Henry. Patty tells Johnny that she would not weep if Henry died, but that will not keep her from caring for him. Patty tells Johnny that Henry thinks Billie ran him down because he thinks she would do anything to get his money and be free to marry Lou Pennyroll. They would have gotten married if they had any money, and Lou wants to go back to college and study botany. When Johnny mentions motive, Patty gets defensive. Patty tells Johnny that Doc felt Henry had cheated him once, and he probably did. Johnny borrows Patty's car and drives back to Nashville. Johnny drives to Lou's apartment, slips the lock and searches it, and finds nothing other than a plant that was all too familiar. Johnny finds a Dr. Bradley who is willing to drive back to Laverne with him. Johnny explains the situation and the possible effects in Henry's heart. When they arrive, Johnny spots Lou and Doc Caroway's car. Patty tells Johnny that Henry has had a heart attack. Johnny runs upstairs and tells Dr. Bradley that if he has an antidote for aconite poisoning to use it. Dr. Bradley asks if he means aconitum napellus, the monks hood plant, and that he should have recognized the symptoms. Downstairs, Johnny tells Billy that Henry will recover. Billy relates that Patty went to her room after the police picked up Lou. Billy asks how Johnny knew, and he tells he tells her had found the monkshood plant in Lou's room, and when Henry had all the rights symptoms it turned out to be aconite poisoning. Johnny tells her that he had put the bomb in his own car and had called Johnny in to cover for him. Now he will have plenty of time to think it over.

"So, here's another one for the courts. I hope they throw the book at Lou. A crooked insurance man is the lowest order of operator in this racket of mine. Thank goodness they come few and far between."

NOTES:
- THE FIRST COMMERCIAL BREAK IS FOR NO-DOZ.
- THE SECOND COMMERCIAL BREAK IS FOR KENT CIGARETTES.
- THE THIRD COMMERCIAL BREAK IS FOR SINCLAIR GASOLINE.
- MUSICAL SUPERVISION IS BY ETHEL HUBER
- THE ANNOUNCER IS ART HANNES
- MONKSHOOD (ACONITUM NAPELLUS) IS DESCRIBED AS ONE OF THE MOST POISONOUS PLANTS OF EUROPEAN FLORA. PLINIUS DESCRIBES IT AS "PLANT ARSENIC." ALKALOIDS ARE RESPONSIBLE FOR ITS POISONOUS EFFECT. THE MAIN ALKALOID IS ACONITINE, WHICH ACTS AS A STIMULANT THAT PARALYZES THE NERVOUS SYSTEM.

Producer: Fred Hendrickson   Writers: Jack Johnstone
Cast: Herb Duncan, Bill Adams, Madeline Sherwood, Vicki Vola, Jackson Beck

◆   ❖   ◆

SHOW: THE VOCIFEROUS DOLPHIN MATTER
SHOW DATE: 7/1/1962
COMPANY: TRINITY MUTUAL INSURANCE COMPANY
AGENT: WILL BURNETT
EXP. ACCT: $531.80

SYNOPSIS: A very perky voice asks if Johnny has been out to sunny southern California lately. Will Burnett needs Johnny's help because of a couple of fish, two mammals Petey and Sue, who are dolphins. Johnny asks if Will has issued a life insurance policy on a couple of dolphins, and Will tells him that an important client wants a policy issued, Will is in favor of it, but the whole fishy deal needs looking into. Johnny thinks Will is nuts. "Dolphins! Well if you are willing to pay the freight, ok. I'll see you sometime tomorrow."

Johnny flies to Los Angeles and Will meets Johnny in the airport with a rental car. Will has a client waiting and cannot go with Johnny to Shelter Point, just north of San Diego. Professor Doctor Yuriantha Euridisee Eswell has her private oceanarium there. She is an eccentric, a non-conformist, an oddball, who once held down chairs of zoology and ichthyology at two important colleges and is an important client. This policy is important if the dolphins can do what she thinks they can, which is un-curl that lip based on scientific knowledge. Johnny drives south and runs into a coastal fog. Just as Johnny reaches Shelter Point a bullet whizzes past his head. Johnny eases towards the marksman in the fog and finds a woman holding the rifle. Johnny tells her who he is, and she is Penelope Wyman, and tells Johnny that she was aiming at some sharks and the bullet must have ricocheted. She asks Johnny if he came here because he was worried about Aunt Yuri too? She tells Johnny that he should be worried.

Penny tells Johnny that she was going swimming but saw a lot of sharks around the pier. She admits that she had the rifle there because of the experiments Aunt Yuri does with the dolphins. Her Aunt is using her money to prove that the dolphins can talk. Penny thinks that someone is trying to stop her and that there have been a number of near accidents lately. She still insists on doing everything in spite of the fact she could afford help. She works all alone except for Penny and Carl Petermill, who handles the recording equipment and was Penny's fiancé. Aunt Yuri comes in with Carl and tells Johnny she is making progress. She tells Johnny that she wants insurance on her children Petey and Sue. Johnny goes to the large tank and watches the dolphins put on a great show while Carl fools with some electronic equipment. Yuri tells Johnny that they are her children, and are completely obedient. Yuri is going to demonstrate that they can talk. Carl holds a mike while Sue is called to the edge of the pool. Yuri tells her to talk to her, and the dolphin emits a series of high-pitched squeals. Yuri tells Johnny that the tape recorders record the dolphins at ultra-high speed the sounds made by the dolphins that the human ear cannot hear properly. Carl puts the tape on another machine that plays the tape back at a lower speed that makes it understandable. Carl plays the tape and Yuri hears a garbled "mother, but Johnny hears a much different word, "murder."

As soon as Johnny questions the words, he is ordered to leave. As he drives past the house, Penny tells Johnny she is going shopping, and Johnny offers to take Penny to dinner at the El Cortez. Johnny phones Will with an update, gets a room and waits for Penny. During dinner Penny tells Johnny that she should not have left her aunt alone. She tells Johnny that she broke off the engagement with Carl because of his lack of formal education and his past working as a barker for a freak show, which is what he hopes to do again. Penny tells Johnny that she will get her aunt's money when she dies, except for the dolphins, which go to Carl. Johnny and Penny do the nightclub thing, and he sends her home at 4 AM. An hour later Penny calls to tell Johnny that Aunt Yuri is dead. Johnny rushes to Shelter Point to find Penny waiting for him at the cut off. She tells Johnny that Carl had been off for the night, and she takes Johnny to the tank where Johnny finds the body floating in the tank, with the dolphins protecting her. Carl runs up and accuses Penny of hitting Yuri on the head and pushing her into the pool to get the money. He tells Johnny that he can prove it with the dolphins that can talk and will tell him who killed Yuri. Carl rigs up a tape and asks one of the dolphins "who killed Yuri." The voice on the tape says, "Me see Murder. Me see Penelope kill." Johnny sends Carl to La Jolla to get the police, and he leaves. Johnny has been thinking about a man that knows every electronic trick, Bob McKenny, an engineer with CBS. Johnny takes the tape and Penny to see Bob at his home. Bob experiments for hours and eventually gets the tape to play at its original speed, and the tape plays the voice of Carl faking the voice of the dolphins. Penny tells Johnny that Carl was going to get the aquarium and the dolphins, and Johnny is sure that he was afraid that Yuri would find out about the electronic tricks, so he killed her to preserve his sideshow and the life he wanted. "But he has booked himself a one-night stand, and its blackout is permanent."

"Thanks to Carl, the police and he were still there at shelter Point waiting for us."

NOTES:
- THE FIRST COMMERCIAL BREAK IS FOR NO-DOZ.
- THE SECOND COMMERCIAL BREAK IS FOR KENT CIGARETTES.
- THE THIRD COMMERCIAL BREAK IS FOR SINCLAIR GASOLINE.
- BOB MCKENNY WAS ALSO IN TWO OTHER PROGRAMS: THE MISSING MISSILE MATTER AND THE WAYWARD KILOCYCLES MATTER
- MUSICAL SUPERVISION IS BY ETHEL HUBER
- THE ANNOUNCER IS ART HANNES

Producer: Fred Hendrickson   **Writers:** Jack Johnstone
Cast: Larry Robinson, Ethel Everett, Joan Lazer, Bill Lipton, Ben Yafee

◆ ❖ ◆

SHOW: THE RILLDOE MATTER
SHOW DATE: 7/8/1962
COMPANY: TRINITY MUTUAL INSURANCE COMPANY
AGENT: WILL BURNETT
EXP. ACCT: $250.00

SYNOPSIS: Will Burnett calls Johnny and is glad that Johnny is still there in San Diego. Will tells Johnny that he cannot leave until he gets a sample of the famous fishing there in San Diego, California. Ted Pfluger knows more about fishing the coast than any one else, so when he heard that Johnny was here, he called Will, who arranged for Johnny to go fishing with Ted. "You fixed me up on the expense account? Just fishing?" Johnny asks. Oh there is one thing Johnny can ask Ted about—Bernard W. Bessom, who is an appliance dealer and a client. Johnny is to ask Ted about Bessom. Ask him if he thinks Bessom is still alive.

Johnny buys gas and drives to Ted Pfluger's place on Emerald Bay. Pfluger is a gruff individual with a heart of gold. They load up Johnny's car with tackle and drive north to Balboa harbor. Johnny is sure he is getting a runaround as he talks to Ted about fishing. In Lonestar Beach, Ted points to a large building, Bessom and Associates the big appliance house. At a red light Johnny points out a gorgeous doll sitting in a convertible outside of the Bessom building. Johnny describes it as the face you see on every beautiful girl from the neck up. The girl asks Johnny what time it is, and Johnny gives the time as 2:50. When Johnny asks if there is anything else she wants, she tells Johnny that he needs to know something: the light has changed! Johnny tells Ted that a girl that pretty should be involved in every one of his cases. Ted tells Johnny that Bernie Bessom is a real fine fellow, but his partners, Tony and Joe Rilldoe are sharpies. They made their money running liquor during prohibition. Ted is sure that they would do anything to get Bernie's part of the business away from him. Ted called Bernie this morning to come fishing and he has not been able to reach him at home or the office. Nor did he show for a poker game last night. But Ted wants to go fishing even though he is his afraid of what else might be out there. Johnny and Ted arrive in Balboa and prepare to take off in Ted's 21-foot boat that is full of tackle. After a final tackle box is hefted aboard, the deck hand Manuel is surprised that Ted is going out after coming in so late last night. Ted tells Johnny to wait until the tide goes out, and he will see what is going on. Johnny and Ted fish off the lee side of San Clemente Island until dusk when Ted starts back. Ted has been waiting for the tide to go all the way down. He tells Johnny that last night he saw a boat drifting, and what the people were doing. He is sure that the boat was the Rilldoe brother's and that Bernie was with them. Johnny rigs up a set of small grappling hooks on a heavy line, and at a large bed of kelp they start to drag around the kelp bed. Ted searches the water as they search for a body. Finally they snag something and bring up a piece of Bernie's jacket. Johnny strips to his shorts and dives in to recover the badly beaten lead-weighted body of Bernie Bessom. The body is brought on board, and Ted tells Johnny that he knew the boat belonged to the Rilldoe brothers, and he saw what they were throwing overboard. Johnny is sure that the Rilldoe brothers will deny everything. A large boat approaches with its spotlight on Ted's boat. Johnny reaches for a .22 Ted keeps on the boat as the larger craft slowly bears down on them.

Johnny and Ted are sitting ducks as the boat approaches. The boat slows and the girl Johnny had seen earlier calls to them, but the boat does not belong to the Rilldoes. She is Molly Boyle and had seen their lights. She asks if they have any spare gas and Ted throws her a line. Johnny goes on board offers to pour the gas as he introduces himself. She in turn introduces her boyfriends, Tony and Joe Rilldoe. Tony tells Johnny to drop his gun and Molly tells Joe it would be easy since she used her own boat. Tony tells Ted he will be in trouble if he meddles with him. They do not know anything about Bessom, but Ted tells them what they have done. Tony tells Johnny that he does not have a case on him but will when he shoots Ted for meddling. As the seas pick up and the boat starts to rock, Tony starts to shoot Ted. Ted pulls Joe overboard and Johnny goes after Tony and the gun. Johnny pulls Ted back on board and they pull a waterlogged Joe onto the boat. Johnny gets another gun from Molly, who tries to tell Johnny that she had nothing to do with the Rilldoes, as she is a nice girl. She tells Johnny that she can be good to Johnny, and that he has to help her.

"Well, it's up to the authorities now. And I do not think they will have any trouble putting those three where they belong. The real reward for all that? A couple of days of great fishing, thanks to Ted Pfluger."

NOTES:
- THE FIRST COMMERCIAL BREAK IS FOR NO-DOZ.
- THE SECOND COMMERCIAL BREAK IS FOR KENT CIGARETTES.
- THE THIRD COMMERCIAL BREAK IS FOR SINCLAIR GASOLINE.
- MUSICAL SUPERVISION IS BY ETHEL HUBER
- THE ANNOUNCER IS ART HANNES

Producer: Fred Hendrickson   Writers: Jack Johnstone
Cast: John Gibson, Hetty Galen, Larry Robinson, Marty Green,
             Ralph Camago, Marty Myers

◆   ❖   ◆

SHOW: THE WEATHER OR NOT MATTER
SHOW DATE: 7/15/1962
COMPANY: TRI-STATE LIFE & CASUALTY INSURANCE COMPANY
AGENT: EARLE POORMAN
EXP. ACCT: $247.92

SYNOPSIS: Earle Poorman calls and Johnny asks how things are in Los Angeles. Earle tells Johnny he is back in Sarasota, but they are thinking about moving back to California. Earle asks Johnny to come down and investigate a murder that has not happened yet, but if Earle can read the signs, there is one in the making.

Johnny flies to Sarasota, Florida, rents a car and drives to the office Earle shares with Don Boomhauer. Over a lunch of shrimp cooked in beer at the Plaza Hotel, Earle tells Johnny about the case. The client is T. Rockway Mayfield, a crazy character who made a pile of money in New England. He retired here and spends his time sunning himself with a jug beside him, shooting at sea gulls with an air pistol and never hitting them. He also throws large parties with lots of pretty girls. He told Earle he came here to get away from his stepchildren Betty and Frank Merriton. He had been supporting the kids while his wife was alive, but when she died he left them flat until he dies. Tomorrow is Mayfield's birthday, and the kids are coming. Earle thinks they are coming to murder him. On the drive to Mayfield's home Earle tells Johnny to keep an eye on Mayfield. And, Earle might even take Johnny fishing afterwards.

Earle drives up to a huge mansion that is guarded by a high wall. The house is concrete and stucco with aluminum and glass surrounded by a large patio complete with a bar and bartender. Johnny is introduced to Mayfield, who makes a bad joke about dollars and cents. Mayfield has been listening to Johnny on the radio for years and orders the bartender to bring Johnny a scotch and soda, a gin and tonic for Earl; and a cognac with root beet and a piece of mint for himself. Mayfield invites Earle and Johnny to his party the next day. Mayfield tells Johnny that the girls always come to get at his money, but they won't succeed until he dies. Mayfield tells Johnny that his stepchildren are arriving the next day and

Johnny volunteers to pick them up. Mayfield shows Johnny his pride and joy—a complete weather station with all the necessary tools. Mayfield tells Johnny he cannot plan a party if he does not know what the weather will be. Mayfield asks Johnny how good a shot he is, and for an hour Johnny and Mayfield feed the birds and shoot at them with an air pistol. Mayfield dismisses Earle and Johnny and goes to make his weather report for the party. Johnny gets a rental car and goes to talk to an old friend, Sgt. Phil Phillips at police headquarters. Sgt. Phillips tells Johnny that if the kids are what Mayfield describes, he needs protection while they are here. Sgt. Phillips tells Johnny that Mayfield has told the police not to show up. If they do he will throw them out, stop the party and get the people down on them. Johnny tells Sgt. Phillips to keep a prowl car near the wall, just in case. Johnny is concerned that the case seems like a waste of time, yet . . . yeah.

The next day Johnny kills time by hitting some golf balls, going to the Jungle Garden, the Ringling Circus Museum and stopping in at station WSPB to talk to the boys. Johnny picks up Betty and Frank. Betty is beautiful with a head on her shoulders. Frank is a weak, wishy-washy, well spoken nothing, with a capitol "N" who tells Betty that it is ridiculous for Mayfield to make him sweat and toil when he has all that money that he does not know what to do with. Betty tells Frank that daddy will be furious when he finds out Frank does not have a job and is chiseling off his friends. He is sure that daddy will give him money, and has a sob story that would melt the heart of a statue; so do not interfere. Betty tells Johnny that she loves parties and asks Johnny to dance with her now and then. At the house Mayfield takes the kids into the library and Johnny goes swimming until dinner. At the party is a bevy of pretty girls, and Johnny dances with Betty and makes plans to meet back up north. The lights go out and Mayfield tells Johnny that it is a gag. Johnny goes to look for the switch box with Betty just as the lights go out and there are three shots from near the weather station. The lights go on again and Johnny and Mayfield discover that Frank is dead from a couple of .38s in the chest. Sgt. Phillips and his men scale the wall and do a complete investigation but cannot find the gun. Johnny has a hunch and kicks himself for not having wised up before. It was Mayfield who had been telling everyone about the kids. And that crazy drink yesterday that Johnny had noticed did not have a drop of liquor in it, and probably the same thing tonight. So Mayfield is sober as a judge. And the gun, the answer is in the weather station, which had a weather balloon large enough to carry a gun out over the Gulf of Mexico, never to be seen again. Johnny tells Mayfield to come with the police to get a paraffin test of his shooting hand, and he admits that he killed Frank. Sgt. Phillips has to admit that using a weather balloon was really clever. "Was it?" Johnny asks.

"So the Mayfield fortune will go to Betty, and I can't think of a more deserving girl, or come to think of it, a prettier one."

NOTES:
- **THE FIRST COMMERCIAL BREAK IS FOR PEPSI.**

- THE SECOND COMMERCIAL BREAK IS FOR NO-DOZ.
- THE THIRD COMMERCIAL BREAK IS FOR KENT CIGARETTES.
- THE FOURTH COMMERCIAL BREAK IS FOR SINCLAIR GASOLINE.
- MUSICAL SUPERVISION IS BY ETHEL HUBER
- THE ANNOUNCER IS ART HANNES

Producer: Fred Hendrickson   **Writers:** Jack Johnstone
Cast: Ian Martin, Bill Kramer, Joe Hardy, Ivor Francis, Constance
             Simons, Karen McCrary

◆ ❖ ◆

SHOW: THE SKIMPY MATTER
SHOW DATE: 7/22/1962
COMPANY: MONO GUARANTEE INSURANCE COMPANY
AGENT: DANNY NIXON
EXP. ACCT: $10.80

SYNOPSIS: Danny Nixon calls Johnny and asks if he remembers Amos Crutchfield. Johnny remembers that he is the former city attorney who retired in a blaze of glory after he clamped a lid on the policy rackets. Danny tells Johnny that Amos also had Skimpy Dingle sent up four years ago and Johnny remembers him. The parole board has released Skimpy for good behavior, and Danny reminds Johnny of the threats Skimpy made to Johnny and Crutchfield. Crutchfield is sure Skimpy was serious, and Danny agrees with him. Danny also has a new policy on Crutchfield's life for $75,000.

Johnny buys gas and drives to the Hartford, Connecticut Parole Office. Johnny is told that Skimpy has not reported in yet, and they have no address for him. Johnny is told that Skimpy's brother, Percy Dingle, is the one who convinced the parole board to release Skimpy. Percy is a psychologist who has kept Skimpy out of jail a number of times and can be very convincing. Johnny gets Percy's address and leaves. Johnny goes to see Crutchfield and notices a new compact car out front. Johnny realizes he should have taken a better look at it as he rings the doorbell and hears shots ring out inside. Johnny breaks in the door to find Crutchfield on the floor.

Crutchfield is still alive and Johnny notices how the assailant had come in and left through an open window. Johnny puts Crutchfield on the couch and hears a car pull away. Johnny calls for a doctor and the police. Doctor Franklin Edwards arrives and patches Crutchfield up, noting that one bullet came very close to his heart. Johnny tells the doctor to stay until the police arrive and he leaves. As Johnny drives back to Hartford, a car driven by Skimpy hits him. Skimpy gets out and shoots at Johnny four times, but only one bullet grazes his arm. Johnny drives home to fix his arm and is about to make a call when Percival Dingle knocks at the door. Johnny drags him in with his gun drawn, and Percy tells Johnny that Skimpy was right; Johnny is a killer. Percy tells Johnny that he wants to talk rationally, so Johnny sits down and holsters his gun. Percy tries to convince

Johnny that he needs to have some sympathy for Peter. Percy tells Johnny that Peter has been in trouble because of a lack of education and guidance, and that Peter had rebelled against authority. Peter feels that Johnny and Crutchfield have been persecuting him and are the only ones who can help him. Percy tells Johnny that he knows Peter's mind and that the last incarceration was a fulcrum that provided the lever to convince Peter of the error of his ways. His release from prison is proof that Peter has reformed. Percy tells Johnny that he can provide help to Peter. Percy feels that Crutchfield is a doddering old fool who only convinced the judge to give Peter an unjust sentence. Johnny tells Percy that the judge should have given Skimpy thirty years. Johnny tells Percy he is full of impractical theories, and Johnny has seen more of Skimpy's kind than Percy ever will. The more he thinks about it he is convinced that Skimpy is rotten all the way through, and that Skimpy got out because of Percy's smart pitch to the parole board, and that Percy is all wrong. Percy is sure that they can work things out. Johnny tells him that it is a plot to get Johnny close to Skimpy, so he can shoot Johnny the way he shot Crutchfield. Percy is shocked that Peter has tried to kill a man so Johnny shows Percy the wound on his arm. Percy is sure that Peter has to see that Johnny is on his side. Percy knows where Peter is and will let Johnny see him, if he agrees to talk to him. Johnny agrees to go see him only to turn him over to the police. Percy tells Johnny that he will go to Peter and tell him that Johnny will talk to him, and if the reaction is proper, Percy will call Johnny.

Johnny takes a nap and orders some food from a nearby restaurant. The phone rings and Percy arranges for Johnny to meet Peter in room 4 of a rooming house at 1217 North Chalma and thanks Johnny. Johnny drives to the decrepit old boarding house and sees Skimpy pacing thoughtfully in the room. Johnny goes in and knocks. Skimpy opens the door and Johnny kicks it in. Skimpy tells Johnny to put his gun away, as his brother has convinced him to talk to Johnny. He admits he was wrong about trying to kill Johnny and hopes Mr. Crutchfield will be ok. He could not believe Johnny would help him. Johnny tells him he is there to take him to the police, and that his brother is living in a dream. Peter agrees that his brother was stupid, stupid enough to get Johnny here where Skimpy cannot miss. Skimpy pulls a gun and shoots once and misses but Johnny fires and hits him. As Johnny reaches for Skimpy's gun on the floor, Skimpy pulls another one and tells Johnny it is aimed at the back of his head. There is a shot and footsteps as Percy comes in and Johnny tells him he had seen him outside, and hoped that Percy would pull the trigger when he saw what Peter was doing. When Percy asks if he killed Peter, Johnny tells him that, "just like your brother, you are a pretty lousy shot."

"Skimpy, and without his brother's support anymore, he will be lucky if he ever gets out of the pen. Percy? Well I hope he never forgets his lesson in practical psychology."

NOTES:
- THE FIRST COMMERCIAL BREAK IS FOR NO-DOZ.
- THE SECOND COMMERCIAL BREAK IS FOR NEWPORT CIGARETTES.

- THE THIRD COMMERCIAL BREAK IS FOR SINCLAIR GASOLINE.
- WALTER OTTO DOES THE SOUND PATTERNS
- MICHAEL SCHOSKIS DOES THE TECHNICAL DIRECTION.
- STUART METZ IS THE ANNOUNCER.
- MUSICAL SUPERVISION IS BY ETHEL HUBER
- JOHNNY IS SHOT FOR THE 13TH TIME.

Producer: Fred Hendrickson   Writers: Jack Johnstone
Cast: Rosemary Rice, Larry Haines, Jack Arthur, Melville Ruick, William Redfield

◆ ❖ ◆

SHOW: THE FOUR IS A CROWD MATTER
SHOW DATE: 7/29/1962
COMPANY: STAR MUTUAL INSURANCE COMPANY
AGENT: DENNIS TAYLOR
EXP. ACCT: $400.00

SYNOPSIS: Dennis Taylor calls Johnny from Colorado Springs. An important client, Melvin Lockerty is spending the summer at a nearby guest ranch. Lockerty is having guests for the week, but he believes that one of his guests is going to try to murder him. Johnny is on his way.

Johnny flies to Denver, Colorado the home of station KLZ, and takes a ferry plane to Colorado Springs where Dennis Taylor meets Johnny and loans him his car while Johnny is in town. Dennis tells Johnny that one of the relatives coming to see Lockerty is going to kill him. The visitors are the children of Lockerty's brother Henry, so Johnny better get to the "No Name Ranch" as quickly as possible. Dennis tells Johnny that Lockerty had hornswoggled his brother out of some mining property just as the properties were beginning to pay off. Dennis is sure that Lockerty is a crook, and was the cause of his brother killing himself. Dennis boils the case down to dollars and cents and does not care what happens to Lockerty. Johnny describes the ranch and his room, which has a view of Pikes Peak. Lockerty visits Johnny and does not want the relatives to know why Johnny is there. He invited them to the ranch to try and make peace with them. Johnny is told that Henry made a promise to him to get even with Lockerty for the stolen money. Lockerty tells Johnny that he has been getting letters threatening his life. Johnny is surprised that any of the guests he sees could kill anyone.

Johnny watches the relatives unload their car. The driver is about 26, tall blonde and beautiful. Another, a couple years younger is a brunette, a real doll with a mischievous sparkle in her eye. The third is a very naturally beautiful girl, in spite of the horn-rimmed glasses, plain dress and hair tied in a bun. Johnny goes out and Kitty Lockerty introduces her self, thinking that Johnny is the manager. Teckla and Marion Lockerty introduce themselves to Johnny, who takes their bags to their cabins and then watches as the girls go to see Lockerty. Johnny hears a lot of yelling and then the girls leave without speaking to each other. Later

Lockerty tells Johnny that he told them that he knew that one of them was going to kill him because Harry made one of his daughters promise to kill him. Lockerty tells Johnny that Teckla is all concerned with her self and Katherine, Kitty is a hot-tempered little lynx while Marion is quiet and smart, but remembers that still waters run deep. Johnny arranges for the girls to go to a barn dance tonight and Lockerty tells Johnny he will be sleeping with a gun. Johnny sashays to the barn dance and manages to take each of the girls outside for a quiet walk. Teckla tells Johnny that Lockerty has a silly notion that they are going to kill him. She tells Johnny about her father and that she would kill Lockerty if her father had asked her to. Johnny agrees to meet her later, and seals the deal with a kiss. Johnny then talks to Kitty who tells him that she wishes someone would kill Melvin. Kitty is really chilly and wants Johnny to warm her up, just as Marion calls for Johnny. Marion has a walk with Johnny and tells him that she knows who Johnny is, and that he is there to protect Uncle Melvin. She tells Johnny that they came up to the ranch to humor Lockerty. Besides, would a secretary like Kitty or a softy like Teckla or herself, an old-maid schoolteacher, kill Uncle Melvin? After the dance, Kitty and Teckla go to town with some boys and Marion goes to her cabin. Johnny visits Lockerty, who is going to stay up all night reading. Johnny agrees to stay until the girls are back when a shot comes through the window and kills Lockerty. Everyone at the ranch rushes to Lockerty's cabin, Kitty and Teckla show up with their boyfriends and Marion shows up in her bathrobe. Johnny asks Kitty and Teckla why they got there so quickly, and Kitty tells him that they and their boyfriends had gone to town for a beer and were just coming back, and Pete Mackenzie tells Johnny she is right. Kitty tells Johnny that she saw Marion's light go on just as they were driving up. Marion tells Johnny that she could not sleep and was going to make some cocoa and read when she heard the shot. Johnny wonders who else could have a motive, as every one seems to have an alibi. Johnny makes a call to Colorado Springs and the only other man who would want Lockerty dead, but Dennis Taylor is at home. The sheriff arrives and convinces Johnny that if the murder weapon were in a murky pond, there would be no fingerprints if it were ever found. Johnny gets a hunch and is sure that since one of the girls recognized him, she would also need and airtight alibi. Johnny remembers that she had told Johnny why the others had come and had tried to defend them, but she was in her cabin when it happened and had just turned on her light. Johnny remembers about the timers people use to turn on their lights and buys one. That night Johnny sits on the porch and talks to the girls and asks them to look at the clock and then to look at his cabin. Johnny asks them to tell him exactly what time he gets to his cabin and turns on the lights. Johnny leaves and later the girls see his lights go on and look at the clock. Johnny comes from around the corner and tells them that he had used an automatic switch, the same way Marion did to turn on his lights. Marion tells Johnny that Lockerty did not deserve to live, but Johnny tells her that nobody deserves to be murdered.

NOTES:

- THE NAME OF THE DEAD BROTHER SEEMS TO CHANGE FROM HENRY TO HARRY HALFWAY THROUGH THE STORY.
- THE FIRST COMMERCIAL BREAK IS FOR NEWPORT CIGARETTES.
- THE SECOND COMMERCIAL BREAK IS FOR SINCLAIR GASOLINE
- MUSICAL SUPERVISION IS BY ETHEL HUBER
- THE ANNOUNCER IS ART HANNES

Producer: Fred Hendrickson   **Writers:** Jack Johnstone
Cast: Bill Smith, Constance Simons, Edgar Stehli, Freddy Chandler, Hetty Galen, Reynold Osborne

◆ ❖ ◆

SHOW: THE CASE OF TROUBLE MATTER
SHOW DATE: 8/5/1962
COMPANY: MID STATES INDUSTRIAL INSURANCE COMPANY
AGENT: TOM BARTLEY
EXP. ACCT: $256.10

SYNOPSIS: Tom Bartley calls Johnny from Des Moines. The Case Paper Products Company is being blown off the maps. There have been fires and explosions in their warehouses, and they have cost Tom $125,000. If there are any more, or if the main plant is hit . . . Johnny agrees to fly out as soon as possible.

Johnny flies to Des Moines, Iowa and circles the tower of station KRNT. Johnny rents a car and goes to Tom Bartley's office where the secretary greets Johnny with a "Yes, Mr. Case." Johnny corrects her and is told that Tom has gone to Indianola where Tom wants Johnny to meet him. Johnny will know where to find Tom. Johnny drives to Indianola and finds a thick pawl of smoke that once was the Case Paper Products Company building. Tom finds Johnny and shows him the results of fire number three that will cost them $50-60 thousand. Tom is sure that the fire is arson, and so are the owners, Albert and Ed Case. Tom tells Johnny that the fires have all started with an explosion, which make Johnny sure that an arsonist with a pattern is at work. Tom takes Johnny to his home for drinks and dinner with his wife Millie. As soon as Millie sees Johnny, she calls him "Ed," and Tom remarks that Johnny does look a little like Ed Case and Tom tells Johnny that Millie used to be singer. Tom tells Johnny that Albert runs the business, and Ed only takes the profits, as he is a black sheep of the family. Albert Case is supposed to drop by after he returns from the site of the last fire. Tom tells Johnny that business has not been good, but disagrees that Albert would ever burn his own buildings. There is a call from Albert and he tells Tom that the fires were set, and he has proof. He tells them not to come over and the phone goes dead. Johnny, Millie and Tom rush to the home of Albert Case and spot him sitting at a desk on the phone. Johnny breaks in the door and they find Albert dead, shot through the forehead.

Tom calls the police and Johnny searches the home. The police arrive and a young police officer asks if Johnny is related to Mr. Case. The policeman finds a bullet hole in the window and tells them to leave. Johnny tells Tom that the bullet came from inside the house and was fired by someone Albert knew or let into the house, which is why the phone went dead. Tom tells Johnny that Albert was not married, and that Ed will inherit the business. Ed lives in Grinnell, just beyond Colfax, and both of the towns have warehouses in them. Johnny gets his car and drives to Colfax. Johnny stops at a fire at a Case Paper Products warehouse. Johnny stumbles over an old man sobbing over the loss of the warehouse. He had told Albert that it would happen as soon as the car came prowling around. The car was a big white Peratti convertible and Albert said he knew who was setting them. As soon as Johnny stands him up the man thinks that Johnny is the man and shoots at him. Johnny takes the man's gun and drives off. Johnny visits the police in Grinnell and talks to Lt. Cal Golden who calls Johnny "Mr. Case." Lt. Golden finally realizes that Johnny is not Ed, and Johnny tells Lt. Golden he thinks Ed Case is the firebug, and the man who killed Albert. Lt. Golden agrees to put out an APB and gives Johnny the address of Ed Case. Johnny goes there and the woman next door mistakes Johnny for Ed Case. Johnny rushes off when he realizes that the neighbor's description of a petite blond with green eyes matches the description of Millie Bartley. Johnny calls Tom, and learns that Millie has gone out. She was talking to Bernice, with whom she used to dance, and left. Johnny goes back to Ed's house, slips the backdoor lock and leaves the door open. Inside, Johnny is stopped by a gun in his back and a voice that tells Ed Case he is trying to stall over the $5,000 just before he slugs Johnny. Johnny wakes up after nightfall when the all too-familiar petite figure of a woman enters the house. She tells Eddie that it must have been Louie getting even because Eddy did not pay him for setting the last fire. She tells Eddie that she saw him kill Albert from outside the house. She tells Eddie that he had to kill Albert. When Johnny calls her Millie and turns on the light, she realizes that Johnny is not Eddie and Johnny realizes that she is not Millie but Bernice. Eddie comes in and Bernice takes Johnny's gun. Ed tells them he heard everything. Ed tries to think of a plan to kill both Johnny and Bernice. Ed takes Johnny's gun to shoot him when there is a knock at the door. Ed slaps Bernice and shoots her, giving Johnny the chance to hit Ed. Millie is at the door, and Johnny tells her not to go into the room, as Ed has killed Bernice. Millie tells Johnny that she came alone to see if she could help Bernice, and Johnny tells her to call Tom and tell him what has happened.

"I guess it is pretty obvious what will happen to Ed Case. Now it's two murders against him. As for the insurance and the estate, Iowa law will have to take care of that."

NOTES:

- THE FIRST COMMERCIAL BREAK IS FOR NEWPORT CIGARETTES.
- THE FINAL COMMERCIAL BREAK IS FOR SINCLAIR GASOLINE
- SOUND PATTERNS ARE BY WALTER OTTO
- TECHNICAL DIRECTION BY FRED CUSICK

- THE ANNOUNCER IS STUART METZ.
- MUSICAL SUPERVISION IS BY ETHEL HUBER
- THIS PROGRAM IS A REMAKE OF THE BURNING CAR MATTER OF 12/9/56, BUT WITH A CHANGE OF VENUE AND BUSINESS.
- GRINNELL IS DUE EAST OF DES MOINES.

Producer: Fred Hendrickson   **Writers:**   Jack Johnstone
Cast: John Seymour, Abby Lewis, Terri Keane, Edgar Stehli, Jack Grimes, Jim Stevens, Gilbert Mack

◆   ❖   ◆

SHOW:	THE OLDEST GAG MATTER
SHOW DATE:	8/12/1962
COMPANY:	STAR MUTUAL INSURANCE COMPANY
AGENT:	LARRY SPANGLER
EXP. ACCT:	$0.00

SYNOPSIS: Larry Spangler calls Johnny from Hartford, Connecticut. Larry has never met Johnny, as he has only been there a year. Larry asks if the name Briscum means anything, and Johnny replies that Lloyd Briscum runs some sort of factory out on the edge of town. Larry tells Johnny that Briscum is an important client and he would like Johnny to come with him to the factory. The business partner has called Larry and told him that Briscum is dead. His housekeeper found him a few minutes ago with a bullet in his head. Since Johnny's apartment is on the way, he will pick Johnny up on the way to the Briscum house.

Johnny describes Larry as a new-age Madison Avenue insurance man with a gray suit, shined shoes and crisp haircut and eager to set the world on fire. Larry has a few ideas as to who killed Briscum, but will wait to see what the police say. John Barber the business partner supposedly called the police. Larry leaves all sorts of clues and hints about things that were supposed to have happened. Larry tells Johnny that Trudy, Briscum's ward, is above suspicion, as Larry is a good friend of hers. Mike Briscum is the adopted son, who lived off of Briscum. Johnny remembers seeing Mike's name in the paper after a fight at a club. The beneficiaries of the insurance are Mike, who gets one third, and Trudy, who will get two thirds, and the business goes to Barber. At the house, Sgt. Danny Gilbert, a "too sure" police officer is in charge. Sgt. Gilbert takes Johnny in to see the body and an old battered .38 in the right hand. Johnny sees the powder burns and no sign of a struggle. Sgt. Gilbert thinks it happened last night and is sure that Briscum committed suicide, but Johnny is not sure. Sgt. Gilbert tells Johnny that business had not been good, and Briscum has had Mike and Trudy living off of him.

Johnny doubts suicide based on what Larry told him. The lab crew can find nothing to prove anything but suicide, but Johnny is sure that Briscum had someone help him pull the trigger. Johnny asks Sgt. Gilbert for the results of the autopsy and goes to talk to the family. Trudy is sure that her father would not commit suicide. She moved away because Briscum was a tyrant and would not even allow her fiancé into the house. Trudy is not upset, and she confirms that with the money she will be free to do as she chooses, which could make her a suspect. Mr. Barber is sure that Briscum did not commit suicide, and that he was not worried about the business. The business was not doing well because of his old-fashioned practices. Barber is free now to make the necessary profitable changes to the factory, which makes him a suspect. Mike is not sorry about Briscum's death as he was not family, and he wished at times he could have helped him on his way to get the insurance money. Johnny tells Mike that there will be no money if it was suicide. Mike tells Johnny that killing himself was against what Briscum believed in. Mike can see anyone in the house killing Briscum and even suggests making a play for Trudy, as they are not really related. But he could never get Trudy away from Larry Spangler.

After the body is removed Sgt. Gilbert lets the beneficiaries leave. As Barber leaves to go to the plant Johnny suggests that he can go now to make the changes he wants, and Mike gets a ride with him so he can go to town and tie one on. Larry starts to take Trudy home and leaves his car with Johnny to take home. Trudy asks Johnny if he thinks it was suicide, and tells him that the insurance is nothing compared to the rest of the estate and she will be satisfied without it. Johnny tells her that it really seems to be adding up to be suicide, which will make Larry happy because the company will not have to pay off. Johnny drives Larry's car and thinks about something Larry had said about the route to the office. Johnny goes to the morgue where Dr. Frandler tells Johnny that it was suicide, and there was only a light bruise on the forehead. Johnny tells a confused doctor that he is sure that Briscum was hit on the forehead and shot where he was hit. Johnny is sure that someone put the gun into Briscum's hand and pulled the trigger while he was unconscious. Johnny also tells Dr. Frandler that his apartment was not close to the route between Larry's office and Briscum's house. It was just an excuse and the suggestions were to cover up the murder if it was not done well enough. Calling Johnny in is the oldest gag in the world, a cover up to take suspicion from Larry, and after all, he had the motive. Johnny realizes that if he tears into Larry, he can get the evidence he needs. Johnny goes to see Larry and tells him that his lack of experience tripped him up and that he left latent prints on the gun, on Briscum's hand and the arm of a chair he sat in. Larry tells Johnny that prints are impossible because he wore a pair of cotton gloves. Opps! Johnny tells him that only the rankest amateur would let himself get tripped up like that.

"And only the rottenest kind of insurance man would have tried a thing like that. Thank heaven there are not that many of them. Expense account total, wait a minute, of course, there isn't any! And you know what? I'm glad there isn't. This kind I wouldn't want to collect on any way."

NOTES:
- THE FIRST COMMERCIAL BREAK IS THE KINGSTON TRIO FOR SEVEN UP

- THE SECOND COMMERCIAL BREAK IS FOR MENTHOLATUM DEEP HEATING RUB.
- THE THIRD COMMERCIAL BREAK IS FOR INSTANT TENDER LEAF ICED TEA.
- WILLIAM MASON IS LARRY, CHARITA BAUER IS TRUDY, RAYMOND EDWARD JOHNSON IS BARBER, IVOR FRANCIS IS DOC, RALPH BELL IS DANNY.
- THE ANNOUNCER IS ART HANNES.
- MUSICAL SUPERVISION IS BY ETHEL HUBER

Producer: Bruno Zirato, Jr.   Writers: Jack Johnstone
Cast: William Mason, Charita Bauer, Raymond Edward Johnson,
             Ivor Francis, Ralph Bell

◆   ❖   ◆

SHOW: THE LORELEI MATTER
SHOW DATE: 8/19/1962
COMPANY: STAR MUTUAL INSURANCE COMPANY
AGENT: ED WILLIAMS
EXP. ACCT: $0.00

SYNOPSIS: Johnny is called and asked if he is that insurance investigator. When Johnny tells the caller that he is a freelance investigator, the man wants the Johnny Dollar who works for the Star Insurance Company. Johnny tells the caller that he works on assignment, so he tells Johnny to get an assignment and get over here right away. When Johnny tells the caller he does not know who he is or where he lives, the caller stumbles and identifies himself as Timothy Jerrad, and tells Johnny to rush over to his apartment. Jerrad tells Johnny to check with the insurance company after he gets there and mentions a murder, but it has not occurred yet. If Johnny does not hurry he will have Johnny fired.

While downtown, Johnny stops and sees Ed Williams in the Star Mutual building. Johnny asks Ed about Jerrad, and Ed tells Johnny that even with the life policy of 2 million, Jerrad is still a crackpot. "All or Nothing Jerrad" was a clever stock manipulator and used to be loaded, but five or six wives have taken care of most of the money. His present wife is young and pretty but sensible. She is Lorelei Lambert, an artist from Quebec who spends a lot of time out of town painting. Johnny tells Ed about the phone call, and Ed tells Johnny that Jerrad has a persecution complex. Ed tells Johnny that Lorelei is the beneficiary, but she is not the type to murder anyone, as Jerrad has taken very good care of her. Ed tells Johnny to go over and keep Jerrad happy, so he will not lose the great big premiums.

Johnny goes to the old fashioned Fleur de Lei apartments in Hartford, Connecticut where two doormen tell Johnny that he is expected. Johnny walks up to suite 3-A and knocks and the most beautiful girl Johnny has ever seen tells Johnny not to bang on the door as she stands there with a purse and attaché case in one hand and a suitcase in the other. Mid-twenties, petite, brown eyes and hair, umm, umm! She introduces herself as Mrs. Jerrad and Johnny tells her who she is. She has been up on Cape Ann painting seascapes and came back today rather than next week because of Timothy. She hands Johnny her bags as she opens the door. When Johnny mentions that she is lovely, she tells Johnny that she would slap his face if he did not know she was married. Johnny tells her that Jerrad wants to see him. Inside she calls for Timothy, and searches the apartment. In the bedroom she finds Timothy in bed, dead. Johnny notes only one solid blow behind the ear by someone who sneaked up and struck once. Lorelei sobs and Johnny calls the police. Johnny calls the doorman up, but he has seen no one come into the building that day except Johnny. Johnny asks about new tenants, and Mr. Bascome is the newest one; he came here in 1937. The police arrive with the doctor and Sgt. Barney Foster and Johnny go over the apartment and find nothing. Sgt. Foster tells Johnny to get Lorelei out of the apartment for a few days. He tells Johnny that the killer must have been somebody Jerrad knew, so he is going to start running down everyone the Jerrads have known for the past five years. Sgt. Foster tells Johnny that he could be the suspect because of the attractive young wife, but Johnny makes light of it. Sgt. Foster is going to seal the apartment and let no one in, but Johnny makes sure he can get back in. Sgt. Foster tells Johnny not to act on any crazy hunches, but to call him if anything comes up. Promise?

Johnny arranges with Betty Lewis to stay at the Staler Hotel with Lorelei. Johnny gets that silly feeling that a hunch is brewing as two days go by with no word from anyone. Finally on the third day he goes back with Lorelei to help the hunch materialize. Lorelei tells Johnny what a good person Betty is and almost breaks down. In the apartment Lorelei tells Johnny about Cape Anne and wants to take her clothes out of the apartment, but Johnny says no. Johnny comments on her name Lorelei and the legendary sirens that enticed men to their deaths. She shows Johnny her sketches and Johnny recognizes the scenes. She tells Johnny that she had never been to the cape before, but will go again. Johnny tells her that she won't. Johnny tells her that she is a destroyer of men as she was the one person who would benefit from her husband's death, and the one person who could get in with a key in the back door without being seen by the doormen. Johnny suspects that she overheard Jerrad talking on the phone to Johnny, and decided to use him as an alibi and left by the back door again. When she insists that Johnny helped her with her luggage, Johnny reminds her that she was not carrying the portfolio full of the sketches she had made. She had to have been in the apartment. Lorelei tells Johnny that she did kill her husband because he was an egotistical, crazy old man. She killed him because of the money with which she can enjoy life, and invites Johnny to join her. "Nice Try, Lorelei, but not this time."

"Oh, why do they do it? Why don't they learn? Don't they know it won't work? That sooner or later they are bound to be found out? And why a lovely little thing like Lorelei? Lorelei. Destroyer of men. Expense account total, who wants it. Who wants anything out of a case like this?"

NOTES:
- THE FIRST COMMERCIAL BREAK IS AN **AFRS** STORY ON THE BENEFITS OF DEMOCRACY.
- THE SECOND COMMERCIAL BREAK IS A CONTINUATION OF THE FIRST COMMERCIAL BREAK.
- RITA LLOYD IS LORELEI, SAM GRAY IS BARNEY, HERB DUNCAN IS ED, ARTHUR KOHL IS JERRAD, GUY REPP IS THE DOORMAN.
- MUSICAL SUPERVISION IS BY ETHEL HUBER
- ART HANNES IS THE ANNOUNCER.
- THE LORELEI IS A LARGE ROCK ON THE RHINE RIVER IN GERMANY. THE RIVER IS DIFFICULT TO NAVIGATE, AND THE MANY WRECKS THERE GAVE RISE TO THE LEGEND OF A SIREN LIKE CREATURE THAT LURED MARINERS TO THEIR DEATHS.

Producer: Bruno Zirato, Jr.   **Writers:**   Jack Johnstone
Cast: Rita Lloyd, Sam Gray, Herb Duncan, Arthur Kohl, Guy Repp

◆ ❖ ◆

SHOW: THE GOLD RUSH MATTER
SHOW DATE: 8/26/1962
COMPANY: GREATER SOUTHWEST INSURANCE COMPANY
AGENT: JAKE WALTON
EXP. ACCT: $700.00

SYNOPSIS: Paul calls Johnny to welcome him to San Francisco and to tell him not to unpack, but to hop over to Virginia City, Nevada. Contact Jake Walton about the new gold rush going on now. This one has all the same old problems, including a couple of murders.

Johnny flies to Reno where he rents a car for the drive to Virginia City. Johnny describes the old Virginia City and the Comstock Lode. Johnny asks an old man for directions to Jake's office and is told that he is not there. Johnny is told not to go there, as Jake and the Sheriff are out at the Scarlet Queen mine. Johnny asks if his car can make the trip, and the man tells him he better get a horse. Johnny is directed to Jake Beckley's stable, but Johnny is warned not to go the mine as there has been another killing, and there will be more. The man tells Johnny that there will be more dynamite accidents like the one that blinded him. Johnny rents a horse and rides up Six-Mile Canyon trail. At the top of a ridge Johnny sees a body being taken from the mine just as a bullet whizzes by his head. Johnny takes cover and circles around a boulder when a girl with a rifle tells Johnny to drop his little lemon squeezer. Johnny is held at gunpoint while the girl calls for Jake. Jake walks up and tells Leona that he will make sure that Johnny will not try any tricks and slugs him.

Just as Jake throws the punch Johnny rolls out of the way, grabs Jake's arm and gets him on the ground. Johnny grabs for the girl's leg and takes her down and gets the rifle. Jake gives Johnny his gun and identifies himself as Jake Walton, just the man Johnny has been looking for. Jake and Leona had been at the mine because of the accident. When Johnny tells them who he is, Jake tells Leona that he is the man Jake has been waiting for. Leona tells Johnny that they thought he was the one causing all the problems. Jake tells Johnny that this was the second killing, and that someone is using dynamite at the wrong time and place. Leona tells Johnny that her Uncle Dave was blown out of the mine and blinded. Johnny realizes that Dave was the man he met in town. Leona asks Johnny whom he was shooting at, and he tells her "just some rattlesnakes." Leona tells Johnny that she almost shot Johnny when she heard the shots. Johnny, Jake and Leona go to the mine, located on the edge of the Comstock Lode. Jake tells Johnny that the mine will not pay off, and Leona tells them that Dave should own the mine, but a crooked lawyer fixed it so that Ski Lambert owns the mine. Jake thinks that the lawyer might have been right. Dave had been working in the mine until the accident. Jake tells Johnny that the mine re-openings are caused by a government rise in the price of gold. All three go into the mine and Johnny catches Leona as she "trips" at the bottom of a ladder, and Johnny tells her he hopes she had fallen on purpose. At the end of the mine is an area shored up with 12x12 timbers and the acrid smell of dynamite. Jake tells Johnny that this is the site there the dynamite went off and killed two people. Johnny asks for the lantern and it breaks as Jake hands it to Johnny, forcing them to climb out in darkness. Back outside the mine, Jake drives Johnny and Leona to town via a shortcut as Leona starts laying plans for a dinner with Johnny. Johnny asks to borrow Jake's jeep to investigate a little idea he has. Johnny wants to go investigate who had shot at him and a second tunnel to the mine mentioned by Jake, and the shortcut, which could have allowed someone from town to get there and shoot at him. But Who? After dinner and apple pie with Jake and Leona, Johnny takes the jeep and a lantern to drives out of town, hearing gunshots on the way. At the mine Johnny finds the hidden second tunnel under some roofing materials. Johnny goes into the mine and looks at the shoring in the tunnel where he finds a hidden door to the second tunnel. Johnny hears someone coming and plants the lantern as a decoy and starts to climb the ladder when a blast goes off. After the blast Johnny hears Leona ask if the blast got him and Dave is not sure. Leona and the old man; all Johnny needs to know!

In a saloon in town Johnny meets Jake and asks him to get a rope and a gun. As Jake drives, Johnny tells Jake what happened at the mine. Johnny knocks at Leona's door, and she is very surprised to see him. Johnny goes in to meet a very nervous Uncle Dave, who recognizes Johnny by his voice. While Leona fixes a drink, Dave talks to Johnny and slowly moves his hand towards a table drawer while Johnny slowly draws his .38. Johnny tells Dave that he went to the mine because of Dave's blindness, blindness that was an act because he had told Johnny what kind of car he was driving. Johnny tells Dave that he told everyone he was blind to back up the story that he was dynamited and that he has been causing the explosions to get the mine back. Johnny tells Dave that his next victim would have been Ski Lambert, the owner. Leona comes in with her rifle and Jake comes in with his rifle and shoots Leona in the hand.

"I do not know if Leona was actually involved in the murders in the mine or not. I hope not, because she was a doll. Then, sometimes, they are the most dangerous kinds. Anyhow, it will be up to the courts again to figure it out."

NOTES:
- THE FIRST COMMERCIAL BREAK IS FOR NO-DOZ.
- THE SECOND COMMERCIAL BREAK IS FOR KENT CIGARETTES.
- THE THIRD COMMERCIAL BREAK IS FOR SINCLAIR DINO GASOLINE.
- GENE SIMES DOES THE MUSICAL SUPERVISION.
- WALTER OTTO DOES THE SOUND PATTERNS.
- MICHEAL SCHOSKIS DOES THE TECHNICAL DIRECTION.
- THE ANNOUNCER IS STUART METZ.

Producer: Fred Hendrickson   Writers: Jack Johnstone
Cast: Cliff Oland, Reynold Osborne, Terri Keane, Leon Janney,
           Rosemary Rice, Sam Raskyn

◆ ❖ ◆

SHOW: THE DONINGER DONINGER MATTER
SHOW DATE: 9/2/1962
COMPANY: NEW JERSEY STATE MUTUAL LIFE INSURANCE COMPANY
AGENT: MAURICE PARKELY
EXP. ACCT: $155.70

SYNOPSIS: Maurice Parkely calls Johnny, and tells him that things are bad. He has $40,000 worth of troubles and Johnny suggests that Maurice just mail him a check. Maurice tells Johnny that a check is not involved, it is all cash, so Johnny will fly down and pick it up. But there is a hitch. The policy beneficiary is Walter P. Doninger, and they cannot find him. Johnny mentions his commission on the $40,000 and Maurice tells Johnny to come down, and they will talk about it.

Johnny flies to Trenton, New Jersey and cabs to Maury's office. Johnny and Maury head of for lunch at Hildebrechts where Johnny fills up on soft-shelled crabs. The client is Walter P. Doninger, VII. Walter the seventh is the last of the line, now that his sister has died and left him the $40,000 "cash in hand" as the policy reads. The money must be paid in cash within 10 days of the death, which is less than a week from now. If they cannot find Walter, the company will have to pay an additional thousand every week or fraction there of. Johnny wonders if Doninger is trying to dodge the company to get more money, and Maury thinks it is a possibility. The policy has had eight addresses for Doninger, and he is not at the last address. Maury has not considered a pattern to the moves. They start in Trenton, then Atlantic City, Bloomfield, Cranford, Dumont, East Rutherford, Franklin, Gibbstown and Highbridge. Johnny realizes that they go in alphabetical order, so the next town should start with an "I." In an atlas, Johnny finds almost a dozen New Jersey towns starting with "I." Maury suggests writing to the towns, but Johnny has a better pattern. Johnny bets Maury that if he cannot find Walter

P. Doninger, VII in Interlaken, Johnny will work for free. If he is there, Maury will add an additional thousand, and he agrees. Johnny tells Maury that the answer is in the atlas.

Johnny explains that the cities are order in descending order of population, so Walter is going up the alphabet and down in population with each move. Johnny is sure he will find Doninger in Interlaken. Johnny rents a car and drives to Interlaken, New Jersey. Johnny ends up at the New York and Long Branch Railroad station and asks for directions to City Hall. A man tells Johnny that he recognizes Johnny's voice. He is Bill McGrogan, and knows everyone in town and is willing to help Johnny for a small fee that Johnny can expense. Johnny tells Bill that he his looking for Walter Doninger. Bill is suddenly quiet and tells Johnny that for $50 he will deliver Walt. After all, Walt is loaded. Bill tells Johnny to get a room at the Larchmont Hotel and he will get Doninger there tonight. Johnny asks if it would not be easier to just tell him where Walter is, but Bill tells Johnny that Walt moves around too much. Johnny gives Bill $25 and promises the rest when Bill delivers Doninger. Johnny visits the police department and Sgt. Holloway tells Johnny that he will try to find Doninger, but he does get around a lot. After he heard his sister died, Doninger has lived in about three different rooming houses. Johnny has dinner and calls Maury. There is a knock on the door and Johnny opens it to find a man with a gun and silencer. The man tells Johnny that he expected to see Johnny on his case, but not this fast. He is Walter "Scrappy" Doninger. Scrappy tells Johnny he is not going to take any chances and is going to kill Johnny.

Scrappy tells Johnny that he pulled a heist up in Hartford, and the goods were insured, so Johnny he knew Johnny would be assigned to the case. But he does not know how Johnny found him so soon. Scrappy tells Johnny that Bill McGrogan set Johnny up for $100. There is another knock at the door that allows Johnny to slug Scrappy. Johnny asks who is and it is Walter P. Doninger, VII. Johnny lets him in and Walter shows Johnny his identification and Walter also admits that he was stalling for time to get more money. Maury calls to tell Johnny that Tri-States in Hartford wants him to work on a big jewelry job, and the crook has the same name as the man Johnny is looking for. Plus there is a $10,000 reward out for him. Johnny tells Maury that he has his man right there. Johnny asks Maury to call Tri-States and tell them their job is done, and to mail the reward to Johnny. "I am up to HERE in Doningers!"

"So for once I got real lucky. Now you can see why I've called this report "The Doninger Doninger Matter." Expense account total, including the trip home with Scrappy Doninger in tow, $155.70, plus commission of course. Plus the extra $1,000 on Walter, VII. Oh, and I couldn't find Bill McGrogan again, so he will never get that other $25, maybe just a jail term some day for the kind of company that he keeps."

NOTES:
- THE FIRST COMMERCIAL BREAK IS FOR NO-DOZ.
- THE SECOND COMMERCIAL BREAK IS FOR KENT CIGARETTES.

- THERE ARE A VARIETY OF SPELLINGS FOR THIS NAME OF THIS STORY. I HAVE CHOSEN "DONINGER" BASED ON THE PRONUNCIATION OF MANDEL KRAMER AS DON'-IN-GER.
- WALTER OTTO DOES THE SOUND PATTERNS.
- EUGENE SIMES DOES THE MUSIC SUPERVISION.
- MIKE SCHOSKIS DOES THE TECHNICAL SUPERVISION.
- ART HANNES IS THE ANNOUNCER.
- THE POPULATION OF THE TOWNS MENTIONED WERE ATLANTIC CITY (60,000+), BLOOMFIELD (49,000), CRANFORD (17,500). APPROXIMATE 2003 POPULATIONS ARE ATLANTIC CITY (41,000), BLOOMFIELD (48,000), CRANFORD (22,500)

Producer: Fred Hendrickson   **Writers:**   Jack Johnstone
Cast: Jack Arthur, Jack Grimes, Ian Martin, Santos Ortega, Melville Ruick, Neil Fitzgerald

SHOW: THE FOUR CS MATTER
SHOW DATE: 9/9/1962
COMPANY: GREATER SOUTHWEST INSURANCE COMPANY
AGENT: ROYAL J. HARKIN
EXP. ACCT: $401.23

SYNOPSIS: Royal J. Harkin calls Johnny from Los Angeles, and tells Johnny that if he flies to New York now, he can get there by 4 AM to be in Royal's office at 9 AM sharp. Johnny tells Roy that he is busy, but Roy is not to be deterred. There is a conspiracy here to commit murder!

Johnny calls Betty Lewis to cancel a date, and she offers to drive him to the airport. As Johnny rushes to catch a flight to Los Angeles, California Betty tells him to look up an old school mate, Doris Crutten, who is planning to go to Europe this fall. Johnny arrives at 8:30 as the plane circles station KNX. Roy meets Johnny and he has a rental car for him. The name of the client is Harvey Crutten, of Three Cs Imports: Crutten, Carding and Callenger. Harvey is the senior partner and he lives on Mulholland Drive and is insured for $250,000, double indemnity. The beneficiary is Doris Crutten but the business will pass to the partners. Royal shows Johnny a newspaper with two articles. One is about Wilbur Carding threatening Harvey Crutten; the other is about Earl R. J. Callenger threatening Harvey Crutten. Roy tells Johnny that both partners threatened Crutten because he is bad for their business. Carding hates him because he will not sell out before the business goes bust, and Callenger hates him because Crutten is a playboy and has gone after his wife. Roy is paged and takes the call. His office tells him that Harvey Crutten is dead.

Roy tells Johnny that Harvey was killed while driving his Minerva-Pechini sports car. The police told Doris that he lost control on Dead Man's Curve and crashed 300 feet to the bottom of the canyon. Harvey was not a wild driver in spite of the car. Roy is sure that he was murdered and driven off the road. Johnny drives to Mulholland Drive and the Crutten home. Johnny reaches Dead Man's Curve just as the car is being lifted out. Johnny goes to the car and meets an old friend, Sgt. Mike Conroy. Sgt. Conroy is sure that the car was in perfect condition, as Mike knows where Crutten lives, and he could not back out without brakes. Sgt. Conroy estimates that the car was doing 90 when it went over and he thinks the accident was suicide. Sgt. Conroy tells Johnny that Doris is a real dish, but she works like a handyman and drives an old jalopy. Johnny arrives at the modest Crutten house that is immaculate. In the garage Johnny spots a 1938 automobile. Doris comes into the garage and tells Johnny that she rebuilt it herself. Johnny introduces himself, and Doris tells Johnny she is a fan of his. While Doris installs a sink, she tells Johnny that fixing things is her hobby. When Johnny mentions that Doris is not upset about the death of her husband, she tells Johnny that she had been waiting for him to die since she married him.

Doris tells Johnny that she stayed married to Crutten to get his money and his insurance. Doris tells Johnny that she was at a poker game with some girls and got home at 1:00 AM to find Harvey's car gone. She had no idea where Harvey was going and asks if Johnny had met Earl Callenger's wife Moira. She tells Johnny that if either Carding or Callenger got to Harvey, she can only say "thanks, or sorry if you're offended." Johnny leaves to call Sgt. Conroy who tells Johnny that the doctors found nothing in the autopsy. Johnny arranges to see the car and then drives to the headquarters of the Four Cs Importers. Earl Callenger is glad Crutten is gone so Moira his wife can come back to her senses. He blames himself for letting Moira be influenced by Crutten. Earl tells Johnny that he and Carding and three salesmen were on a train coming from San Francisco when the accident happened, and the police will confirm that. Wilbur Carding and the salesmen give Johnny the same story, but Johnny is stuck with a motive for the killing. Johnny asks about the four C's name and realizes that there is a fourth "C" and leaves. This is no hunch, as Johnny remembers what Betty had said about her friend Doris going to Europe this fall, alone. Sgt. Conroy shows him the special metric tools in a toolkit in the trunk of the car. Johnny notices that one tool is missing, the wrench that bleeds the brake lines. Johnny thinks he knows where the wrench is. Back at the Crutten home Johnny goes to the garage and searches for the missing metric wrench. Doris walks in and tells Johnny that she expected to find him back at the garage. She admits that she used the special wrench to fix the car's brakes. Johnny tells her that she loosened the bleeder valve so that the brake would be useless when Harvey got to Dead Man's Curve. She had waited so long for someone else to do it, and they didn't, so she had to do it herself. "I shouldn't have, I guess." "No, you shouldn't have."

"So once again it's up to the courts. I suppose if she hadn't done it somebody else would, likely in the mistaken belief that he could have gotten away with it."

NOTES:

- THE FIRST COMMERCIAL BREAK IS FOR NO-DOZ.
- THE SECOND COMMERCIAL BREAK IS FOR KENT CIGARETTES.

- The third commercial break is for Sinclair Dino gasoline.
- Music supervision is by Ether Huber .
- Walter Otto does the sound patterns.
- Technical supervision by Fred Turner.
- Art Hannes is the announcer.

Producer: Fred Hendrickson   **Writers:** Jack Johnstone
Cast: Grace Matthews, Mercer McLeod, Frank Milano, Walter Kinsella, Vivian Smolen, Robert Dryden, Joseph Boland, Barbara Wipple, Larry Robinson

◆ ❖ ◆

Show: The No Matter Matter
Show Date: 9/16/1962
Company: Eastern Liability and Trust
Agent: Raymond Tilotton
Exp. Acct: $0.00

Synopsis: Raymond Tilotton calls Johnny around 11 PM and wants Johnny to come to his apartment immediately. There is no matter to investigate, but he has to see Johnny immediately and hangs up.

Johnny does not know Tilotton, but Eastern Liability was an old and generous client, so Johnny dresses and drives to the Kearnsley Arms Apartments in Hartford, Connecticut. At the end of a dingy hallway Johnny rings at 4-A but gets no answer. Johnny opens the door to find a dead girl sitting by a window with an ugly hole in her blouse. Johnny goes to the bedroom to use the phone and a man tells Johnny he should not have come and slugs Johnny. Around dawn Johnny wakes up and calls the police and faints. Johnny wakes up again and washes his face when the police arrive. Johnny tells the officer there has been a murder and points to the dead girl, but she is gone. Johnny explains what happened and the officer asks what really happened, as there is no evidence of a woman ever being there. The officer asks about the absence of cordite smell and asks Johnny what is really going on. Johnny talks to the building super who tells him that Tilotton rents apartment 4-A. Johnny drives to a drugstore and then to the offices of Tilotton. Johnny tells Tilotton who he is, but Tilotton denies calling Johnny; he was in New Haven last night visiting his mother on her birthday. Johnny tells him something is very wrong. Johnny is sure that Tilotton's voice was the one on the phone and in the apartment. Johnny takes a train to New Haven, Connecticut and cabs to the home of Tilotton's mother. Mrs. Tilotton invites Johnny in and tells him it was nice to have one of her sons there for her 87th birthday. Raymond is in insurance, and is doing very well. She tells Johnny that he stayed until after supper, but Johnny notes that would still allow time for him to get back to Hartford and call him.

As Johnny hails a cab, Johnny sees a car drive up, and the driver is a dead ringer for the dead girl in the apartment, except she is a blond. She tells Johnny that she is Clara, an old friend of the family. When Johnny tells her who he is, she is glad to meet him, as she has something very important to talk to Johnny about. She suggests that they go to Danny's, and talk over a drink. In the very dark bar there is one lone customer and no bartender. Johnny asks how Clara just happed to show up when he was leaving, but Clara does not know what Johnny is talking about. Johnny asks about the blouse with the phony bullet hole, but Clara is confused. Johnny tells her that her hair is probably a wig, and she pulls a .25 automatic on Johnny. Clara calls for Tilly, and the man at the bar comes over and slugs Johnny. When Johnny wakes up a policeman is slapping him. He had gone through Johnny's pockets and knows who he is. He had heard a shot from across the street and came over, because Danny's is supposed to be closed. He was suspected to be partners with that guy Tilotton. Tilly, the guy they will nab for pushing drugs around here. Johnny leaves and goes back to Hartford. Johnny goes back to the apartment and Tilotton is there. He is glad to see Johnny because of the things Johnny had said earlier, and because of a call from the building super saying that the police had been there. Johnny tells him about visiting his mother and Tilotton tells Johnny that he had visited someone else that evening and had spent the night in a hotel. Johnny tells Tilotton he came back to Hartford and set up the phony murder scene with the brunette who is mixed up in the narcotics racket with him. Johnny tells him about the trip to New Haven. Tilotton can only repeat the name Warren, his twin brother called "Tilly." Johnny mentions that Tilotton's mother had told him that Warren was dead, but Ray tells Johnny that he had gone to see Warren once more to plead with him to straighten his life out. He tells Johnny that to his mother, Warren is dead. That way she can reject him the way her religion, her beliefs and her heart tells her she must reject him. Ray has tried to help him, but Warren is mad about the money their mother will leave to him and not to Warren. Ray swears that what he has said is true, but Johnny is confused about what has happened. Ray tells Johnny that the act was a plot to make it look like Ray had killed the girl so that his mother would cut him off. Then Warren would be happy, because he had told Ray that if he were out of the will, Ray would be too. He would get Ray involved into a scandal somehow. Johnny realizes that he was called so that the police would not be there and they could work out their plot. Warren comes in to Ray's office with Clara and tells them Johnny is right. Ray tries to reason with Warren, but Warren tells them that they have the guns, including Johnny's gun they got in New Haven. Warren tells Johnny that he will kill Ray with Johnny's gun and Johnny with Clara's gun, but only Johnny and Ray's prints will be on the guns. Clara gets anxious for Warren to shoot and Johnny rushes her. Warren turns and shoots Clara and Johnny then slugs Warren. Well, this time she really is dead. Ray tells Johnny he took an awful chance rushing Clara, and Johnny tells him "I have never seen a girl who was fast on the trigger, and I hope I never do."

"You know something else? The part I am really grateful about is that one more dope peddler is out of business. And Warren is, you can be sure of that. Expense account total, $11.45, so forget it."

NOTES:
- THE ONLY COMMERCIAL IS FOR SINCLAIR DINO GASOLINE.
- ETHEL HUBER DOES THE MUSIC.
- SOUND PATTERNS BE WALTER OTTO
- MIKE SCHOSKIS DOES THE TECHNICAL SUPERVISION.
- ART HANNES IS THE ANNOUNCER.

Producer: Fred Hendrickson **Writers:** Jack Johnstone
Cast: Richard Keith, Guy Repp, Arthur Kohl, Ethel Everett, Evelyn Juster, Bill Lipton, Constance Simons

◆ ❖ ◆

SHOW: THE DEADLY CRYSTAL MATTER
SHOW DATE: 9/23/1962
COMPANY: WORLD MUTUAL INSURANCE COMPANY
AGENT: LES WALTERS
EXP. ACCT: $100.00

SYNOPSIS: Les Walters calls and he is ready to blow a gasket. Les has $300,000 in troubles and will pick Johnny up at his apartment. Les tells him only to think about his commission on 300 Gs.

Johnny is picked up and taken to the airport to go to New York. Les has just come back from Bronxville, New York, where Mrs. Gurney Dahlrimple Weatherwell lives at 1263 Birchbrook Road. Today is the servant's day off, and she wears $300,000 in jewels at all times to remind herself of when she was poor. She only takes the jewels off when she takes a bath, and she took a bath two weeks ago today. She left the jewels on a dressing table and they were gone when she was finished. The police were not called and Les only knows what he has told Johnny. She wants Johnny, and only Johnny to handle the case. As Johnny is given a list of the items, Les almost hits a car with a good-looking girl in it. The most valuable piece is a 23 carat ruby pendant. Johnny flies to New York, and sitting next to him the girl Les almost hit. She is Lynn Peters and not friendly. Johnny drives to Bronxville where Mrs. Weatherwell tells Johnny that her jewels were taken while she was "taking her tub." There was no sign of forced entry, and the servants are above suspicion. The doorbell rings, and Lynn gives Johnny a package from Charley. The package contains the jewels. Johnny helps close the latch as Mrs. Weatherwell puts on the ruby when he would rather follow Lynn. Johnny is told the case is closed and the door is shut on his back. Johnny is sure that something fishy is going on and that Mrs. Weatherwell will give him no more information. So there is only the girl to go on.

Johnny drives into town to see Randy Singer, who does not recognize the name. Johnny looks at the mug books for ten hours and fifteen minutes. Suddenly Johnny finds the right picture, with the name Ruth Balachay. Randy knows Ruth as "The Quick Dip," a former pickpocket who is clean now. Johnny gets the address and cabs to 2120 W 94th. Ruth opens the door and recognizes

Johnny and slams the door in his face. Johnny cases the apartment for three days and finally calls Les to ask who the insurance beneficiary is. The answer is Charles Weatherwell, a stepson who lives in New York and will get the insurance immediately upon Mrs. Weatherwell's death, half a million's worth. Les tells Johnny that as soon as she dies, Charles will be pounding on his door demanding the money. Mrs. Weatherwell hates Charles but he is her only heir. Les also tells Johnny that Mrs. Weatherwell is ready to die. The doctor is there and he cannot figure what is causing her anemia. Johnny goes to the apartment and asks for Charlie, who comes out with a gun and a hypo. Lynn rolls up Johnny's sleeve so that Charlie can give him a shot that will put him out for about five days. He did not study chemistry for nothing. Johnny gets the shot in his muscles and Charlie tells Lynn that by the time Johnny wakes up, they will have the money and the ruby and be in Europe.

Johnny remembers that the best action sometimes is to play possum. Johnny sterilizes his pocketknife with a match and makes an X shaped cut over the needle mark and squeezes for dear life. Johnny is giddy, but does not pass out. Johnny gets a drink at a bar and has a doctor work on his arm. Johnny drives back to Bronxville and is met at the door by Dr. Harmon Briarly. Johnny asks if Mrs. Weatherwell is wearing the ruby pendant. Johnny is sure that the ruby has been switched with something else. On her chest is a pinkish mark that causes the doctors to treat Mrs. Weatherwell for one of the most a fiendish poisons ever known. Thirty-six hours later doctors Briarly, Radford and Wilson are sure Mrs. Weatherwell will recover. The doctors ask Johnny why he suspected the poison potassium peradichromate, which caused the red corpuscles deteriorate. Johnny tells them that earlier that year a young student had made some jewelry from various crystals made in the lab. There was a furor in the press because some of the crystals that looked like jewels were actually poisons that would bring about the exact symptoms of Mrs. Weatherwell. Johnny tells them that when he said he had the ruby, he must have substituted a deadly crystal for the real jewel. When the doctors ask if Johnny knows the name of the man, he tells them "I certainly do." Mrs. Weatherwell does recover and, after calling Les, Johnny goes home. The next day Les tells Johnny that the article about Mrs. Weatherwell dying was published, and a retraction will be printed the next day. So Johnny is waiting for Charlie to arrive. The intercom buzzes, and Charlie is there. Charlie comes in and is somewhat speechless when he sees Johnny. Charlie asks how Johnny got there, and Les tells Charlie that he had a call from his stepmother, and can return it if he wishes. When Charlie tells Les that she is dead, Les mentions the erroneous article in the paper. Charlie tells them that it is true, it has to be, and Johnny asks if it is true because he poisoned her. He tells them that it is a trick and pulls a gun and fires. Johnny slugs Charlie and takes his gun.

"Lynn Peters, nee Ruth Balachay had made the mistake of waiting for Charlie outside in a car. So, she'll have her day in court too. And the original ruby, the real one, we found it sewed into the lining of Charlie's coat."

NOTES:

- MANDEL KRAMER URGES EVERY ONE TO LISTEN TO NEXT WEEK'S PROGRAM. YOU MAY BE SORRY IF YOU MISS IT. I CALL IT "THE CASE OF THE TIP-OFF MATTER."
- NEXT WEEK'S PROGRAM IS THE LAST IN THE SERIES, AND ALONG WITH SUSPENSE WHICH WOULD END THE SAME DAY, THE END OF RADIO DRAMA.
- THE ONLY COMMERCIAL IS FOR SINCLAIR DINO GASOLINE.
- ETHEL HUBER DOES THE MUSIC.
- SOUND PATTERNS BE WALTER OTTO
- TECHNICAL SUPERVISION IS BY LARRY SOLOW.
- ART HANNES IS THE ANNOUNCER.

Producer: Fred Hendrickson   **Writers:** Jack Johnstone
Cast: Carl Frank, Olive Deering, Elsbeth Eric, Sam Gray, Casey Allen, Dean Carlson, Renee Santoni

◆　❖　◆

SHOW: THE TIP-OFF MATTER
SHOW DATE: 9/30/1962
COMPANY: NORTHEAST INDEMNITY ASSOCIATION
AGENT: GEORGE HARDY
EXP. ACCT: $349.40

SYNOPSIS: George Hardy calls Johnny and asks him to write down "130-07-05-83." "Got it! So?" Johnny is told that he wants to see you at the state prison. If it is who George thinks it is, Johnny will be going to the commission over $100,000.

Johnny buys gas for his car and drives to the state prison in Weathersfield, Connecticut where the father of our country once planned the historic battle of Yorktown. In other words, George Washington slept there. Johnny is taken to the hospital ward to see a thirty-year old man who looks like he was 200. The man is Turner McGackie, up for safe cracking. Mac tells Johnny that he is supposed to get out, but instead he is lying there dying. He sent for Johnny to stop a killing. Mac tells Johnny that the money from his last job was never recovered. Mac tells Johnny that he is the only one Mac respects. He hated Johnny's guts until the warden told him what Johnny had done for his kid brother Tommy, getting him into a foster home and getting him a good education. Johnny tells Mac that his brother just graduated from high school with honors. Mac is thankful that Johnny led his brother to believe that he was killed, so he would have nothing to live down. Mac tells Johnny to listen as he explains where the money from the robbery is. Mac tells Johnny about Joe Perelli, an old friend who is posing as a fisherman, and living in Mac's old cottage where there is a safe in the basement to which Joe knows only half the combination. The other half was given to Danny Russelloff who is in the pen with Mac. Mac would not have given Danny the combination if he had known what Johnny had done for

Tommy. Mac is sure that Danny will kill Joe. Mac agrees to give Johnny the combination so that he can have the money and save Joe's life. Mac also tells Johnny that Danny is being released today, so Johnny has to act fast. As Mac tries to give the combination to Johnny, he dies. The warden tells Johnny that Danny has been released and good riddance. Johnny rents charter plane and flies south and lands on a beach near Cutchaw where Johnny walks to a gas station and rents a car. Johnny gets directions to Joe's place and is told that if no one answers to go in, as Joe is probably drunk. Johnny gets to Joe Pirelli's place and a drunken voice tells him to come in, and Johnny sees that Joe has a gun and takes a shot at Johnny. Johnny takes the gun from him and Joe calls Johnny "Danny," thinking he is Russelloff. Johnny tells Joe that he came to get the money in the safe. Joe tells Johnny that the money belongs to Mac, and Johnny tells him that Mac is dead. Joe realizes that Johnny is an insurance dick. Johnny tells him he is there to get the money and save his life. He promised Mac to save Joe's life, and he tells Joe that Danny has the other half of the combination. Johnny is sure that Danny would take the money and kill Joe. Johnny tells Joe that if he does not want Johnny's help Johnny will send him to prison if Danny does not kill him. Johnny tells Joe he is moving in to wait for Danny. Johnny goes to the gas station to wait. Johnny gives the gas station attendant $100 to use his car and make some calls. Johnny calls George and tells him what is going on. George tells Johnny that maybe Danny is playing smart and reporting to his parole officer. Johnny is sure that Danny will act quickly. Johnny asks George to get Pete Larkin, a detective to watch for Danny. Johnny will check back with George each day. Johnny goes back and verifies that the safe is still there. Joe tells Johnny his part of the combination. Johnny hears a car approaching and turns off the lights. Joe tells Johnny that it is Danny and gets anxious, so Johnny slugs him. Johnny waits for the man to come to the house and Johnny swings open the door to find Jimmy, the gas station attendant. He gives Johnny the key to the trunk and tells him that he thinks Johnny is "the most." Johnny tells Jimmy that if any one knew that Johnny Dollar was there, Johnny Dollar might end up real dead. Understand? Jimmy understands and leaves. Johnny waits for three days and calls George every day only to learn that Danny is sitting tight in Hartford. On the fourth day George tells Johnny that Danny got away from Pete Larkin and they do not know where he is. Jimmy tells Johnny that a car went down the road and came back. Johnny gives him a sawbuck and goes back to Joe's, but changes his mind and goes down a side road to an old fishing camp where he sees Danny's car and footprints leading to Joe's. Johnny crawls to Joe's place and hears nothing. Johnny looks in to see Mike Perelli dead on the floor. So Danny will have to blow the safe. As soon as the safe blows, Johnny rushes in and tells Danny to freeze. Danny waves a bottle of nitro at Johnny and throws it.

"I had heard of such things, but never thought them possible. But so help me, when I picked my self up on the edge of the wreckage of that cottage most of my clothes were blown completely off. And yet by some miracle I suffered no more than a couple of bruises and a slight headache. As for Danny, well lets not go into that. He's paid for all his crimes. Expense account total $349.40. And don't forget my commission, in spite of the fact that a lot of bits and pieces of the money had to be pasted back together."

NOTES:
- THE FINAL COMMERCIAL IS FOR SINCLAIR DINO GASOLINE.
- THE MUSIC SUPERVISION IF BY ETHEL HUBER.
- SOUND PATTERNS BY WALTER OTTO.
- HALF WAY THROUGH THE PROGRAM, JOE PERELLI BECOMES MIKE PERELLI.
- THE CAST LISTINGS FOR THIS PROGRAM HAVE BEEN SLICED ONTO THE END OF MOST COPIES OF "THE WINDSOME WIDOW MATTER."

Producer: Fred Hendrickson   **Writers:** Jack Johnstone
Cast: Jackson Beck, Joseph Julian, Jack Grimes, Bob Maxwell, Peter Fernandez

With the ending of this program, the Golden Age of Radio ended, and radio changed forever.

Section 7: Audition Programs

The catalog of Yours Truly Johnny Dollar contains six audition programs. The program chosen changed for each of the actors, although the title was the same for several.

The audition actors include two regular Johnny Dollars (John Lund and Charles Russell) as well as two major stars (Gerald Mohr and Dick Powell) that auditioned for the part and opted to accept other shows.

There is an audition by Bob Bailey, but I am unable to verify that the program I have of "The Ellen Dear Matter" is the actual audition or the broadcast program, but it is included here to complete the catalog.

The following are the audition programs for Yours Truly, Johnny Dollar.

DICK POWELL

SHOW:	MILFORD BROOKS III
SHOW DATE:	12/7/1948
COMPANY:	EAST COAST UNDERWRITERS
AGENT:	AUSTIN FARNSWORTH
EXP. ACCT:	$1,182.23

SYNOPSIS: Mr. Brooks is trying to jump out of the window at the insurance company. He wants to kill himself (there is no suicide clause.) to get the 2 Million from the policy because he cannot get a $500,000 loan to give to Harold Hatcher—a known gangster. To keep Perry out of trouble, Johnny goes to New York City with Perry to visit "Butter"—a girlfriend. While Johnny "entertains" Butter, Perry disappears. After an hour-long search, Johnny calls Lt. Fisher at missing persons and reports Perry missing. The police report finding Perry's topcoat and ID on the 125th street ferry, and a matchbook with "HH" on it. At Hatcher's club, bar girl Genelle points Johnny to Harold's office. After a short talk, the police show up. Genelle spills the beans about a personal note Hatcher has for Perry's debt to him. The personal note is found in one of Hatcher's suits. Then Johnny follows Genelle to a garage apartment where Perry is. Then Hatcher shows up. It seems Genelle was putting Perry up to faking the suicide and framing Hatcher and running away with her. After a fight and the police, Perry is in the hospital and makes a full statement of insurance fraud.

NOTES:

- AUDITION ONLY; POWELL NEVER DID THE SERIES.
- POWELL NOTES, "HE CAN PAD AN EXPENSE ACCOUNT WITH THE BEST OF THEM."
- HIS SUIT SIZE IS 42, SHIRT SIZE IS 15 1/2 X 33 AND A HAT SIZE OF 7 3/8—EXCEPT AFTER A CASE WHEN IT IS 7 1/2.
- $1 TIPS TO TAXI AND SHOESHINE.
- PERRY HAS A CREW HAIR CUT.
- $18 FOR BRANDY TO CALM PERRY DOWN.
- PERRY GIVES THREE CHEERS FOR DEAR OLD ELI AS THEY DRIVE PAST YALE.
- JOHNNY TELLS BUTTER HE FOUND PERRY IN A BOX OF CRACKER JACKS—DRESSED IN A BROOKS BROTHERS SUIT.
- BOURBON AND SODA IS THE DRINK AT BUTTER'S.
- JOHNNY STARTS TO SING "SLOW BOAT TO CHINA."
- POWELL STAMMERS SEVERAL TIMES, ONCE OVER "EAST COAST."
- EXPENSE ACCOUNT INCLUDES A $318 BRACELET FOR BUTTER.
- NEXT WEEK "SPECIAL INVESTIGATION SINGAPORE!"

Producer: **Writers:**
Cast: William Conrad

◆   ❖   ◆

CHARLES RUSSELL

SHOW: THE ROBERT PERRY CASE
SHOW DATE: 1/14/1949
COMPANY: AMERICAN CONTINENTAL LIFE INSURANCE
AGENT:
EXP. ACCT: $1,263.00

SYNOPSIS: A bomb blast welcomes Johnny to Mr. Perry's New York City import office exactly at 9:00 AM when Susan the receptionist buzzes him in. Mr. Perry had thought his life was in danger. His next appointment was to be with his partner Van Brooten, who would pick up a check dissolving the partnership. Christine the wife was due later to finalize the upcoming divorce.

Van Brooten picks up the check after the explosion. A trip to see the wife ends up with a boy friend, Al Donovan in the apartment. Everyone seems to have been at the Club Caprice the previous night—everyone except Al Donovan. After a row with Christine, Al and Christine leave the apartment and Johnny on the floor.

After a car ride with the wife, Al heads for a police precinct where he makes a full confession to bombing the office.

A search of Perry's office shows the Van Brooten was bald and had been getting toupees from Perry for years; Al was Perry's former bodyguard and Susan the receptionist was a former ordinance technician.

A visit to Susan's apartment ends up in her being shot through the door. Susan knows the man in the office was a phony and she was shot because she was trying to blackmail him.

Johnny goes looking for the phony Van Brooten in his hotel and gets him out of the room with a phony fire drill. ($1000 fine, by the way) The real Van Brooten was drugged in the next room. The phony Van Brooten had drugged Perry and set up the bomb to get the money. It seems the phony Van Brooten had black hair—Perry was sending his partner red wigs!

NOTES:
- (AUDITION) SEE PROGRAM OF 3/4/49

Producer:	**Richard Sanville**	**Writers:**	**Paul Dudley, Gil Doud**
Cast:	**Unknown**		

GERALD MOHR

SHOW:	THE TRANS-PACIFIC MATTER PART 1
SHOW DATE:	8/29/1955
COMPANY:	CORINTHIAN LIABILITY & RISK
AGENT:	AL HARPER
EXP. ACCT:	$0.00

SYNOPSIS: Al Harper at Corinthian has a job for Johnny, but he won't like it. However the commission will be big. The policy is for $200,000 and Johnny will have to travel to Hong Kong, and Johnny is not scared yet. The policyholders are people they have had trouble with before. "Remember the Trans-Pacific Import Export outfit?" "Yeah, I sent flowers to the widow." Johnny is scared, but he will take a crack at it.

Johnny flies to Hong Kong and finds Honk Kong a city with simplicity with shortages in everything. The city is full of immigrants as Johnny makes his way to the American Consulate. A secretary tells Johnny that life is very difficult in Hong Kong, and asks if life is like this in America. Mr. Grover meets with Johnny, who tells him why he is here. Grover remembers the company run by Will Meadows that was burned to the ground last month. Grover has met Meadows and realizes Johnny is there because he suspects fraud. Johnny tells him of the similar fire in Shanghai where Trans-Pacific made a lot of money. Johnny asks for introductions to the fire department and police and Grover tells him that he will do what he can. Grover comments on the elections and asks for his hotel. Johnny tells him he does not have a room, and Grover tells him to talk to Miss

Vedras his secretary as her father runs a hotel and might have a room. Grover asks about the case in Shanghai, and Johnny tells him that the investigator was killed before he could build a case. The death was blamed on war conditions. Miss Vedras arranges for a room and Johnny's room looks out over an alley with few amenities. That night Johnny is visited by Miss Vedras who tells Johnny that Mr. Harrison of the fire control office will see him the next day. Vedras asks why Johnny is here and tells Johnny he has been followed. Johnny looks out and spots the man in the shadows, and Vedras tells him that she recognizes the man. Johnny asks her about the music, which is a love song. She knows many Americans and wants to marry one that will take her from China, as there is no good here. She thinks that Americans are very impatient people, yet they live better than the Chinese do. Johnny is disturbed by the pleading in Vedras' eyes, the sounds and smells of the restless crowed city, and the watcher on the street. Johnny is concerned because everyone is a potential assassin. Next morning a different man follows Johnny to the office of Mr. Harrison, who was not able to meet with Johnny. Johnny goes to visit William Meadows and tells him who he is. Meadows asks them what is wrong with the insurance company, and Johnny tells him that this case is too similar to the previous one, and Meadows tells Johnny that careless people die every day in Hong Kong. Johnny tells him he came to get a reaction, and Meadows is on the defensive and having him followed, so Meadows must have a reason and is afraid of Johnny. Meadows tells Johnny that Corinthian means nothing, and the company is going to pay. Johnny has a platform to build a suspicion on and a veiled threat about the other agent who had been killed. Johnny is sure that Meadows is telling Johnny that this is his town, and people who get in his way can get hurt. A real nice situation. Johnny goes back to his hotel and watches the window that night.

"Tomorrow night, a complicated lesson on how to get shot at by your best friend and like it."

NOTES:
- THIS AUDITION USED THE MUSIC USED IN THE BOB BAILEY SERIES.
- GEORGE WALSH IS THE ANNOUNCER.

SHOW:	THE TRANS-PACIFIC MATTER PART 2
SHOW DATE:	8/29/1955
COMPANY:	AGENT:
EXP. ACCT:	$4,515.00

SYNOPSIS: Superintendent Clyde calls, and Johnny tells him he had a bird in his room that is ready to sing. He just scalped the two-bit thug William meadows had on him and Meadows is next. Clyde warns Johnny that he will be arrested if he does anything illegal. Johnny tells Clyde to send a wagon for the thug, as he has a knife and a gun and tried to kill Johnny. Clyde will send some one over.

After five days Johnny reports additional expenses. Johnny is working over the thug in his room when Inspector Clyde arrives and takes his gun. Clyde knows the man as Pen Lu. Johnny tells Clyde that he got his information about Meadows by duress and gets very angry at Clydes' inaction. Clyde tells Johnny that his evidence against Meadow is only circumstantial. Clyde tells Johnny that he has checked on Johnny and discovered that Johnny has an enviable reputation in the states, but the case is complex and must be investigated cautiously. He will question the man and tell Johnny what he learns. Clyde warns Johnny not to do anything rash or he will be arrested. Johnny rents a 1935 Packard and has difficulty driving in the crowded streets, but the horn worked beautifully. Johnny drives to Meadow's house and the houseboy tells Johnny that Meadows is not there and that he will be back next week. Johnny forces the houseboy to tell Johnny that Meadows is in Kowloon, but after a little more convincing, Johnny is told that Meadows is in Repulse Bay, on the other side of the island where he has a cottage. The houseboy dials the number and Johnny hears Meadow's voice. Johnny gets to the cottage as the police arrive. Clyde tells Johnny that they are there because the houseboy had called and told them what Johnny had done to him. Clyde tells Johnny that he is hot headed and impetuous, but he was right about Pen Lu who admitted he had been hired by Meadows to kill Johnny. His gun was checked and found to be the one that killed Luisa Vedras but Clyde does not know why Meadows had Vedras killed. Johnny tells him that Pen Lu thought that Vedras was Johnny. He tells Clyde that he had gotten to know Vedras and that this is a bad job for his nerves. Johnny tells him that she came there each night until she was killed waiting for Johnny to come back. Clyde asks if Johnny is there to get Meadows for the company or for Luisa, and Johnny tells him that Luisa was a lovely girl. Clyde tells Johnny to make his play. Johnny walks to the cottage and tells Meadows that he knows that he is still alive and that he had killed the girl. Johnny wants him to make a statement and tells him he had gotten the statement from the punk sent to kill him. Johnny is invited in and shot at. Johnny returns fire and Meadows is shot and falls down the stairs. Meadows tells Johnny that he knew he would not take him. Johnny tells him he is hit in the arm, and Meadows says it should have been his stomach. Meadows refuses to make a statement and dies. The police arrive and tell Johnny to have his arm looked at.

"Expense account item 16, $43 even for medical fees and hospital charges. I don't suppose it could be called hewing to the niceties of jurisprudence since Meadows was dead and he refused before dying to speak or write his confession. But there were two police carloads of expert witnesses who took the fact that he had opened fire as acceptable admission of guilt. The same thing cleared me legally on the grounds of self-defense. I had hoped it would clear my mind, but it hasn't. Luisa Vedras is still there. I guess she always will be."

"Monday night, the story of a ship, the Marley K. Destination: Davey Jones locker. Join us won't you?"

NOTES:
* AUDITION PROGRAM

- **GEORGE WALSH IS THE ANNOUNCER.**

Producer: Jack Johnstone   **Writers:**   E. Jack Neuman, Gil Doud

Cast: Lillian Buyeff, Will Wright, Tony Barrett, Harry Bartell, Ben Wright

◆ ❖ ◆

JOHN LUND

SHOW: THE TRANS-PACIFIC MATTER PART A
SHOW DATE: 11/28/1952
COMPANY: CORINTHIAN LIABILITY & RISK
AGENT: AL HARPER
EXP. ACCT:

SYNOPSIS: Al Harper at Corinthian has a job for Johnny, but he won't like it. However the commission will be big. The policy is for $200,000 and Johnny will have to travel to Hong Kong, and Johnny is not scared yet. The policyholders are people they have had trouble with before. "Remember the Trans-Pacific Import Export outfit?" "Yeah, I sent flowers to the widow." This is their Hong Kong outfit. Johnny is scared, but he will take a crack at it.

Johnny finds Honk Kong a city of difficulties with shortage in everything. The city is full of immigrants as Johnny makes his way to the American Consulate. A secretary tells Johnny that life is very difficult in Hong Kong, and asks if life is like this in America. Mr. Grover meets with Johnny, who tells him why he is here. Grover remembers the company run by Will Meadows that was burned to the ground last month. Grover has met Meadows and realizes Johnny is there because he suspects fraud. Johnny tells him of the similar fire in Shanghai where Trans-Pacific made a lot of money. Johnny asks for introductions to the fire department and police and Grover tells him that he will do what he can. Grover comments on the elections and asks for his hotel. Johnny tells him he does not have a room, and Grover tells him to talk to Miss Vedras his secretary as her father runs a hotel and might have a room. Grover asks about the case in Shanghai, and Johnny tells him that the investigator was killed before he could build a case. The death was blamed on war conditions. Miss Vedras arranges for a room and Johnny's room looks out over an alley with few amenities. That night Johnny is visited by Miss Vedras who tells Johnny that Mr. Harrison of the fire control office will see him the next day. Vedras asks why Johnny is here and tells him he has been followed. Johnny looks out and spots the man in the shadows, and Vedras tells him that she recognizes the man. Johnny asks her about the music, which is a love song. She knows many Americans and wants to marry one who will take her from China, as there is no good here. She thinks that Americans are very impatient people, yet they live better than the Chinese do. Johnny is disturbed by the pleading in Vedras' eyes, the sounds and smells of the restless crowed city, and the watcher on the street. Johnny is concerned because everyone is a potential assassin. Next morning a different man follows Johnny to the office of Mr. Harrison, who was not able to meet with Johnny. Johnny goes to visit William Meadows and tells him who he is. Meadows asks them what is wrong with the insurance company, and Johnny tells him that this case is too similar to the previous one, and Meadows tells Johnny that careless people die every day in Hong Kong. Johnny tells him he came to get a reaction, and Meadows is on the defensive and having him followed, so Meadows must have a reason and is afraid of Johnny. Meadows tells Johnny that Corinthian means nothing, and the company is going to pay. Johnny has a platform to build a suspicion on and a veiled threat about the other agent who had been killed. Johnny is sure that Meadows is telling Johnny that this is his town, and people who get in his way can get hurt. A real nice situation. Johnny goes back to his hotel and watches the window that night.

NOTES:
- JOHN LUND CAN BE SEEN IN THE PARAMOUNT PICTURE "JUST ACROSS THE STREET."
- DAN CUBBERLY IS THE ANNOUNCER.

Producer: Jaime del Valle   **Writers:** E. Jack Neuman
Cast: Unknown

SHOW:	THE TRANS-PACIFIC MATTER PART B
SHOW DATE:	11/24/1952
COMPANY:	CORINTHIAN LIABILITY & RISK
AGENT:	AL HARPER
EXP. ACCT:	$4,515.00

SYNOPSIS: Grover at the consulate calls and tells him that Superintendent Clyde of the Police is upset at Johnny's attitude and Grover told him he had talked to Johnny and told him to be careful. Johnny tells him that he had been cautious and has just scalped the thug Meadows had following him. Johnny is going after Meadows next and tells Grover that the claim is no good, Miss Vedras was killed in his room for no reason. Johnny agrees to come over and talk.

After five days Johnny rents a 1935 Packard and has difficulty driving in the crowded streets, but the horn worked wonderfully. In Grover's office Johnny tells him that he had forced the man with the gun to tell him that Meadows had hired him. Grover asks if his actions are for the insurance company or for Miss Vedras. Johnny tells him he came to know Miss Vedras very well, and she was there in his room and he talked to her. She was there each night until she was killed waiting for Johnny to come back. Johnny complains that he cannot get the police to do anything, and Johnny tells him he has to go after Meadows. Johnny drives to Meadow's house and the houseboy tells Johnny that Meadows is not there and that he will be back next week. Johnny forces the house boy to tell Johnny that Meadows is in Kowloon, but after a little convincing, Johnny is told that

Meadows is in Repulse Bay, on the other side of the island where he has a cottage. The houseboy dials the number and Johnny hears Meadow's voice. Johnny calls the police superintendent and tells him that Meadows is going to confess, and tells him to have his men there in an hour. Johnny gets to the cottage and the police arrive. Clyde tells Johnny that they are there to make sure that nothing unnecessary happens and will arrest Johnny if he does anything illegal, as his case is mostly circumstantial. Clyde is very cautious and tells Johnny to make his play. Clyde tells Johnny that he has checked on Johnny, and he has a very good reputation in the states. Johnny walks to the cottage and tells Meadows that he knows that he is still alive and that he had killed the girl. Johnny wants him to make a statement and tells him he had gotten the statement from the punk. Johnny is invited in and shot at. Johnny returns fire and Meadows is shot and falls down the stairs. Meadows tells Johnny that he hit him in the arm but it should have been his stomach. Meadows refuses to make a statement and dies. The police arrive and tell Johnny to have his arm looked at.

"Expense account item 15, $43 even for medical fees and hospital charges. I don't suppose it could be called hewing to the niceties of jurisprudence since Meadows was dead and he refused before dying to speak or write his confession. But there were two police carloads of expert witnesses who took the fact that he had opened fire as acceptable admission of guilt for the crimes accused. The same thing cleared me legally on the grounds of self-defense. I'd hoped it would clear my minds, but it hasn't. Luisa Vedras is still there. I guess she always will be. Nothing good came out of this assignment except saving your company some money it didn't know it had."

NOTES:
- **AUDITION SHOW**

Producer:	Jaime del Valle	**Writers:**	E. Jack Newman
Cast:	Unknown		

BOB BAILEY

SHOW:	THE ELLEN DEAR MATTER
SHOW DATE:	1/6/1957
COMPANY:	WESTERN MARITIME & PROPERTY
AGENT:	ARTHUR ARTHUR
EXP. ACCT:	$453.95

SYNOPSIS: Pat McCracken calls about the sleek lovely Ellen Dear. She is loaded with $325,000 in jewels. Johnny is interested until he finds out that it is a boat. Pat wants Johnny to find out what is going on.

Johnny cabs to Pat's office and Pat is not smiling. Johnny is to bill Western Maritime and Property. Pat tells Johnny about Randolph Berman, whom everyone thinks is a crook, but seems to handle some of the finest jewels in the world. He is involved with the Bettenhouse collection out of Hungary. A man in Mexico sold the collection to Berman. The boat is a 72 ft. motor cruiser and was sailing in the pacific. When he heard of the jewels he bought them. He had Western Maritime insure the jewels after they had them appraised by a Jacque Jampiere in Guadalajara. So far there is no problem, but there have been incidents in the past, but he got out of them. Western is worried and Johnny is to watch the jewels until they get to the states. The boat is in Mazatlan undergoing some engine work.

Johnny flies to Los Angeles, California where he is paged in the airport. Johnny goes to the Pan Am desk and meets Arthur Arthur, the local Western Maritime agent, and Jacque Jampiere who had appraised the Bettenhouse collection in Mexico. Jampiere has bad news. He had tried to buy pieces of the collection, and knows all of the stones. In Mexico he watched a friend, Garcia Hernandez, work on a mount for a stone from the Bettenhouse collection. He is sure of the identity of the stone. Arthur thinks that maybe the jewels are not on the boat. Berman is now on his way to Los Angeles, but he is not sure where he will dock. Johnny and Arthur drive to the Berman office and Johnny notices a vault in the wall of the office. Johnny meets Mr. Carrillo and he gives Arthur a revision to the policy to exclude the Calabar Diamond, which has been sold. Carrillo tells Johnny that the boat is due in San Pedro tonight, and he arranges to go with Carrillo to meet the boat. The phone rings and Carrillo learns that the Ellen Dear has sunk in 600 feet of water.

Johnny cabs to Coast Guard headquarters and meets Capt Barney Thorson. Thorson tells Johnny that the passengers have been rescued and brought in to the Coast Guard. They had received a call and the boat was sinking when they got there. The engine was too big and broke loose and destroyed the boat. There was a big safe on board and the owner was crying like a baby over the loss. The only thing Berman saved was two hats, a fishing rod, some nylons and a hatbox. They are staying at the Beverly Wilshire hotel.

Johnny calls the police in Mazatlan to make sure the jewels were on board when they left. Johnny cabs back to Berman's office and they have not been there, but are due in soon, and Berman has asked for claim forms to be brought in. Johnny gets a wild idea about something that happened when the Andrea Doria sank—the passengers were brought in without going through customs. Johnny wonders if he could think of it, maybe Berman could too. Johnny calls Thorson who tells him that the Bermans did not go through customs. Johnny calls Arthur and tells him to get to Berman's office make sure that Berman does not bring in the jewels; and keep him there as long a possible. Johnny goes to the hotel and watches Berman leave, and then goes to his suite on the 9th floor. Vy Berman opens the door, and tells Johnny to leave, as Randy does not want anyone in. Johnny tells her that Hernandez sent him and she lets him in. Johnny tells her that Randy had sold Hernandez the wrong stone, and she tells Johnny that he gave Hernandez the diamond so he could make a legitimate change to the policy. Johnny tells her that he has to switch diamonds when Randy gets there. Johnny tells her about the other diamonds in the hatbox and she asks if he read about the Andrea Doria too. Vy starts to wise up and Johnny forces his way into the apartment to search it and threatens to call the police if she continues to scream. Vy tells Johnny the jewels are in the closet and Johnny gets them. There is a knock at the door and Berman tells Vy to open it. Johnny opens the door and tells Berman who he is and why he is there. Berman pulls a gun and threatens to kill Johnny and Vy, "that dizzy blonde." Vy runs out with a bottle and hits Berman as he tries to shoot her.

By way of getting off as easily as possible, Vy sang like a canary and cleared up several other shady deals as well. By the time his prison sentence runs out, Berman will be too long dead to collect on the yacht.

NOTES:

- THE STAR OF CAPETOWN DIAMOND AND KAMANDU EMERALD ARE MENTIONED. THE STAR OF CAPETOWN WAS FEATURED IN A FIVE PART SERIES THE PREVIOUS YEAR.
- $245 WAS SPENT FOR A COUPLE OF DAYS OF RELAXATION IN THE CALIFORNIA SUN. NOW THAT IS PADDING THE EXPENSE ACCOUNT!
- THE ANDREA DORIA WAS AN ITALIAN OCEAN LINER BUILT IN GENOA AND LAUNCHED IN 1951. ON WEDNESDAY, JULY 25TH 1956 SHE COLLIDED WITH THE MV STOCKHOLM NEAR NANTUCKET, MASSACHUSETTS AT 11:10 PM ON A DARK AND FOGGY NIGHT. 46 PASSENGERS AND 5 CREWMEN WERE KILLED.

Producer: Jack Johnstone   Writers: Jack Johnstone
Cast: Virginia Gregg, Lawrence Dobkin, Howard McNear, Jay Novello, Jack Edwards, Barney Phillips, Raymond Burr

So, Who Was the Best Johnny Dollar?

Invariably, this question always seems to come up in any discussion of Yours Truly Johnny Dollar. And for the most part, the answer is pretty much decided.

Most serious discussions will always put Bob Bailey at the top of the "Best" category for the character, and rightly so. Bob was a veteran radio actor who was able to take a character that had grown dull and predictable, and infuse life into it. When Bob was angry, you knew he was angry. When his heart was ready to melt, you melted with him. Bob was the consummate actor playing a part that was, in a sense, written for him.

For the role of second place, most assign Mandel Kramer to that position. Mandel was an excellent radio voice, and was able to continue to bring life and credibility to the character. However, when I sit down to listen to Johnny Dollar, more often than not, I will listen to my favorite number two: Charles Russell.

Many will dismiss Charlie for the very reason that I enjoy listening to him. He was sarcastic, irreverent, droll, and somewhat lecherous. Hardly a sentence goes by without some sort of offhanded remark, some of which I feel are very witty. These qualities seem, for some Freudian reason perhaps, to appeal to me, and I enjoy them. Charlie was a good actor, and portrayed a character who was in his infancy. Everyone built his character portrayals on Charlie, knowingly or otherwise. Given that many of the writers who wrote for Charlie also wrote for other Johnny Dollars, the personality would have to come through.

The rest of the Johnny Dollars: Edmond O'Brien, John Lund, Robert Readick, while accomplished actors, all claim third place in the race for the best Johnny.

In reality though, for the programs to have continued to hold a place in the hearts of the old time radio audience some forty to fifty years after the actors walked up to the microphone and intoned "Johnny Dollar" to the sound of a ringing phone, they had to have some sort of staying power. There had to be some magic there.

So in the final analysis, maybe the best Johnny Dollar should be the one that you are listening to at the moment.

REPORTS

After reviewing over seven hundred Yours Truly Johnny Dollar programs, each in the form of an expense report, it would be a shame not to include a series of reports here.

EXPENSES BY ACTOR

Each Johnny Dollar program included the various expenses incurred during the investigation and ended with an expense account total. Each of the stories outlined in the above sections includes the total expenses, if available.

Because these expenses were incurred during a different century than the one in which this book was written, the totals may not necessarily make sense. So for each of the actors who portrayed Johnny Dollar, I have listed the total expenses obtained from the various programs. That total is then converted to current (2006) dollars using information available from the Federal Reserve Bank of Minneapolis web site.

When you look at the total expenses incurred, the numbers can be alarming. To consider that Bob Bailey expensed over $800,000 in six years gives new meaning to the term "incidentals" that was used so often to pad the expense account.

ACTOR	ACTUAL EXPENSES	EXPENSES ADJUSTED FOR INFLATION
BOB BAILEY TOTALS	$135,311.86	$963,852.20
BOB READICK TOTALS	$4,403.20	$29,759.13
CHARLES RUSSELL TOTALS	$40,500.68	$343,127.00
DICK POWELL TOTAL	$1,182.23	$9,894.43
EDMOND O'BRIEN TOTALS	$70,319.90	$570,509.32
GERALD MOHR TOTAL	$4,515.00	$33,980.43
JOHN LUND TOTALS	$42,650.39	$321,715.92
MANDEL KRAMER TOTALS	$16,345.42	$109,568.98
GRAND TOTALS	**$315,228.68**	**$2,382,407.40**

Employers & Agents

Over the run of the program, Johnny Dollar worked for a number of insurance companies, and a few individuals. The table below lists each of the employers and the cases assigned by them. Also included are the agents (if known) and the expenses for the cases.

BOB BAILEY	BB
MANDEL KRAMER	MK
JOHN LUND	JL
EDMOND O'BRIEN	EO
ROBERT READICK	RR
CHARLES RUSSELL	CR

ALL STATES INSURANCE COMPANY

THE BALTIMORE MATTER	DON FREED	JL	$294.60
	COMPANY EXPENSES		**$294.60**

ALLIANCE BONDING COMPANY

THE CALGARY MATTER		EO	$1,180.00
	COMPANY EXPENSES		**$1,180.00**

ALLIED ADJUSTMENT BUREAU

THE LANCER JEWELRY MATTER	PAT CORBETT	JL	$70.25
THE UNDERWOOD MATTER	RED EAGAN	JL	$491.50
THE ROCHESTER THEFT MATTER		JL	$155.42
	COMPANY EXPENSES		**$717.17**

ALLIED CASUALTY & INSURANCE COMPANY

THE MACORMACK MATTER	ED BARTH	BB	$265.91
	COMPANY EXPENSES		**$265.91**

AMALGAMATED LIFE ASSOCIATES

THE CRYSTAL LAKE MATTER	TOM WILKINS	BB	$423.00
THE WAYWARD GUN MATTER	ADOLPH DORFMAN	MK	$0.00
	COMPANY EXPENSES		**$423.00**

AMALGAMATED LIFE ASSOCIATION

THE JIMMY CARTER MATTER	WALDO BOTTOMLY	BB	$117.00

THE NEGLIGENT NEPHEW MATTER	LEONARD TILLSON	BB	$10.50
THE MORNING AFTER MATTER	TIMOTHY HANDLEY	RR	$0.00
THE PHILADELPHIA MISS MATTER	GEORGE CALDWELL	MK	$485.75
	COMPANY EXPENSES		**$613.25**

AMBASSADOR LIFE & CASUALTY INSURANCE COMPANY

BODYGUARD TO ANNE CONNELLY	FRANKLIN HALEY	CR	$845.30
	COMPANY EXPENSES		**$845.30**

AMERCON NORTHERN TRUST COMPANY

THE MATTER OF REASONABLE DOUBT	BEN GUARDLEY	BB	$596.25
	COMPANY EXPENSES		**$596.25**

AMERICAN CONTINENTAL INSURANCE COMPANY

THE DIAMOND PROTECTOR MATTER	ROBERT FERRY	CR	$1,142.89
	COMPANY EXPENSES		**$1,142.89**

AMERICAN CONTINENTAL LIFE INSURANCE

THE ROBERT PERRY CASE		CR	$1,263.00
THE ROBERT PERRY CASE	MR. GORDON	CR	$1,263.00
	COMPANY EXPENSES		**$2,526.00**

AMERICAN FEDERATED LIFE INSURANCE COMPANY

HAITI ADVENTURE MATTER	HARVARD HUNTINGTON	CR	$424.70
	COMPANY EXPENSES		**$424.70**

AMERICAN PIONEER LIFE INSURANCE

THE CASE OF BARTON DRAKE	W. K. GREEN	CR	$1,482.63
	COMPANY EXPENSES		**$1,482.63**

AMERICAN VOLUNTEER LIABILITY INSURANCE COMPANY

DR. OTTO SCHMEDLICH	HOMER SHALLY	CR	$1,211.69
	COMPANY EXPENSES		**$1,211.69**

APEX & GREAT NORTHERN BONDING COMPANY

THE MISSING CHINESE STRIPPER MATTER	PHINEAS PERCH	CR	$611.44
	COMPANY EXPENSES		**$611.44**

ASSOCIATED INSURANCE COMPANIES OF NEW ENGLAND

THE HENRY J. UNGER MATTER	CAL PORTER	EO	$50.39
	COMPANY EXPENSES		**$50.39**

ASSURED EQUITY & TRUST COMPANY

THE MEEK MEMORIAL MATTER	MAX GREEN	BB	$98.30
	COMPANY EXPENSES		**$98.30**

ATHENA LIFE & CASUALTY COMPANY

THE MAYNARD COLLINS MATTER	ED GRIMM	EO	$310.00
	COMPANY EXPENSES		**$310.00**

ATLAS INDEMNITY INSURANCE COMPANY

THE INDEPENDENT DIAMOND TRADERS MATTER	ERIC CARLSON	JL	$64.20
	COMPANY EXPENSES		**$64.20**

BALTIMORE LIABILITY & TRUST

THE EMILY BRADDOCK MATTER	FRANK PRESTON	JL	$738.32
	COMPANY EXPENSES		**$738.32**

BAY STATE BONDING & LIABILITY

THE MISSING MASTERPIECE	DOUG STRAND	EO	$68.30
	COMPANY EXPENSES		**$68.30**

BRITANNIA INSURANCE COMPANY

THE PAUL BARBERIS MATTER	AD MEYERS	EO	$160.30
	COMPANY EXPENSES		**$160.30**

BRITANNIA LIFE INSURANCE COMPANY

THE HOWARD CALDWELL MATTER	MR. NATHAN	EO	$1,050.00
THE DAVID ROCKY MATTER		EO	$840.75
THE JARVIS WILDER MATTER		EO	$540.00
THE SODERBURY, MAINE MATTER		EO	$84.90
	COMPANY EXPENSES		**$2,515.65**

BRITIANNIA CASUALTY & LIFE

STUART PALMER, WRITER		EO	$635.24
	COMPANY EXPENSES		**$635.24**

BRITTANIA LIFE INSURANCE COMPANY

THE MORGAN FRY MATTER		EO	$136.65
	COMPANY EXPENSES		**$136.65**

BRITTANIA UNDERWRITERS ASSOCIATION

THE CIRCUS ANIMAL SHOW MATTER		CR	$152.70
	COMPANY EXPENSES		**$152.70**

CAMDEN LIFE & FIDELITY COMPANY, LTD.

THE BERLIN MATTER	DAVE HOPKINS	JL	$693.03
	COMPANY EXPENSES		**$693.03**

CITY OF NEW BEDFORD POLICE DEPARTMENT

THE NEW BEDFORD MORGUE MATTER		EO	$213.30
	COMPANY EXPENSES		**$213.30**

CLAYSON MUTUAL ASSURANCE COMPANY

THE HAROLD TRANDEM MATTER	JACK BARTON	EO	$706.82
	COMPANY EXPENSES		**$706.82**

COLUMBIA ACCIDENT & LIFE INSURANCE COMPANY

THE CHICAGO FRAUD MATTER	NILES HARTLEY	JL	$219.77
	COMPANY EXPENSES		**$219.77**

COLUMBIA ALL RISK INSURANCE COMPANY

THE WOODWARD MANILA MATTER	RALPH WEADEN	EO	$3,940.00
THE MONTH-END RAID MATTER		EO	$396.50
THE FAIRWAY MATTER	SAM HARRIS	EO	$0.00
THE PROTECTION MATTER	PHILLIP MARTIN	EO	$101.92
THE BIRDY BASKERVILLE MATTER	PHILLIP MARTIN	EO	$137.27
THE YOUNGSTOWN CREDIT GROUP MATTER		EO	$195.20
THE ALMA SCOTT MATTER		EO	$572.00
THE BIRDY BASKERVILLE MATTER	PHILLIP MARTIN	JL	$137.27
THE EMIL CARTER MATTER		JL	$572.00
THE SHAYNE BOMBING MATTER		JL	$123.70
THE NANCY SHAW MATTER	PHILLIP MARTIN	JL	$604.65
THE NELSON MATTER	PHILLIP MARTIN	JL	$301.01
THE LESTER MATSON MATTER	PHILLIP JAMES	JL	$154.50
THE ALFRED CHAMBERS MATTER	PHILLIP MARTIN	JL	$114.05
THE FAIRWAY MATTER	SAM HARRIS	JL	$25.95
THE WOODWARD MANILA MATTER	RALPH WEADON	JL	$2,611.80
	COMPANY EXPENSES		**$9,987.82**

COLUMBIA ALL-RISK INSURANCE COMPANY

THE EMIL LOVETT MATTER		EO	$93.45
THE JANET ABBE MATTER	BOB RUDD	EO	$2,796.00
THE WILLIAM POST MATTER	RAY KEMPER	JL	$78.05
	COMPANY EXPENSES		**$2,967.50**

COMMONWEALTH MUTUAL ASSURANCE COMPANY

THE DAN FRANK MATTER	JIM BATES	JL	$194.90
	COMPANY EXPENSES		**$194.90**

CONCOURSE MUTUAL LIFE INSURANCE COMPANY

THE JONES MATTER	GEORGE DEAN	JL	$418.40
	COMPANY EXPENSES		**$418.40**

CONSOLIDATED INDEMNITY COMPANY
THE ROAD-TEST MATTER	MR. KING	JL	$217.40
	COMPANY EXPENSES		**$217.40**

CONSTANT SUN TRADING COMPANY
THE EXPIRING NICKELS AND THE EGYPTIAN JACKPOT		CR	$5,350.40
	COMPANY EXPENSES		**$5,350.40**

CONTINENTAL ADJUSTMENT BUREAU
THE LESTER JAMES MATTER	ED TALBOT	JL	$151.22
THE FORBES MATTER	MR. TURNER	BB	$363.51
	COMPANY EXPENSES		**$514.73**

CONTINENTAL ASSURANCE COMPANY
THE FELICITY FELINE MATTER	HENRY PARKER	BB	$407.20
	COMPANY EXPENSES		**$407.20**

CONTINENTAL FIRE & CASUALTY COMPANY
THE UPJOHN MATTER	MATT BRANDON	JL	$293.65
	COMPANY EXPENSES		**$293.65**

CONTINENTAL INSURANCE & TRUST COMPANY
THE DESALLES MATTER	HILLARY FUKES	BB	$416.00
THE FROWARD FISHERMAN MATTER	CLARK THORNESS	BB	$181.00
THE WAYWARD RIVER MATTER	LEE HARKINS	BB	$100.00
THE WAYWARD KILLER MATTER	PAUL HEMPLE	BB	$315.17
THE TELLTALE TRACKS MATTER		BB	$0.00
THE LIFE AT STAKE MATTER	BILL FERGUSON	BB	$0.00
THE DEADLY CHAIN MATTER	BILL FERGUSON	BB	$27.35
THE MYSTERY GAL MATTER	FRED MELCHIOR	BB	$0.00
THE BACK TO THE BACK MATTER	ED BARRENGER	BB	$25.80
	COMPANY EXPENSES		**$1,065.32**

CONTINENTAL INSURANCE COMPANY
THE LOSS OF MEMORY MATTER	LES CRUTCH	BB	$95.00
THE VILLAGE OF VIRTUE MATTER	BEN ORLOFF	BB	$100.00
THE VIRTUOUS MOBSTER MATTER	BEN ORLOFF	BB	$174.00
THE FATAL FILET MATTER		BB	$0.00
THE DEEP DOWN MATTER		BB	$131.50
THE PAPERBACK MYSTERY MATTER	FRED BRISCOE	RR	$70.00
	COMPANY EXPENSES		**$570.50**

CORINTHIAN ALL RISK INSURANCE COMPANY
THE ARTHUR BOLDRICK MATTER		EO	$77.30
	COMPANY EXPENSES		**$77.30**

CORINTHIAN ALL-RISK INSURANCE COMPANY

THE ADOLPH SCHOMAN MATTER	HAROLD WARNER	EO	$150.80
THE MONOPOLY MATTER	MR. BRANDT	EO	$63.80
THE BYRON HAYES MATTER		EO	$180.80
THE CUMBERLAND THEFT MATTER		EO	$834.75
THE AMELIA HARWELL MATTER	GEORGE PARKER	EO	$122.35
THE MONOPOLY MATTER	MR. BRANDT	JL	$62.20
	COMPANY EXPENSES		**$1,414.70**

CORINTHIAN INSURANCE COMPANY

THE RADIOACTIVE GOLD MATTER	ED TRASK	JL	$165.45
THE HAMILTON PAYROLL MATTER	BILL FEDDERSON	JL	$417.65
	COMPANY EXPENSES		**$583.10**

CORINTHIAN LIABILITY & BONDING COMPANY

OUT OF THE FIRE INTO THE FRYING PAN		CR	$1,463.00
	COMPANY EXPENSES		**$1,463.00**

CORINTHIAN LIABILITY & RISK

THE TRANS-PACIFIC EXPORT MATTER	AL HARPER	EO	$3,544.00
THE TRANS-PACIFIC MATTER	AL HARPER	JL	
THE TRANS-PACIFIC MATTER	AL HARPER	JL	$4,515.00
THE TRANS-PACIFIC MATTER	AL HARPER	GM	$0.00
THE TRANS-PACIFIC MATTER	AL HARPER	GM	$4,515.00
	COMPANY EXPENSES		**$12,574.00**

CORINTHIAN LIFE & LIABILITY INSURANCE COMPANY

THE RICHARD SPLAIN MATTER	BRUCE HARVARD	EO	$375.00
	COMPANY EXPENSES		**$375.00**

CORINTHIAN LIFE INSURANCE COMPANY

THE ABEL TACKETT MATTER		EO	$4,077.80
THE JOAN SEBASTIAN MATTER	MR. SEMPLIN	EO	$356.75
THE JEANNE MAXWELL MATTER	MR. SEMPLIN	JL	$266.85
THE JEANNE MAXWELL MATTER	MR. SEMPLIN	JL	$265.85
	COMPANY EXPENSES		**$4,967.25**

COSMOPOLITAN ALL-RISK INSURANCE COMPANY

THE HARTFORD ALLIANCE MATTER	BARTON KEEFE	EO	$180.00
	COMPANY EXPENSES		**$180.00**

COSMOPOLITAN BONDING & INSURANCE CORPORATION

THE BRISBANE FRAUD MATTER		JL	$286.20
	COMPANY EXPENSES		**$286.20**

COUNTY COURT, KINGS COUNTY

THE RUDY VALENTINE MATTER		EO	$10.85
THE RUDY VALENTINE MATTER		JL	$10.85
	COMPANY EXPENSES		**$21.70**

DELAWARE MUTUAL LIFE INSURANCE COMPANY

THE WALTER PATTERSON MATTER	MR. ELGIN	JL	$610.13
	COMPANY EXPENSES		**$610.13**

DELTA LIABILITY

THE FATHOM FIVE MATTER	RALPH STEEDLER	BB	$684.95
	COMPANY EXPENSES		**$684.95**

DR. LUDWIG GOYA

THE EDITH MAXWELL MATTER		EO	$0.00
	COMPANY EXPENSES		**$0.00**

EAST COAST UNDERWRITERS

MILFORD BROOKS III AUSTIN FARNSWORTH DICK POWELL			$1,182.23
THE PARAKOFF POLICY		CR	$1,230.20
THE SIDNEY RYKOFF MATTER	EDWARD HOLEY	EO	$982.28
THE VIRGINIA BEACH MATTER	CARL BREWSTER	EO	$855.75
	COMPANY EXPENSES		**$4,250.46**

EASTERN ALLIED CASUALTY INSURANCE COMPANY

THE SQUARED CIRCLE MATTER	PAUL KENDRICK	BB	$491.20
	COMPANY EXPENSES		**$491.20**

EASTERN CASUALTY & TRUST COMPANY

THE CALLICLES MATTER	DAVE BLAINE	BB	$1,100.59
	COMPANY EXPENSES		**$1,100.59**

EASTERN FIRE & CASUALTY COMPANY

THE MAGNOLIA AND HONEYSUCKLE MATTER	GIL RANDALL	JL	$176.45
	COMPANY EXPENSES		**$176.45**

EASTERN INDEMNITY & FIRE COMPANY

THE PUNCTILIOUS FIREBUG MATTER	JEFF CONNORS	JL	$309.25
	COMPANY EXPENSES		**$309.25**

EASTERN INDEMNITY & INSURANCE COMPANY

THE KING'S NECKLACE MATTER	MARTY FENTON	JL	$348.60
THE MILK AND HONEY MATTER	MITCHELL	JL	$1,480.20

THE UNCUT CANARY MATTER	MR. HARRISON	JL	$373.25
THE CLASSIFIED KILLER MATTER	TED ALBRIGHT	JL	$191.15
THE BILKED BARONESS MATTER	BEN TURNER	JL	$50.45
THE PATTERSON TRANSPORT MATTER	TOM BENSON	JL	$184.45
THE JAN BREUGEL MATTER	TOM LESLIE	JL	$135.85
THE CARBONIFEROUS DOLOMITE MATTER	BILL WESLEY	JL	$2,074.05
	COMPANY EXPENSES		**$4,838.00**

EASTERN INDEMNITY INSURANCE COMPANY

THE UNDRIED FIDDLE BACK MATTER	TOM HARRISON	JL	$480.30
THE SULPHUR AND BRIMSTONE MATTER	PHILIP MARTIN	JL	$585.60
	COMPANY EXPENSES		**$1,065.90**

EASTERN INSURANCE COMPANY

THE FIREBUG HUNTER MATTER	ARNOLD WHELAN	CR	$410.00
	COMPANY EXPENSES		**$410.00**

EASTERN LIABILITY & TRUST COMPANY

THE PEARLING MATTER	MARTIN SCOTMAN	BB	$714.35
THE HOLLYWOOD MYSTERY MATTER	HAL SPIDLE	BB	$0.00
THE ONLY ONE BUTT MATTER	FRED WAKELY	BB	$25.55
THE MAN WHO WAITS MATTER	TED BESSEM	BB	$0.00
	COMPANY EXPENSES		**$739.90**

EASTERN LIABILITY & TRUST INSURANCE COMPANY

THE ONE TOO MANY MATTER	HAL KEMPER	MK	$4.80
	COMPANY EXPENSES		**$4.80**

EASTERN LIABILITY AND TRUST

THE NO MATTER MATTER	RAYMOND TILOTTON	MK	$0.00
	COMPANY EXPENSES		**$0.00**

EASTERN LIFE & TRUST COMPANY

THE THELMA IBSEN MATTER	MILTON DEFRANCO	JL	$84.15
	COMPANY EXPENSES		**$84.15**

EASTERN MARITIME & INSURANCE COMPANY

THE AROMATIC CICATRIX MATTER	JAMES HARRINGTON	JL	$196.10
	COMPANY EXPENSES		**$196.10**

EASTERN SEABOARD CASUALTY INSURANCE COMPANY

THE PLANTAGENT MATTER		BB	$702.13
	COMPANY EXPENSES		**$702.13**

EASTERN TRUST & INSURANCE COMPANY

THE ELEVEN O'CLOCK MATTER		BB	$21.40
THE BASKING RIDGE MATTER	STUART SMITH	BB	$29.55
THE HAPLESS HAM MATTER		BB	$100.00
	COMPANY EXPENSES		**$150.95**

EASTERN TRUST INSURANCE COMPANY

THE BRODERICK MATTER	ROBERT STEEL	BB	$1,132.14
	COMPANY EXPENSES		**$1,132.14**

EMPLOYEE COOPERATIVE GROUP INSURANCE COMPANY

THE SYNDICATE MATTER	WILBUR RUNION	JL	$236.04
	COMPANY EXPENSES		**$236.04**

ESTATE OF E. P. WATKINS

THE HAPPY FAMILY MATTER		BB	$73.00
	COMPANY EXPENSES		**$73.00**

ETERNITY MUTUAL INSURANCE COMPANY

THE CONFIDENTIAL MATTER	MORT PARKINSON	BB	$1,912.61
THE RAT PACK MATTER	GEORGE FRANKLIN	RR	$0.00
THE WRONG IDEA MATTER	TIM HARRINGTON	MK	$229.57
	COMPANY EXPENSES		**$2,142.18**

FEDERAL INSURANCE & CLAIMS ADJUSTERS

THE COSTAIN MATTER		JL	$227.50
	COMPANY EXPENSES		**$227.50**

FEDERAL LIFE INSURANCE COMPANY

THE SARAH DEARING MATTER	ED GROSS	JL	$372.25
	COMPANY EXPENSES		**$372.25**

FEDERAL UNDERWRITERS INC.

THE DAMERON MATTER		JL	$551.10
	COMPANY EXPENSES		**$551.10**

FINANCIAL SURETY

THE WELDON BRAGG MATTER	JIM WALDO	EO	$65.80
THE STANLEY SPRINGS MATTER	ED BEST	EO	$0.00
	COMPANY EXPENSES		**$65.80**

FINANCIAL SURETY COMPANY

THE HATCHET HOUSE THEFT MATTER		EO	$1,182.75
	COMPANY EXPENSES		**$1,182.75**

FINE ARTS SECURERS

STOLEN PORTRAIT	FREDERICK KIMBLE	CR	$1,563.40
	COMPANY EXPENSES		**$1,563.40**

FLOYDS OF ENGLAND

THE MISSING MOUSE MATTER	GEORGE REED	BB	$38.20
THE MAD HATTER MATTER	GEORGE REED	BB	$870.40
THE MING TOY MURPHY MATTER	GEORGE REED	BB	$225.70
THE MICHAEL MEANY MIRAGE MATTER	GEORGE REED	BB	$420.10
THE FUNNY MONEY MATTER	GEORGE REED	BB	$171.25
THE JPD MATTER	GEORGE REED	BB	$204.80
THE SILVER BELLE MATTER	GEORGE REED	BB	$317.10
THE HOPE TO DIE MATTER	GEORGE REED	BB	$0.00
THE BORON 112 MATTER	GEORGE REED	BB	$2,431.00
THE DURANGO LARAMIE MATTER	GEORGE REED	BB	$1,460.00
THE DOTING DOWAGER MATTER	GEORGE REED	BB	$17.80
THE BLUE MADONNA MATTER	GEORGE REED	BB	$620.00
THE FAIR WEATHER FRIEND MATTER	GEORGE REED	BB	$203.50
THE CAUTIOUS CELIBATE MATTER	GEORGE REED	BB	$1,053.45
THE TWIN TROUBLE MATTER	GEORGE REED	BB	$0.00
THE NIGHT IN PARIS MATTER	GEORGE REED	BB	$5,870.00
THE EMBARCADERO MATTER	GEORGE REED	BB	$1,174.00
THE MISSING MISSILE MATTER	GEORGE REED	BB	$0.00
THE WRONG MAN MATTER	GEORGE REED	BB	$1.00
THE NUCLEAR GOOF MATTER	GEORGE REED	BB	$0.00
THE ALVIN'S ALFRED MATTER	GEORGE REED	BB	$0.00
THE COLLECTOR'S MATTER	GEORGE REED	BB	$371.20
THE TWISTED TWIN MATTER	GEORGE REED	BB	$196.55
THE KILLER KIN MATTER	GEORGE REED	BB	$0.00
THE TOO MUCH MONEY MATTER	GEORGE REED	BB	$0.00
THE EMPTY THREAT MATTER	GEORGE REED	BB	$2,561.00
THE SHIFTY LOOKER MATTER	GEOFFREY REED	MK	$4.40
	COMPANY EXPENSES		**$18,211.45**

FOUR STATE FIRE & CASUALTY INSURANCE COMPANY

THE FIRE IN PARADISE MATTER	FRED HANLEY	BB	$241.28
	COMPANY EXPENSES		**$241.28**

FOUR STATE FIRE INSURANCE CORPORATION

THE BENNET MATTER	ANDREW CORD	BB	$1,140.37
	COMPANY EXPENSES		**$1,140.37**

FOUR STATE INSURANCE COMPANY

THE TODD MATTER	DON FREED	BB	$1,095.00
THE EVAPORATED CLUE MATTER	HENRY BASCOME	BB	$574.00

THE HOOD OF DEATH MATTER	LUTHER PENNYROLL	MK	$200.00
	COMPANY EXPENSES		$1,869.00

FOUR STATE MUTUAL INSURANCE COMPANY

THE PEERLESS FIRE MATTER	HENRY WILLOWBY	BB	$14.46
THE PRICE OF FAME MATTER		BB	$2,341.00
THE BOLT OUT OF THE BLUE MATTER	HARRY MCQUEEN	BB	$171.50
THE YAAK MYSTERY MATTER	STEVE YOKUM	RR	$207.75
	COMPANY EXPENSES		**$2,734.71**

GLOBAL CASUALTY

THE PICTURE POSTCARD MATTER	TOM WILKINS	BB	$1,723.00
	COMPANY EXPENSES		**$1,723.00**

GRAND EAST ALL RISK INSURANCE COMPANY

THE ADAM KEGG MATTER	AL BEGNEY	EO	$230.40
	COMPANY EXPENSES		**$230.40**

GRAND EAST LIFE & LIABILITY INSURANCE COMPANY

THE ARROWCRAFT MATTER	MILLARD SNELL	EO	$940.20
	COMPANY EXPENSES		**$940.20**

GRAND INDUSTRIAL INSURERS

THE DEAD FIRST-HELPERS	BILL HUDSON	EO	$520.25
	COMPANY EXPENSES		**$520.25**

GREAT CHESAPEAKE FIDELITY INSURANCE COMPANY

THE STORY OF THE BIG RED SCHOOLHOUSE	PAUL MCGRAW	EO	$3,227.00
	COMPANY EXPENSES		**$3,227.00**

GREAT COLUMBIAN LIFE INSURANCE COMPANY

DEATH TAKES A WORKING DAY	HARRY DELHUBBEL	CR	$823.00
THE LOYAL B. MARTIN MATTER		EO	$823.00
	COMPANY EXPENSES		**$1,646.00**

GREAT CORINTHIAN LIFE INSURANCE COMPANY

THE DISAPPEARANCE OF BRUCE LAMBERT		EO	$496.90
ALEC JEFFERSON, THE YOUTHFUL MILLIONAIRE	BOB DOUGLAS	EO	$711.00
	COMPANY EXPENSES		**$1,207.90**

GREAT EAST INSURANCE COMPANY

THE SINGAPORE ARSON MATTER		JL	$2,112.10
	COMPANY EXPENSES		**$2,112.10**

GREAT EASTERN FIDELITY & LIFE INSURANCE COMPANY

THE SAN ANTONIO MATTER	ED QUIGLEY	JL	$573.49
	COMPANY EXPENSES		**$573.49**

GREAT EASTERN FIRE & CASUALTY

THE ELLIOTT CHAMPION MATTER	DON VICKERS	JL	$516.54
	COMPANY EXPENSES		**$516.54**

GREAT EASTERN INSURANCE COMPANY

THE PORT O'CALL MATTER	BOB REDDEN	EO	$450.60
THE LLOYD HAMMERLY MATTER		EO	$2,350.00
THE WILLARD SOUTH MATTER	LOU CREAGER	EO	$373.00
THE NEAL BREER MATTER		EO	$556.70
THE DOUGLAS TAYLOR MATTER	MR. NIBLEY	EO	$181.20
	COMPANY EXPENSES		**$3,911.50**

GREAT EASTERN LIFE INSURANCE COMPANY

THE NORA FAULKNER MATTER	JIM MORRIS	EO	$1,120.40
THE GEORGE FARMER MATTER	MR. MITCHELL	EO	$33.65
THE BAXTER MATTER	LUTHER BISHOP	EO	$324.10
THE ALLEN SAXTON MATTER	STANLEY MITCHELL	JL	$119.93
THE NATHAN GAYLES MATTER	MR. BISHOP	JL	$235.00
THE NATHAN SWING MATTER	MR. MITCHELL	JL	$176.45
	COMPANY EXPENSES		**$2,009.53**

GREAT NORTHERN BONDING & SURETY

THE LILLIS BOND MATTER		EO	$308.90
	COMPANY EXPENSES		**$308.90**

GREAT PLAINS GUARANTY COMPANY

THE OPEN TOWN MATTER	RALPH KEARNS	BB	$516.20
	COMPANY EXPENSES		**$516.20**

GREATER SOUTHWEST INSURANCE & LIABILITY COMPANY

THE MIDAS TOUCH MATTER	JAKE KESSLER	BB	$978.35
THE MOJAVE RED MATTER	JAKE KESSLER	BB	$0.00
THE MOJAVE RED MATTER	JAKE KESSLER	BB	$307.00
	COMPANY EXPENSES		**$1,285.35**

GREATER SOUTHWEST INSURANCE COMPANY

THE ALLANMEE MATTER	FRED BRINKLEY	BB	$341.10
THE FRISCO FIRE MATTER		BB	$923.91
THE WINSOME WIDOW MATTER	HERB SHILLING	BB	$250.00
THE BIG H. MATTER	ROY HARKINS	BB	$447.45
THE FRANTIC FISHERMAN MATTER	ROY HARKINS	BB	$650.85
THE WILL AND A WAY MATTER	JAKE KESSLER	BB	$3,280.00
THE RED ROCK MATTER	JAKE KESSLER	BB	$496.25
THE VERY FISHY MATTER	THEODORE JARVIS	RR	$245.50
THE CAPTAIN'S TABLE MATTER	BARTON H.B. HOLLISTER	RR	$438.00
THE MAD BOMBER MATTER	HANK PARNELL	MK	$350.00
THE DO IT YOURSELF MATTER	ROY HARKINS	MK	$833.70
THE GOLDEN DREAM MATTER	JAKE KESSLER	MK	$451.80
THE GOLD RUSH MATTER	JAKE WALTON	MK	$700.00
THE FOUR CS MATTER	ROYAL J. HARKIN	MK	$401.23
	COMPANY EXPENSES		**$9,809.79**

GREATER SOUTHWEST LIFE INSURANCE COMPANY

THE SIDEWINDER MATTER	JAKE KESSLER	BB	$345.40
	COMPANY EXPENSES		**$345.40**

GUARANTEE TRANSPORT INSURANCE COMPANY

THE FLIGHT SIX MATTER	PETE CARDLEY	BB	$608.10
	COMPANY EXPENSES		**$608.10**

HARTFORD POLICE

THE GLEN ENGLISH MATTER		EO	$0.00
	COMPANY EXPENSES		**$0.00**

HARTFORD POLICE BUNKO SQUAD

THE HENRY PAGE MATTER		EO	$53.00
	COMPANY EXPENSES		**$53.00**

HARTFORD POLICE DEPARTMENT

THE MICKEY MCQUEEN MATTER		EO	$0.00
THE MICKEY MCQUEEN MATTER		EO	$0.00
	COMPANY EXPENSES		**$0.00**

HEMISPHERIC INSURANCE COMPANY

THE KAY BELLAMY MATTER	BERT WELCH	JL	$135.40
	COMPANY EXPENSES		**$135.40**

HEMISPHERIC LIFE INSURANCE COMPANY

THE ENOCH ARDEN MATTER	HENRY GRANT	JL	$1,879.80
	COMPANY EXPENSES		**$1,879.80**

HIGHWORTHY INSURANCE UNDERWRITERS ASSOCIATION
THE CASE OF THE $100,000 LEGS HARVEY ANTHONY CR $948.76
COMPANY EXPENSES **$948.76**

HONESTY LIFE INSURANCE UNDERWRITERS
MILFORD BROOKS III MATTER AUSTIN FARNSWORTH CR $1,182.23
COMPANY EXPENSES **$1,182.23**

INDUSTRIAL INSURERS INCORPORATED
THE DEPARTMENT STORE EVAN STEVENS CR $511.50
SWINDLE MATTER
COMPANY EXPENSES **$511.50**

INTER ALLIED INSURANCE COMPANY
THE BLOOMING BLOSSOM MATTER PAUL BRANNON BB $61.55
COMPANY EXPENSES **$61.55**

INTER ALLIED LIFE INSURANCE COMPANY
THE CURSE OF KAMASHEK MATTER JIMMY SAYER BB $985.00
THE KILLER'S LIST MATTER PAT CUMMINGS BB $146.50
COMPANY EXPENSES **$1,131.50**

INTER-ALLIED INSURANCE COMPANY
THE MONTICELLO MYSTERY MATTER HENRY FOREMAN MK $71.70
COMPANY EXPENSES **$71.70**

INTER-COASTAL MARITIME & LIFE
THE MARLEY K. MATTER BYRON KAY BB $81.00
COMPANY EXPENSES **$81.00**

INTER-COASTAL MARITIME & LIFE INSURANCE COMPANY
THE MEG'S PALACE MATTER BYRON KANE BB $221.60
THE CHARMONA MATTER BYRON KAYE BB $103.80
THE SILVER QUEEN MATTER BYRON KAYE BB $58.35
COMPANY EXPENSES **$383.75**

INTERCOMMERCIAL INSURANCE COMPANY OF AMERICA
THE CALIGIO DIAMOND MATTER HENRY GLACEN EO $65.34
COMPANY EXPENSES **$65.34**

INTERCONTINENTAL BONDING & INDEMNITY
THE GINO GAMBONA MATTER ROGER STERN JL $112.07
COMPANY EXPENSES **$112.07**

INTERCONTINENTAL INDEMNITY & BONDING COMPANY

THE CUBAN JEWEL MATTER	ROGER STERN	EO	$708.83
	COMPANY EXPENSES		**$708.83**

INTERCONTINENTAL INDEMNITY & BONDING CORPORATION

THE JONATHAN BELLOWS MATTER	ROGER STERN	JL	$208.60
THE JAMES FORBES MATTER	ROGER STERN	JL	$148.48
	COMPANY EXPENSES		**$357.08**

INTERCONTINENTAL MARINE INSURANCE COMPANY

THE FISHING BOAT AFFAIR		CR	$1,264.28
THE S.S. MALAY TRADER SHIP		EO	$0.00
	COMPANY EXPENSES		**$1,264.28**

INTERNATIONAL CASUALTY & LIFE INSURANCE COMPANY

THE HARRIED HEIRESS MATTER	BERT LARKIN	BB	$7,604.25
	COMPANY EXPENSES		**$7,604.25**

INTERNATIONAL INSURANCE & BONDING COMPANY

THE VOODOO MATTER	NELSON PRICE	JL	$461.40
	COMPANY EXPENSES		**$461.40**

INTERNATIONAL INSURANCE CORPORATION

THE MADISON MATTER	PAUL DUPREE	JL	$525.39
	COMPANY EXPENSES		**$525.39**

INTERNATIONAL LIFE & CASUALTY COMPANY

THE WINNIPESAUKEE WONDER MATTER	CHRISTIAN ALBECK	BB	$0.00
	COMPANY EXPENSES		**$0.00**

INTERNATIONAL LIFE & CASUALTY INSURANCE COMPANY

THE PHONY PHONE MATTER	ART INGLES	BB	$1.35
THE TWINS OF TAHOE MATTER	MICHAEL J. KENDRY	BB	$416.00
THE THREE FOR ONE MATTER	CHRISTIAN ALBECK	MK	$81.50
	COMPANY EXPENSES		**$498.85**

KEYSTONE MUTUAL ASSURANCE COMPANY

THE BEN BRYSON MATTER	ED MURPHY	JL	$823.82
	COMPANY EXPENSES		**$823.82**

KING HART

THE CASE OF BONNIE GOODWIN		CR	$0.00
	COMPANY EXPENSES		**$0.00**

LAKESIDE LIFE & CASUALTY INSURANCE COMPANY

THE INDESTRUCTIBLE MIKE MATTER	PETER BRANSON	BB	$1,126.50
	COMPANY EXPENSES		**$1,126.50**

LLOYDS UNDERWRITERS ASSOCIATION

THE RACEHORSE PILEDRIVER MATTER		CR	$1,449.22
	COMPANY EXPENSES		**$1,449.22**

MARIGOLD POLICE DEPARTMENT

THE MARIGOLD MATTER	WALT YOUNGER	JL	$4.00
	COMPANY EXPENSES		**$4.00**

MARINE & MARITIME CASUALTY, LTD.

THE MOLLY K MATTER	DAVE BORGER	BB	$547.60
	COMPANY EXPENSES		**$547.60**

MASTERS INSURANCE & TRUST COMPANY

THE POOR LITTLE RICH GIRL MATTER	BERT MAJOR	BB	$317.75
THE DIAMOND DILEMMA MATTER	BERT MAJOR	BB	$284.30
THE UGLY PATTERN MATTER	BARRY WINTERS	BB	$101.00
THE CURLEY WATERS MATTER		BB	$0.00
THE DATE WITH DEATH MATTER	BERT WELLS	BB	$47.00
THE DOUBLE EXPOSURE MATTER	FREDERICK KEELEY	BB	$17.20
THE WAYWARD FIREMAN MATTER	HARRISON HADLEY	RR	$227.00
	COMPANY EXPENSES		**$994.25**

MAURIE STRAND BAIL BOND

THE TOM HICKMAN MATTER	MAURIE STRAND	EO	$2,204.06
	COMPANY EXPENSES		**$2,204.06**

MAX KRAUSE BAIL BOND & INSURANCE

WITNESS, WITNESS, WHO'S GOT THE WITNESS	MAX KRAUSE	CR	$500.71
	COMPANY EXPENSES		**$500.71**

MID STATES INDUSTRIAL INSURANCE COMPANY

THE CASE OF TROUBLE MATTER	TOM BARTLEY	MK	$256.10
	COMPANY EXPENSES		**$256.10**

MID-EASTERN INDEMNITY CORPORATION

THE TEMPLETON MATTER	LUD BARLOW	BB	$413.28
THE P.O. MATTER	HARRY McQUEEN	BB	$397.70
	COMPANY EXPENSES		**$810.98**

MID-EASTERN LIFE & CASUALTY COMPANY

THE MARY GRACE MATTER	BEN PERRIN	BB	$0.00
	COMPANY EXPENSES		**$0.00**

MID-STATES INDUSTRIAL INSURANCE COMPANY

THE PRIMROSE MATTER	BRAD TAYLOR	BB	$914.15
	COMPANY EXPENSES		**$914.15**

MISS MELANIE CARTER

THE MELANIE CARTER MATTER		CR	$0.00
	COMPANY EXPENSES		**$0.00**

MONARCH LIFE INSURANCE COMPANY

THE BARBARA JAMES MATTER	FRANK GARBER	EO	$344.59
	COMPANY EXPENSES		**$344.59**

MONO GUARANTEE INSURANCE COMPANY

THE SILVER BLUE MATTER	RALPH DEAN	BB	$541.25
THE DELECTABLE DAMSEL MATTER	RALPH SINGLE	BB	$230.00
THE RHYMER COLLECTION MATTER	FRED PORTER	BB	$35.50
THE BAD ONE MATTER	CULPEPPER WALKER	BB	$231.20
TOO MANY CROOKS MATTER	FREDDIE FREIDKIN	MK	$0.00
THE DOUBLE-BARRELED MATTER	PHIL EASTERDAY	MK	$760.00
THE BURMA RED MATTER	JIMMY BARTELL	MK	$0.00
THE SKIMPY MATTER	DANNY NIXON	MK	$10.80
	COMPANY EXPENSES		**$1,808.75**

MUTUAL LIABILITY

THE EIGHTY FIVE LITTLE MINKS	ED BONNER	EO	$384.16
	COMPANY EXPENSES		**$384.16**

NATIONAL ALL RISK INSURANCE COMPANY

THE BLACKMAIL MATTER	PHILLIP SHORE	JL	$22.68
THE BLACK DOLL MATTER	PHILLIP SHAW	JL	$467.67
	COMPANY EXPENSES		**$490.35**

NATIONAL ALL-RISK INSURANCE COMPANY

THE BISHOP BLACKMAIL MATTER	PHILLIP SHAW	JL	$46.35
	COMPANY EXPENSES		**$46.35**

NATIONAL FIDELITY LIFE INSURANCE COMPANY

MR. AND MRS. ARBUTHNEL TRUMP		EO	$763.90
	COMPANY EXPENSES		**$763.90**

NATIONAL LIFE & CASUALTY COMPANY

THE OSCAR CLARK MATTER	DON MAYNARD	JL	$168.59
	COMPANY EXPENSES		**$168.59**

NATIONAL LIFE & CASUALTY INSURANCE COMPANY

THE ISABELLE JAMES MATTER	DON MAYNARD	JL	$335.04
THE PHILIP MOREY MATTER	DON MAYNARD	JL	$99.38
	COMPANY EXPENSES		**$434.42**

NATIONAL MARINE INDEMNITY

THE HOLLYWOOD MATTER	ABE SANDSTROM	BB	$618.45
	COMPANY EXPENSES		**$618.45**

NATIONAL MEDICAL & HOSPITALIZATION INSURANCE COMPANY

THE BOBBY FOSTER MATTER	WALTER JACKSON	JL	$196.96
	COMPANY EXPENSES		$196.96

NATIONAL SURETY & LIFE INSURANCE COMPANY

HOW MUCH BOURBON CAN FLOW UNDER THE BRIDGEWORK		CR	$2,063.00
	COMPANY EXPENSES		**$2,063.00**

NATIONAL UNDERWRITERS

THE LATOURETTE MATTER		JL	$219.50
	COMPANY EXPENSES		**$219.50**

NATIONAL UNDERWRITERS ASSOCIATION

THE LONG SHOT MATTER	JIM DARRELL	BB	$490.80
	COMPANY EXPENSES		**$490.80**

NEW BRITAIN INSURANCE COMPANY

THE VALENTINE MATTER	ROY VICKERS	BB	$1,290.38
	COMPANY EXPENSES		**$1,290.38**

NEW BRITAIN MUTUAL INSURANCE COMPANY

THE WAYWARD HEIRESS MATTER	AL TURNER	BB	$10.00
THE PARADISE LOST MATTER	AL TURNER	BB	$50.00
	COMPANY EXPENSES		**$60.00**

NEW ENGLAND MUTUAL TRUST & CASUALTY

THE NEW CAMBRIDGE MATTER	DAVE TAYLOR	JL	$125.00
	COMPANY EXPENSES		**$125.00**

New Jersey Fire & Casualty Insurance Company

The Smokey Sleeper Matter	Fred Larkin	BB	$130.49
The Terrible Torch Matter	Fred Larkin	MK	$1,500.00
	Company Expenses		**$1,630.49**

New Jersey State Mutual Life Insurance Company

The Heatherstone Players Matter	Garrett Reynolds	BB	$51.25
The Short Term Matter	Bill Tilton	RR	$82.80
The Doninger Doninger Matter	Maurice Parkely	MK	$155.70
	Company Expenses		**$289.75**

New York Mutual

The James Clayton Matter	Chet Graham	JL	$56.35
	Company Expenses		**$56.35**

New York Police Department

The Jane Doe Matter		EO	$0.00
	Company Expenses		**$0.00**

Northeast Fidelity & Bonding

The Alvin Summers Matter	Fred Wilkins	BB	$923.00
	Company Expenses		**$923.00**

Northeast Indemnity Affiliates

The Big Scoop Matter	Joe McNab	BB	$187.40
	Company Expenses		**$187.40**

Northeast Indemnity Affiliates

The Earned Income Matter	Toby Tetrick	BB	$418.15
	Company Expenses		**$418.15**

Northeast Indemnity Associates

The Imperfect Alibi Matter	Joe McNab	BB	$192.40
The Grand Canyon Matter	Bill Walker	MK	$550.00
	Company Expenses		**$742.40**

Northeast Indemnity Association

The Tip-Off Matter	George Hardy	MK	$349.40
	Company Expenses		**$349.40**

NORTHEASTERN FIDELITY & BONDING COMPANY

THE TWO-FACED MATTER	NICK WALTERS	BB	$9.80
	COMPANY EXPENSES		**$9.80**

NORTHEASTERN INDEMNITY ASSOCIATION

THE WAYWARD MONEY MATTER	FRED NORWOOD	BB	$104.70
	COMPANY EXPENSES		**$104.70**

NORTHWEST INDEMNITY ALLIANCE

THE AMY BRADSHAW MATTER	GEORGE ATKINS	BB	$185.20
THE CRATER LAKE MATTER	PETER WILKERSON	BB	$495.60
	COMPANY EXPENSES		**$680.80**

NORTHWEST SURETY COMPANY

THE LONELY HEARTS MATTER	DAVE ELWOOD	BB	$416.40
THE MIDNIGHT SUN MATTER	BILL CHADWICK	BB	$600.00
	COMPANY EXPENSES		**$1,016.40**

NUTMEG STATE CASUALTY & BONDING COMPANY

MURDER IS A MERRY-GO-ROUND		CR	$692.18
	COMPANY EXPENSES		**$692.18**

NUTMEG STATE LIABILITY UNDERWRITERS

WHO TOOK THE TAXIS		CR	$1,100.00
	COMPANY EXPENSES		**$1,100.00**

NYPD HOMICIDE

THE LUCKY COSTA MATTER		EO	$0.00
	COMPANY EXPENSES		**$0.00**

OLD CALEDONIA INSURANCE COMPANY

THE SKULL CANYON MINE	OSCAR WHEATON	CR	$947.99
	COMPANY EXPENSES		**$947.99**

OLD CALEDONIA SECURITY INSURANCE COMPANY

HOW I TURNED A LUXURY LINER INTO A BATTLESHIP	CR		$2,747.27
	COMPANY EXPENSES		**$2,747.27**

ORIENTAL WEST CARGO BONDING COMPANY

THE SLOW BOAT FROM CHINA	MR. FUNDY	CR	$1,407.00
	COMPANY EXPENSES		**$1,407.00**

PARAMOUNT INSURANCE ADJUSTERS

THE HENDERSON MATTER	TIM CONNORS	BB	$802.50
THE DENVER DISBURSAL MATTER	PERRY JAIMERSON	BB	$391.80
	COMPANY EXPENSES		**$1,194.30**

PHILADELPHIA MUTUAL LIABILITY & CASUALTY COMPANY

THE RICARDO AMERIGO MATTER	HARRY BRANSON	BB	$182.65
THE LAIRD DOUGLAS-DOUGLAS OF HEATHERSTONE MATTER	HARRY BRANSON	BB	$1,113.40
THE WAYWARD WIDOW MATTER	HARRY BRANSON	BB	$365.50
THE CASK OF DEATH MATTER	HARRY BRANSON	BB	$101.20
THE DOUBLE DEAL MATTER	HARRY BRANSON	BB	$2,044.45
	COMPANY EXPENSES		**$3,807.20**

PHILADELPHIA MUTUAL LIABILITY & CASUALTY INSURANCE COMPANY

THE INGENUOUS JEWELER MATTER	HARRY BRANSON	BB	$181.00
THE INFORMER MATTER	HARRY BRANSON	RR	$115.20
THE LATRODECTUS MATTER	HARRY BRANSON	RR	$111.35
	COMPANY EXPENSES		**$407.55**

PHILADELPHIA MUTUAL LIFE & CASUALTY INSURANCE COMPANY

THE CLEVER CHEMIST MATTER	HARRY BRANSON	BB	$84.35
THE MOONSHINE MURDER MATTER	HARRY BRANSON	BB	$299.50
THE MONOXIDE MYSTERY MATTER	CLARKE BENDER	BB	$74.65
THE REAL SMOKEY MATTER	HARRY BRANSON	BB	$621.00
	COMPANY EXPENSES		**$1,079.50**

PHILADELPHIA MUTUAL LIFE CASUALTY INSURANCE COMPANY

THE LARSON ARSON MATTER	HARRY BRANSON	BB	$79.75
	COMPANY EXPENSES		**$79.75**

PIEDMONT MUTUAL LIFE INSURANCE COMPANY

THE PEARL CARRASA MATTER	BOB CASE	EO	$712.55
	COMPANY EXPENSES		**$712.55**

PLYMOUTH INSURANCE COMPANY

THE LELAND BLACKBURN MATTER	BOB HALL	EO	$345.75
THE VIVIAN FAIR MATTER		EO	$150.00
THE VIRGINIA TOWNE MATTER		EO	$270.00
THE MILLARD WARD MATTER	WILLARD DUNHILL	EO	$419.95
THE HANNIBAL MURPHY MATTER		EO	$734.40
THE PAUL GORRELL MATTER	GEORGE POST	JL	$369.80
	COMPANY EXPENSES		**$2,289.90**

PLYMOUTH LIFE INSURANCE COMPANY

THE RUM BARREL MATTER		EO	$43.55
	COMPANY EXPENSES		**$43.55**

PLYMOUTH MUTUAL INSURANCE COMPANY

THE BEAUREGARD MATTER	DAVE BRACE	JL	$203.40
	COMPANY EXPENSES		**$203.40**

PREMIER LIFE & CASUALTY COMPANY

HERE COMES THE DEATH OF THE PARTY		CR	$1,434.67
	COMPANY EXPENSES		**$1,434.67**

PROVIDENTIAL ASSURANCE COMPANY

THE MELANCHOLY MEMORY MATTER	BERT McGRAW	BB	$579.12
THE MASON-DIXON MISMATCH MATTER	BERT McGRAW	BB	$319.00
THE DIXON MURDER MATTER	BERT McGRAW	BB	$968.20
THE CONFEDERATE COINAGE MATTER	BERT McGRAW	BB	$405.10
THE HAND OF PROVIDENTIAL MATTER	ERNEST L. WHITEMAN	BB	$0.00
THE MOONSHINE MATTER	CLARK TRACY	BB	$340.00
THE DEADLY SWAMP MATTER	CHARLES KINGSLEY SINCLAIR	BB	$161.60
	COMPANY EXPENSES		**$2,773.02**

PROVIDENTIAL FIRE & MARINE

THE ROYAL STREET MATTER	C. D. BINFORD	BB	$517.20
	COMPANY EXPENSES		**$517.20**

PROVIDENTIAL LIFE & CASUALTY

THE GOLDEN TOUCH MATTER	STEVE KILMER	BB	$240.00
	COMPANY EXPENSES		**$240.00**

PROVIDENTIAL LIFE & CASUALTY INSURANCE COMPANY

THE SHANKAR DIAMOND MATTER	STEVE KILMER	BB	$50.00
	COMPANY EXPENSES		**$50.00**

PROVIDENTIAL PROPERTY INSURANCE COMPANY

THE CANNED CANARY MATTER	JACK PRICE	BB	$1,121.00
	COMPANY EXPENSES		**$1,121.00**

RICHARD PORTER

THE SHEPHERD MATTER	RICHARD PORTER	BB	$485.00
	COMPANY EXPENSES		**$485.00**

SAMUEL RUBEN & ASSOCIATES

THE SALT CITY MATTER	SAMUEL RUBEN	BB	$3,262.00
	COMPANY EXPENSES		**$3,262.00**

Seaboard Mutual Life Insurance Company

The Great Bannock Race Matter	Bill Blake	JL	$1,207.90
	Company Expenses		**$1,207.90**

Seven Seas Maritime Underwriters Association

The South Sea Adventure	Enos McCartle	CR	$3,286.44
	Company Expenses		**$3,286.44**

Shipper's Indemnity

The Story Of The 10:08	Harry Poulden	EO	$312.00
	Company Expenses		**$312.00**

Sierra All Risk

The Jackie Cleaver Matter		EO	
	Company Expenses		

Special Program

The Five Down Matter		BB	$0.00
	Company Expenses		**$0.00**

Star Mutual Insurance Company

The Shady Lane Matter	Pete Carlson	BB	$186.60
The Sick Chick Matter		BB	$0.00
The Hair Raising Matter	Fritz Melchior	BB	$47.50
The Touch-Up Matter	Terry Holmes	RR	$0.00
The Four Is A Crowd Matter	Dennis Taylor	MK	$400.00
The Oldest Gag Matter	Larry Spangler	MK	$0.00
The Lorelei Matter	Ed Williams	MK	$0.00
	Company Expenses		**$634.10**

State Unity Life

The Silent Queen Matter	Vic Carson	BB	$436.25
	Company Expenses		**$436.25**

State Unity Life Insurance Company

The Ghost To Ghost Matter	Oscar M. Trimley	BB	$31.50
The Lone Wolf Matter	Harvey Wakeman	RR	$88.40
The Imperfect Crime Matter	Lou Little	MK	$0.00
The Well Of Trouble Matter	Lou Little	MK	$0.00
The All Wet Matter	Lawrence Penworthy Thurston	MK	$300.00
The Blue Rock Matter	Phil Unknown	MK	$200.00
	Company Expenses		**$619.90**

STROOL BAIL BOND

THE JACK MADIGAN MATTER	MANNY STROOL	EO	$2,720.00
	COMPANY EXPENSES		**$2,720.00**

SURETY MUTUAL & TRUST COMPANY

THE CRONIN MATTER	JOE PARKER	BB	$263.30
THE SUNTAN OIL MATTER	DAVE LAWLER	BB	$474.84
	COMPANY EXPENSES		**$738.14**

SURETY MUTUAL INSURANCE COMPANY

THE RING OF DEATH MATTER	DON PINKLEY	RR	$389.00
THE TOP SECRET MATTER	LEN WALKER	MK	$993.70
	COMPANY EXPENSES		**$1,382.70**

SURETY MUTUAL INSURANCE, LTD.

THE CUI BONO MATTER	DON HANCOCK	BB	$382.65
THE SATURDAY NIGHT MATTER	PETER H. FILLMORE	BB	$301.01
THE IVY EMERALD MATTER	BOB BAKER	MK	$0.00
	COMPANY EXPENSES		**$683.66**

SURETY MUTUAL LTD.

THE BLINKER MATTER	FRED WILLS	BB	$434.50
	COMPANY EXPENSES		**$434.50**

SWANSON INDUSTRIAL INSURANCE CORPORATION

THE BELLO-HORIZONTE RAILROAD	GEORGE DONNELLY	EO	$1,492.54
	COMPANY EXPENSES		**$1,492.54**

TRANSWORLD FIDELITY COMPANY

THE LORKO DIAMOND'S MATTER	BEN TYLER	BB	$1,214.60
	COMPANY EXPENSES		**$1,214.60**

TRI WESTERN LIFE INSURANCE

THE UNWORTHY KIN MATTER	FRANK HARMON	BB	$500.00
	COMPANY EXPENSES		**$500.00**

TRI-EASTERN INDEMNITY ASSOCIATES

THE STAR OF CAPETOWN MATTER	JOE MCNAB	BB	$1,283.60
THE HOT CHOCOLATE MATTER	HARVEY WELLER	MK	$49.35
	COMPANY EXPENSES		**$1,332.95**

TRI-MUTUAL INSURANCE COMPANY

THE WRONG SIGN MATTER	HARLEY TILSON	RR	$129.30
THE LOW TIDE MATTER	FREDERICK BENNOM	MK	$0.00
	COMPANY EXPENSES		**$129.30**

TRI-MUTUAL INSURANCE COMPANY, LTD.

THE HAPLESS HUNTER MATTER	JERRY HOLLAND	BB	$13.13
	COMPANY EXPENSES		**$13.13**

TRI-MUTUAL INSURANCE LTD.

THE NICK SHURN MATTER	DON WILKINS	BB	$486.20
	COMPANY EXPENSES		**$486.20**

TRI-SATE LIFE & CASUALTY COMPANY

THE RECOMPENSE MATTER	DON BOOMHAUER	BB	$0.00
	COMPANY EXPENSES		**$0.00**

TRI-STATE ASSURANCE COMPANY, LTD

THE PINEY CORNERS MATTER	BOB CRALE	JL	$120.70
	COMPANY EXPENSES		**$120.70**

TRI-STATE GUARANTY COMPANY

THE KRANESBURG MATTER	BOB LAUDER	BB	$409.10
	COMPANY EXPENSES		**$409.10**

TRI-STATE INSURANCE COMPANY

THE YANKEE PRIDE MATTER	CARL BUSH	EO	$2,686.00
THE QUEEN ANNE PISTOLS MATTER	WILLIAM CARTER	EO	$365.35
THE YANKEE PRIDE MATTER	CARL BUSH	EO	$2,686.00
	COMPANY EXPENSES		**$5,737.35**

TRI-STATE INSURANCE GROUP

THE EDWARD FRENCH MATTER		EO	$2,739.50
THE ALONZO CHAPMAN MATTER		EO	$672.08
THE LELAND CASE MATTER		EO	$496.13
THE TOLHURST THEFT MATTER	JIM MADISON	EO	$77.60
	COMPANY EXPENSES		**$3,985.31**

TRI-STATE INSURANCE UNDERWRITERS

THE MCCLAIN MATTER	DON TAYLOR	BB	$768.60
	COMPANY EXPENSES		**$768.60**

TRI-STATE LIFE & CASUALTY COMPANY

THE BLOOD RIVER MATTER		EO	$740.00
THE PARLEY BARRON MATTER	EARLE POORMAN	BB	$421.50
THE THREE SISTERS MATTER	EARLE POORMAN	BB	$351.20
THE EASTERN-WESTERN MATTER	EARLE POORMAN	BB	$207.00
THE DOUBLE TROUBLE MATTER	EARLE POORMAN	BB	$178.70
THE CLOUDED CRYSTAL MATTER	EARLE POORMAN	BB	$168.50
THE NET OF CIRCUMSTANCE MATTER	EARLE POORMAN	BB	$151.50

THE FALSE ALARM MATTER	EARLE POORMAN	BB	$151.00
THE WAYWARD KILOCYCLES MATTER	EARLE POORMAN	RR	$400.00
	COMPANY EXPENSES		**$2,769.40**

TRI-STATE LIFE & CASUALTY INSURANCE COMPANY

THE SEARCH FOR MICHELLE MARSH		CR	$786.00
THE BURNING CAR MATTER	EARLE POORMAN	BB	$385.26
THE KIRBEY WILL MATTER	DANNY NEWCUM	BB	$331.25
THE WAYWARD MOTH MATTER	EARLE POORMAN	BB	$204.00
THE SALKOFF SEQUEL MATTER	EARLE POORMAN	BB	$0.00
THE LUCKY 4 MATTER	EARLE POORMAN	BB	$224.95
THE GRUESOME SPECTACLE MATTER	ED BARRETT	BB	$148.00
THE GRUESOME SPECTACLE MATTER	ED BARRETT	BB	$148.00
THE BAYOU BODY MATTER	EARLE POORMAN	BB	$168.65
THE FANCY BRIDGEWORK MATTER	EARLE POORMAN	BB	$200.00
THE DEADLY DEBT MATTER	DON BOOMHAUER	BB	$200.00
THE WHAT GOES MATTER	EARLE POORMAN	BB	$368.50
THE BIG DATE MATTER	DON BOOMHAUER	RR	$20.00
THE FIDDLE FADDLE MATTER	EARLE POORMAN	MK	$681.80
THE WRONG ONE MATTER	EARLE POORMAN	MK	$0.00
THE GUIDE TO MURDER MATTER	EARLE POORMAN	MK	$85.00
THE WEATHER OR NOT MATTER	EARLE POORMAN	MK	$247.92
	COMPANY EXPENSES		**$4,199.33**

TRI-STATE LIFE INSURANCE COMPANY

THE EARL CHADWICK MATTER	LELAND SCARF	EO	$1,575.00
	COMPANY EXPENSES		**$1,575.00**

TRI-WESTERN INDEMNITY COMPANY

THE WAYWARD TRUCK MATTER	TED ORLOFF	BB	$501.05
	COMPANY EXPENSES		**$501.05**

TRI-WESTERN INSURANCE COMPANY

THE BUM STEER MATTER	HAL VERSKI	BB	$0.00
	COMPANY EXPENSES		**$0.00**

TRI-WESTERN LIFE & CASUALTY COMPANY

THE GLACIER GHOST MATTER	WALTER BASCOMB	BB	$431.60
THE IMPOSSIBLE MURDER MATTER	WALT BASCOMB	BB	$516.25
	COMPANY EXPENSES		**$947.85**

TRI-WESTERN LIFE INSURANCE COMPANY

THE HIRED HOMICIDE MATTER		BB	$0.00
THE UNHOLY TWO MATTER	JACK PRICE	BB	$287.20
THE STOPE OF DEATH MATTER	HAL BARKER	BB	$248.75

THE SIMPLE SIMON MATTER	FRANK FRANCIS	RR	$450.00
THE PERILOUS PADRE MATTER	JACK PRICE	MK	$485.00
THE WRONG DOCTOR MATTER	JACK PRICE	MK	$532.40
THE MEDIUM RARE MATTER	JACK PRICE	MK	$465.30
THE IKE AND MIKE MATTER	JACK PRICE	MK	$0.00
THE SKIDMORE MATTER	JACK PRICE	MK	$276.28
	COMPANY EXPENSES		**$2,744.93**

TRI-WESTERN PROPERTY & CASUALTY INSURANCE COMPANY

| THE DOUBTFUL DIARY MATTER | PETER HARDY | BB | $418.00 |
| | **COMPANY EXPENSES** | | **$418.00** |

TRINITY MUTUAL INSURANCE COMPANY

THE ONE MOST WANTED MATTER	BOB TANK	BB	$3,995.00
THE PHONY PHONE MATTER	BERT HELFER	MK	$0.00
THE VOCIFEROUS DOLPHIN MATTER	WILL BURNETT	MK	$531.80
THE RILLDOE MATTER	WILL BURNETT	MK	$250.00
	COMPANY EXPENSES		**$4,776.80**

TRINITY MUTUAL INSURANCE COMPANY, LTD.

| THE CAYLIN MATTER | WALT ALBRIGHT | BB | $596.85 |
| | **COMPANY EXPENSES** | | **$596.85** |

TWIN STATE INSURANCE COMPANY

| THE STARLET MATTER | KEN RALSTON | JL | $366.05 |
| | **COMPANY EXPENSES** | | **$366.05** |

U.S. TREASURY DEPARTMENT

| THE LONDON MATTER | MARK NELSON | EO | $1,580.20 |
| | **COMPANY EXPENSES** | | **$1,580.20** |

UNION STATES CASUALTY COMPANY

| THE LAUGHING MATTER | ED RENZER | BB | $791.55 |
| | **COMPANY EXPENSES** | | **$791.55** |

UNION STATES CASUALTY INSURANCE COMPANY

| THE NUGGET OF TRUTH MATTER | TED NEWBERRY | MK | $20.00 |
| | **COMPANY EXPENSES** | | **$20.00** |

UNITED ADJUSTMENT BUREAU

| THE CLINTON MATTER | AL DAVIES | BB | $2,385.03 |
| | **COMPANY EXPENSES** | | **$2,385.03** |

UNIVERSAL ADJUSTERS

THE OKLAHOMA RED MATTER	FRANK AHERN	JL	$286.45
	COMPANY EXPENSES		**$286.45**

UNIVERSAL ADJUSTMENT BUREAU

THE CHESAPEAKE FRAUD MATTER	PAT KELLEHER	BB	$1,124.98
THE LANSING FRAUD MATTER	JIM CARTER	BB	$1,121.13
THE DUKE RED MATTER	NILES PEARSON	BB	$802.65
THE JOLLY ROGER FRAUD MATTER	PAT MCCRACKEN	BB	$523.23
THE LA MARR MATTER	PAT MCCRACKEN	BB	$0.00
THE MATTER OF THE MEDIUM-WELL DONE	PAT MCCRACKEN	BB	$892.90
THE TEARS OF NIGHT MATTER		BB	$405.16
THE SEA LEGS MATTER	PAT MCCRACKEN	BB	$841.95
THE PHANTOM CHASE MATTER	PAT MCCRACKEN	BB	$1,723.00
THE RASMUSSEN MATTER		BB	$1,965.00
THE YOURS TRULY MATTER	PAT MCCRACKEN	BB	$528.00
THE KILLER'S BRAND MATTER	PAT MCCRACKEN	BB	$528.00
THE IDEAL VACATION MATTER	PAT MCCRACKEN	BB	$115.20
THE MODEL PICTURE MATTER	PAT MCCRACKEN	BB	$103.00
THE SHY BENEFICIARY MATTER	PAT MCCRACKEN	BB	$410.00
THE SUNNY DREAM MATTER	PAT MCCRACKEN	BB	$12.00
THE CARMEN KRINGLE MATTER	PAT MCCRACKEN	BB	$0.00
THE LATIN LOVELY MATTER	PAT MCCRACKEN	BB	$0.00
THE TIME AND TIDE MATTER	PAT MCCRACKEN	BB	$403.50
THE WAYWARD TROUT MATTER	PAT MCCRACKEN	BB	$815.00
THE ROLLING STONE MATTER	PAT MCCRACKEN	BB	$146.00
THE LIMPING LIABILITY MATTER	PAT MCCRACKEN	BB	$1,020.20
THE JOHNSON PAYROLL MATTER	PAT MCCRACKEN	BB	$526.50
THE MISSING MATTER MATTER	PAT MCCRACKEN	BB	$0.00
THE CLOSE SHAVE MATTER	PAT MCCRACKEN	BB	$383.20
THE PERILOUS PARLEY MATTER	PAT MCCRACKEN	BB	$8.00
THE DEADLY DOUBT MATTER	PAT MCCRACKEN	BB	$41.00
THE LOVE SHORN MATTER	PAT MCCRACKEN	BB	$377.00
THE LAKE MEAD MYSTERY MATTER	PAT MCCRACKEN	BB	$196.45
THE WAYWARD SCULPTOR MATTER	PAT MCCRACKEN	BB	$26.15
THE REALLY GONE MATTER	PAT MCCRACKEN	BB	$401.05
THE BACKFIRE THAT BACKFIRED MATTER	PAT MCCRACKEN	BB	$450.00
THE LITTLE MAN WHO WAS THERE MATTER	PAT MCCRACKEN	BB	$12.34
THE BUFFALO MATTER	PAT MCCRACKEN	BB	$0.00
THE FURTHER BUFFALO MATTER	PAT MCCRACKEN	BB	$1,800.00
THE DOUBLE IDENTITY MATTER	PAT MCCRACKEN	BB	$20.00
THE SUDDEN WEALTH MATTER	PAT MCCRACKEN	BB	$38.25

THE RED MYSTERY MATTER	PAT MCCRACKEN	BB	$0.00
THE BURNING DESIRE MATTER	PAT MCCRACKEN	BB	$874.20
THE MERRY-GO-ROUND MATTER	PAT MCCRACKEN	BB	$0.00
THE LOOK BEFORE THE LEAP MATTER	PAT MCCRACKEN	BB	$9,570.00
THE WHOLLY UNEXPECTED MATTER	PAT MCCRACKEN	BB	$0.00
THE MAGNANIMOUS MATTER	PAT MCCRACKEN	BB	$0.00
THE SUPER SALESMAN MATTER	PAT MCCRACKEN	BB	$189.95
THE BEE OR NOT TO BEE MATTER	PAT FULLER	MK	$471.00
THE LUST FOR GOLD MATTER	PAT FULLER	MK	$0.00
	COMPANY EXPENSES		**$28,865.99**

UNIVERSAL BONDING & INDEMNITY COMPANY

THE BARTON BAKER MATTER	CHARLIE MAXWELL	JL	$604.15
	COMPANY EXPENSES		**$604.15**

UNKNOWN

THE BLIND ITEM MATTER		EO	$1,074.00
	COMPANY EXPENSES		**$1,074.00**

WASHINGTONIAN INSURANCE COMPANY

THE MONTEVIDEO MATTER	BILL BRANDON	EO	$1,650.00
THE MARIE MEADOWS MATTER	BILL BRANDON	EO	$110.40
	COMPANY EXPENSES		**$1,760.40**

WASHINGTONIAN LIFE INSURANCE COMPANY

THE CELIA WOODSTOCK MATTER	SAM MILLER	EO	$73.60
THE MALCOLM WISH, MD MATTER		EO	$577.40
THE HORACE LOCKHART MATTER		EO	$583.85
THE MERRILL KENT MATTER	MR. LAVERY	EO	$378.40
THE CELIA WOODSTOCK MATTER	MR. MILLER	JL	$73.60
THE HARPOONED ANGLER MATTER	PHILLIP MARTIN	JL	$1,043.90
THE TERRIFIED TUAN MATTER	TOM BENSON	JL	$2,296.45
THE FRUSTRATED PHOENIX MATTER	MR. BRADLEY	JL	$153.50
THE TEMPERMENTAL TOTE BOARD MATTER	BEN GORDON	JL	$354.95
THE SARAH MARTIN MATTER	ED REYNOLDS	JL	$318.05
	COMPANY EXPENSES		**$5,853.70**

WEST COAST UNDERWRITERS

THE LITTLE MAN WHO WASN'T THERE	BRADFORD L. COATES	CR	$942.08
	COMPANY EXPENSES		**$942.08**

WESTERN INDEMNITY COMPANY

THE FLASK OF DEATH MATTER	PAUL PETERS	BB	$431.00
THE SHADOW OF A DOUBT MATTER	TED ORLOFF	MK	$450.00
THE ALL TOO EASY MATTER	TED ORLOFF	MK	$491.34
	COMPANY EXPENSES		**$1,372.34**

WESTERN INDEMNITY COMPANY, GREATER SOUTHWEST INSURANCE COMPANY, UNIVERSAL ADJUSTMENT BUREAU

THE WHO'S WHO MATTER	TED BECKHAM	RR	$306.25
	COMPANY EXPENSES		**$306.25**

WESTERN LIFE & TRUST COMPANY

THE MARKHAM MATTER	ED PORTER	BB	$968.20
	COMPANY EXPENSES		**$968.20**

WESTERN LIFE & TRUST INSURANCE COMPANY

THE ALKALI MIKE MATTER	BILL KEMPER	BB	$525.00
THE FATAL SWITCH MATTER	ART BASCOMB	BB	$386.21
	COMPANY EXPENSES		**$911.21**

WESTERN MARITIME & LIFE INSURANCE COMPANY

THE CHUCK-A-NUT MATTER	LUCIEN PETERSON	MK	$351.18
THE TWO STEPS TO MURDER MATTER	PETE BRENAMAN	MK	$511.80
THE ZIPP MATTER	PETE BRENAMAN	MK	$200.00
	COMPANY EXPENSES		**$1,062.98**

WESTERN MARITIME & PROPERTY

THE ELLEN DEAR MATTER	ARTHUR ARTHUR	BB	$453.95
	COMPANY EXPENSES		**$453.95**

WESTERN MARITIME & PROPERTY INSURANCE COMPANY

THE MALIBU MYSTERY MATTER	PETER HANLEY	BB	$101.50
THE WAYWARD DIAMONDS MATTER	PETER HANLEY	BB	$218.00
THE BALDERO MATTER	ARTHUR ARTHUR	BB	$0.00
	COMPANY EXPENSES		**$319.50**

WORLD INSURANCE & INDEMNITY COMPANY

THE STANLEY PRICE MATTER	HANDLEY CONRAD	JL	$113.40
THE ANITA BUDDHA MATTER	HANLEY CONRAD	JL	$527.15
THE HOWARD ARNOLD MATTER	HANLEY CONRAD	JL	$123.66
	COMPANY EXPENSES		**$764.21**

WORLD MUTUAL INSURANCE COMPANY

THE DEADLY CRYSTAL MATTER	LES WALTERS	MK	$100.00
	COMPANY EXPENSES		**$100.00**

WORLDWIDE MARITIME & INSURANCE COMPANY

THE HAMPTON LINE MATTER	JACK LORING	JL	$158.55
	COMPANY EXPENSES		**$158.55**

WORLDWIDE MUTUAL INSURANCE COMPANY

THE ALDER MATTER	VIC KELLY	BB	$833.14
THE CARSON ARSON MATTER	JIM PARIS	BB	$56.90
THE NOXIOUS NEEDLE MATTER	WALDO R. WESTBURY	BB	$61.20
THE MEI-LING BUDDHA MATTER	MARTY BRUCE	BB	$300.00
THE LOST BY A HAIR MATTER	FRED STARKEY	BB	$162.70
THE LEUMAS MATTER	LES WALTERS	BB	$89.50
THE TWO'S A CROWD MATTER	PAUL FERRIS	RR	$379.50
THE STOCK-IN-TRADE MATTER	RIP TEETER	RR	$325.00
THE BUYER AND THE CELLAR MATTER	DON REAGLE	MK	$477.30
THE CINDER ELMER MATTER	CHARLIE WARREN	MK	$377.80
THE CAN'T BE SO MATTER	LES WALTERS	MK	$0.00
THE TAKES A CROOK MATTER	LES WALTERS	MK	$0.00
THE MIXED BLESSING MATTER	CHARLIE WARREN	MK	$0.00
	COMPANY EXPENSES		**$3,063.04**

Index

VOLUME ONE: PAGES 1–414
VOLUME TWO: PAGES 415–995
VOLUME THREE: PAGES 996–1203

B

BACKGROUND

C

CASE LOCATIONS

CAST MEMBERS

CATALOGED STORIES

H
HOME ADDRESS

HOTELS USED

M

MARITAL STATUS

MUSIC SUPERVISION

P

PHONE NUMBER

POISONS USED

R

RECURRING CHARACTERS

Made in the USA
Middletown, DE
20 November 2018